Nature

Nature

Western Attitudes since Ancient Times

PETER COATES

Polity Press

First published in 1998 by Polity Press
in association with Blackwell Publishers Ltd.

Editorial office:
Polity Press
65 Bridge Street
Cambridge CB2 1UR, UK

Marketing and production:
Blackwell Publishers Ltd
108 Cowley Road
Oxford OX4 1JF, UK

ISBN 0-7456-1655-0
ISBN 0-7456-1656-9 (pbk)

A catalogue record for this book is available from the British Library.

Typeset in 10 on 12 pt Palatino
by Best-set Typesetter Ltd., Hong Kong
Printed in Great Britain by MPG Books, Bodmin, Cornwall

This book is printed on acid-free paper.

Contents

Preface and Acknowledgements

It has been a terrific educational experience to read so many books and articles in my research for this book. I have never formally studied ancient history and had not given much thought to the Middle Ages since I was freshman at the University of St Andrews, where I recall sweating over an essay on the twelfth-century renaissance. (I don't think I even mentioned 'Nature' – which may explain the poor mark it received.) I then became an Americanist to escape the remorseless and increasingly stale diet of British and European history I had been fed between the ages of 11 and 20. But over the past few years (as I hope this book demonstrates), I have recovered my appetite for 'old world' history.

At first I thought I might undertake a global study. But the anonymous reader who vetted the original proposal thought that, despite the brag, it sounded suspiciously like Western history 'with occasional discussions of the "rest"'. So 'better to be honest and modest'. That was excellent advice, and this is now essentially a history of the Western world. Yet even within these geographical and cultural constraints, it has been necessary to restrict my coverage largely to Britain and the United States, sometimes venturing into France, Germany and Italy.

Some historians will consider a transnational perspective reckless enough. Others may be even more alarmed by the broad timescale. I can think of no better defence than Felipe Fernandez-Armesto's retort to those biased towards narrow chronological coverage. In the preface to *Millennium*, he envisages some future galactic museum, in which 'Diet-Coke cans will share with coats of chain mail a single small vitrine marked "Planet Earth, 1,000–2,000, Christian Era" . . . The distinctions apparent to us, as we look back on the history of our thousand years from just inside it, will be obliterated by the perspective of long time and vast distance.'[1]

This book assumes no previous knowledge on the part of its readers and makes no claim to original scholarship. *Nature* is a synthesis that aims to provide undergraduates and the general reader with an accessible introduction to some of the central features and debates of environmental history, confirming (I hope) its status as one of the most enthralling and worthwhile current pursuits within historical studies.

I am extremely grateful to my colleagues Tony Antonovics, Christopher Clay, Tim Cole and Ian Wei for taking the time to review various portions of the manuscript that fell within their areas of expertise. Sensitive to the introductory nature of the book and my need to maintain a central argument uncompromised by too much qualification and attention to messy detail, they offered comments and suggestions that were invariably helpful. The manuscript also benefited from Janet Moth's astute copy-editing. Any errors of fact or judgement that remain are of course entirely my own responsibility. I should also like to thank the inter-library loan staff at Bristol University Library for procuring a steady stream of materials, as well as the Department of Historical Studies for granting a period of study leave in the autumn of 1996 that advanced the project substantially.

Over the past seven years I have come to know and cherish a variety of local spots in addition to the distant places (such as Alaska) that I usually focus on but to which I get much less frequently these days. Writing this book has helped me develop a sense of place here in the West Country. I am fortunate to live in a region sprinkled with some of the places that feature in my account. Our children Giuliana and Ivana accompanied us on all our excursions, though doubtless there were times when they would have preferred to stay at home watching a Disney video. And, once we got there, they were obviously far more interested in the earwigs, fox droppings, dewy spider webs, white heather and dripping fiddleheads of bracken than in their father's musings as to whether the grassy sheep tracks of the Quantock hills above Holford had changed much since Coleridge and Wordsworth strolled there in the summer of 1797, a time Wordsworth recalled in *The Prelude*: 'That summer, under whose indulgent skies, upon smooth Quantock's airy ridge we roved, unchecked, or loitered 'mid her sylvan combs.'[2] But when our daughters, to whom I dedicate this book, are old enough to read Coleridge and Wordsworth, I hope they will remember their childhood visits to this inspirational place.

Peter Coates

1

The Natures of Nature

An elemental juxtaposition of nature and culture is deep-seated and pervasive in Western thought, with 'nature' frequently serving as shorthand for the natural world and the physical environment. This polarity is enshrined in many book titles, witness George Perkins Marsh's *Man and Nature* (1864) and Arthur Ekirch's *Man and Nature in America* (1963). Nature is often presumed to be an objective reality with universal qualities unaffected by considerations of time, culture and place, an assumption especially evident in appeals to nature as a source of external authority (witness the ever popular saying 'Nature knows best'). This elementary character is encapsulated in an advertisement for water-filter cartridges that shows a tumbling waterfall. The caption reads, 'like nature, Brita is beautifully simple'.

Twenty years ago, however, Raymond Williams called 'Nature' 'perhaps the most complex word in the [English] language'. 'I've previously attempted to analyse some comparable ideas, critically and historically', he had reflected a few years earlier; 'among them were culture, society, individual, class, art, tragedy. But I'd better say at the outset that, difficult as all those ideas are, the idea of nature makes them all seem comparatively simple.' 'Any full history of the uses of nature', he warned, 'would be a history of a large part of human thought.'[1] In 1938 Ernest Robert Curtius listed fourteen ways in which a single aspect of nature, its personification as the goddess Natura, operated in Latin allegorical poetry alone.[2] The layers have never ceased to accumulate since Roman times and the strata of meaning are now bewilderingly dense and convoluted.

There is evidently a vibrant cultural history of nature that belies its deceptive simplicity and ahistorical charm. That we are becoming increasingly aware of it is suggested by recent titles such as Alexander Wilson's *The Culture of Nature: North American Landscapes from Disney to the Exxon Valdez* (1992), I. G. Simmons's *Interpreting Nature: Cultural Constructions of the Environment* (1993) and William Cronon's *Uncommon Ground: Toward Reinventing Nature* (1995). Accordingly, nature has been variously considered both part of us and quite apart from us, nurturing and dangerous, animate and machine-like, spiritual and material. Nature, like us, has a history.

I have tried to render this introductory survey for the non-specialist manageable by restricting its focus to the Western world, crudely defined as Western Europe and North America. (If we discount coverage of ancient Greece and Rome, however, European coverage effectively shrinks to Britain and Germany.) Even within these geographical and intellectual confines, it has proved impossible to follow a sequence that gives equal attention to each region and era. Initial chapters are chronologically organized. Thereafter, while remaining reasonably faithful to chronology, I have opted for a more thematic approach.

This introductory chapter outlines the major categories of meaning that have informed Western thought about nature since ancient times and which will be pursued in various historical contexts. It moves on to delineate the various ideological and material factors that have influenced human perceptions of, attitudes to and uses of nature, notably religion and ethics, science, technology, economics, gender and ethnicity. This is undertaken with specific reference to the establishment of human control over the natural world, the stages in the emergence of dualistic, or so-called 'homocentric' and 'anthropocentric', thinking (i.e. the separation of people and culture from nature, and culture's elevation above nature) and, not least, the attribution of responsibility for our contemporary ecological predicament.

Historians of attitudes to nature face many of the issues confronting other historians of ideas. Lynn White's famous essay of 1967 on the role of the Judaeo-Christian tradition in shaping Western attitudes to nature drew an explicit connection between belief and behaviour.[3] But how far do intellectual transformations precipitate material changes? Moreover, do seminal thinkers stand apart, or do they essentially express the views of the less articulate? Then I examine another cluster of themes: the evolution of an appreciation and admiration of and affection for certain aspects of the natural world in various non-monetary senses; the growth of an awareness of how people can alter the natural world for the worse as well as for the better; and the expression of dismay and concern over the consequences of these actions – not to mention the formulation and execution of remedial action. The final section explores the historiography of writing about nature.

Interpretations and representations of 'nature': towards a historical nature

Understandings of nature in the Western world can roughly be divided (with some inevitable overlap) into five historically important categories: nature as a physical place, notably those parts of the world more or less unmodified by people (as in 'unspoiled nature') – and especially those threatened by human activity; nature as the collective phenomena of the world or universe, including or excluding humans; nature as an essence, quality and/or principle that informs the workings of the world or universe; nature as an inspiration and guide for people and source of authority governing human affairs; and, finally, nature as the conceptual opposite of culture.

The essential starting-point, therefore, is to recognize that 'nature' has both concrete and abstract meanings. The next vital step is to appreciate that, for the larger part of Western history, the first meaning – nature as a physical place, which is also currently the dominant one – has been subordinate to the others. You do not need to have heard of the government organization English Nature, nor to have visited one of its properties, to figure out that this is a body charged with the conservation of England's natural environment. Our basic understanding of nature today derives from the Romantic 'nature poets' of the late eighteenth and early nineteenth centuries, who took nature to mean, in Raymond Williams's phrase, 'what man has not made, though if he made it long enough ago – a hedgerow or a desert – it will usually be included as *natural*'.[4]

Nature in this sense is usually thought of in tandem with 'poetry', 'lover' and 'conservation'. Recent surveys of the British public's taste in poetry have revealed the tenacity of nature poetry's appeal. The top ten British poems (based on a BBC TV poll of 7,500 people), compiled as part of National Poetry Day in October 1995, included William Wordsworth's 'Daffodils' (1815), which was ranked as the fifth favourite, followed by John Keats's 'Ode to Autumn', with Wordsworth still Britain's third favourite poet. A poll of 1,790 Classic FM listeners in 1997 confirmed the popularity of Wordsworth's 'Daffodils', placing it in top position.

Moreover, the British poet James Thomson's characterization of 'gay' green as 'Nature's universal robe' in 'The Seasons' (1730) has been

adopted, if unwittingly, by the entire Western environmental movement: note the names of political parties established on ecological principles – Greens, Grünen, Vertes. Many laypeople may be surprised to
learn that *Nature* (founded in 1869) is not the organ of an environmental
organization but the leading journal of the Western scientific community. (Yet even in this instance Wordsworth was influential. The first
issue took its epigraph from the poet's lines 'To the solid ground of
Nature trusts the Mind that builds for aye.')[5]

Reflecting recent preoccupations, books with the phrase 'nature conservation' are those most frequently encountered when searching a
library database using 'nature' as the keyword. By becoming identified
with Wordsworth's daffodils and a synonym for physical environments and ecosystems (as in Robert Ricklefs's *The Economy of Nature: A
Textbook in Basic Ecology* (1976)), 'nature' has been impoverished. This
overview seeks to recover some of nature's richness and complexity by
heeding a wider and older history of attitudes and approaches.

The definition of nature as material creation in its entirety informs
a leading work produced before the advent of the 'age of ecology' in
the 1960s: R. G. Collingwood's *The Idea of Nature* (1945). Collingwood's
idea of nature as the universe and the cosmos in the broadest possible
sense can be traced to ancient Greece and Rome. The intellectuals
Collingwood discusses took their cue from Titus Lucretius, the Roman
poet and philosopher (99–55 BC), who, in his *De Rerum Natura* (On the
Nature of Things), conceived of nature as the cosmic setting for human
life – from the firmament to the changing seasons. This Lucretian
approach can also be found in C. F. Von Weizsäcker's *The History of
Nature* (1951), a work of astronomy by an atomic physicist, with chapters on infinity, the heavens and the stars, and the age and spatial
structure not only of the universe, earth and life but also of the soul.
The ancients were engrossed by the relationship between the laws of
nature and the laws of God (asking questions such as 'does each blade
of grass represent a separate divine act?') rather than by the impact of
human activities on nature as we understand it.

By the fifth century in Greece, a personified nature (Natura) had
become an object of piety in its own right, endowed with a moral
purpose and meaning independent of mankind.[6] Nature was also personified as the creative force within the universe – the immediate cause
of phenomena. Sometimes the ancient Greeks personified nature more
explicitly in female form, a practice still evident in our invocation of
'Mother Nature'. These are the origins of a singular, capitalized Nature,
indicating how closely nature as essence or principle is related to
nature in the plural as the totality of matter. That the Lucretian view

remained at the heart of scientific understanding is suggested by the definitions of nature favoured by the seventeenth-century British chemist Robert Boyle: 'that on whose account a thing is what it is' and 'the phenomena of the universe/or/of the world'.[7] And, as is suggested by the title of a book about the atomic physicist Niels Bohr and the philosophy of quantum physics – *The Description of Nature* (1987) – and confirmed by the aforementioned title of the premier science periodical, it remains integral.

In Lucretius's view, man's body made him part of nature, but his mind set him apart and equipped him to investigate nature's workings. The difficulty of distinguishing clearly between humans and other animate life forms was highlighted by the use of nature to refer to innate qualities. This sense of the word is still conveyed in expressions such as 'the nature of the beast'. But the idea of nature as essence often extended to human characteristics such as an individual's disposition, as in the characterization of a person as 'good-natured'. This understanding could be extended to shared physiological features or mental attributes, as in 'human nature'. The latter usage in particular conveys the sense of nature as a generic, unalterable feature and fixed order; thus we speak of 'natural' (i.e. born) leaders or of someone gifted at sport or music as 'a natural'. Accordingly, to 'denature' something means to change or remove its essential qualities, though in practice we usually only speak of the adulteration of alcohol in this sense.

The equally venerable idea of nature as instructor was evoked in the 1790s by the sign that hung over the front door to Charles Willson Peale's natural history museum in Philadelphia, introducing 'the great school of nature'. At the museum's back entrance, another sign referred to 'the book of Nature open . . . a solemn Institute of laws eternal'.[8] In this respect, nature has become part of a Manichaean division of the world into good and evil. This privileging of nature as superior 'other', a place of escape from the overbearing 'works of man', cultivated by the pastoralists of the classical world and perfected by the eighteenth-century Romantics, suggested that everything would work out fine and everyone would be happy if only we obeyed nature's unambiguous instructions.

Nature is in some senses an irrevocable dictate: we have little choice but to respond to 'the call of nature'. Nature is also incontrovertibly indifferent to human fate. But the 'laws of nature' are formulated by certain groups for specific purposes. Nature has been attributed with approved human values and ideals to validate and raise above debate particular visions and ideologies. The Nazis, for instance, regarded war as society's natural state, while a naturist recruitment film of the 1950s was entitled *Naked, as Nature Intended*. During the 1992 campaign for the Republican Party's presidential nomination in the United States, Pat Buchanan described the AIDS disease as 'nature's retribution' against what he saw as a strikingly unnatural practice. Buchanan was reiterating the thirteenth-century views of Thomas Aquinas, for whom homosexual intercourse was unnatural because animals did not engage in it. Yet over the past few decades scientists have monitored instances of same-sex attraction in the animal kingdom.[9]

If, following the original Greek definition in all its catholicity, nature is deemed to be everything material that exists, then, strictly speaking, nothing can be unnatural. However, the distinction between the natural and the unnatural (or artificial) is invariably made and, while nature has no conceptual opposite, we usually think of it as human culture. Indeed, without a concept of culture as the works of humankind, there can be no concept of nature. Many ancient Greek thinkers assumed that the original condition of mankind prior to social and political organization was a state of nature governed by natural laws. Depending on your standpoint, humanity had either fallen from this state of grace, where it had been unencumbered by institutions, or had risen beyond its barbaric confines through the salutary mechanisms of culture and human laws.

A fundamental issue for Aristotle in the *Physics* was the distinction between natural entities whose essence is innate – things that do what they do themselves – and artificial entities whose essence derives from an external source: the artist who sculpts a rock, the stonemason who builds a house. Hence the difference between a marble cliff and a statue, a stone and a doorstep. The nineteenth-century American transcendentalist writer Ralph Waldo Emerson summarized this broad division of the world into the created and the creative (culture and man) on the one hand and the uncreated (nature) on the other: '*Nature*, in the common sense, refers to the essences unchanged by man; space, the air, the river, the leaf. *Art* is applied to the mixture of his will with the same things, as in a house, a canal, a statue, a picture.' Emerson sought a further distinction, however, derived from German idealism, between 'me' (spirit, soul, mind, maker, i.e. consciousness) and 'not me' (world, body, matter, the made, i.e. phenomena): 'Philosophically considered, the universe is composed of Nature and the Soul. Strictly speaking, therefore, all that is separate from us, all which Philosophy distinguishes as the NOT ME, that is, both nature and art, all other men and my own body, must be ranked under this name, NATURE.'[10]

The various meanings of nature discussed so far, with the exception of Emerson's, are all more or less predicated on nature's essentialism, the separation of nature and culture, and nature's superiority or inferiority to culture. But precisely which aspects of culture are most responsible for setting people apart from nature? The answer for the ancient Greeks was reason; for Christians it has traditionally been spirit. Early twentieth-century existentialist philosophy, by attributing supreme freedom and autonomy to the individual, posited the widest distance between people and nature. Yet commentators since ancient Greek times have also been alert to the ambiguities in this relationship. Humans are part of nature in so far as we rely on it for food, water and shelter and have the same bodily functions as other creatures. Moreover, gradations of the natural and the cultural have been established, not least by European conquerers, who situated the indigenous peoples of Africa and the Americas much closer to nature than themselves, classifying them as 'natural' because of the absence, to the European eye and mind, of civil polity and other trappings of a universally defined civilization.

The suburban lawn may seem an unlikely choice but it illustrates nicely the clumsiness of the received categories of nature and culture. We might conclude that, while grass seed and blades of grass are part of nature, they enter the realm of artifice through their collective identity as a lawn. Yet the seeds themselves are completely domesticated, bred for shade tolerance, for instance. Does the lawn become more natural, however, if dandelions, daisies and moss – the spontaneous 'products of nature' – establish themselves?

Furthermore, many ostensibly natural features are products of human choice. We actively manage nature to keep it in a desired state. On Dolebury Warren, a National Trust property in Somerset's Mendip hills, scrub is hacked down to maintain grassland. Lose the open cover and grazing sheep, and wildflowers and butterflies will disappear. We wish to enshrine what is in fact a transitional ecosystem, not because nature has endowed grassland with special significance, but because we prefer this particular version of nature. The internal dynamic is working to restore a wild condition – not a pleasing prospect for most visitors.

Other environments perceived to be unaltered are the less deliberate outcome of human agency. Discussing the impact of felling and grazing on upland tree cover, the Chinese philosopher Mencius (c.372–289 BC), declared: 'To these things is owing the bare and stripped appearance of the mountain, and when people now see it, they think it was never finely wooded. But is this the nature of the mountain?'[11] Those Germans who tour the Scottish highlands and islands in search of Western Europe's 'last wilderness' are usually unaware that 'the nature' (*die Natur*) is the product of environmental degradation. Much of today's moorland once supported the great Caledonian forest, which survives only in patches. Samuel Johnson appreciated this during his Scottish tour in the eighteenth century, drawing attention to a plantation of ash trees at Armadale on Skye 'because it proves that the present nakedness of the *Hebrides* is not wholly the fault of Nature'.[12]

The Norfolk Broads, one of England's most treasured recreational and ecological resources, also emerged from unlikely beginnings. Scholars used to think they were an original feature (as many vistors may continue to believe). Prior to the early 1950s, the Broads were considered the relic estuaries of rivers clogged with silt and peat. They are really an industrial landscape gone wild – a flooded pit. The sheerness of the sides of the waterways indicates that the Broads were a series of enormous holes (turbaries) left by 300 years of peat extraction, while the irregular chains of islets represent baulks of peat that separated the diggings, and served as footpaths.[13] Documentary evidence has confirmed these origins; there was precious little woodland to serve the fuel needs of this densely populated part of thirteenth-century England. A rise in sea level towards the end of the thirteenth century was a likelier reason for their abandonment than a fall in peat demand.

Not that the Broads are now static. The waterways are gradually filling in – a natural process of siltation exacerbated by the erosion from motorboat wash – and returning to woodland. Nature's dynamism and redemptive tendencies raise profound questions for those seeking to preserve nature. If such beauty and ecological value can come of such unpromising beginnings, why worry about environmental desecration? And if change is the only constant in the natural world as well as in human society, where is the urgency or sense in trying to preserve in perpetuity something both relatively recent and likely to change of its own accord anyhow?

Some natural environments are so carefully contrived that casual observers often fail to appreciate the degree of cultural selection involved. This is especially true of the parkscapes crafted in eighteenth-century England, when an ideal vision was imposed on nature's provisional arrangements. Man-made nature – nature as artefact, scenery and landscape – is the main focus of chapter 6.

John Stuart Mill once referred to the word 'unnatural' as 'one of the most vituperative epithets in the language'.[14] Conceptions of what is natural have been reinforced by recent innovations in agribusiness. During the BSE (mad cow disease) crisis that afflicted the British cattle industry in 1996, it was not only advocates of organic farming like

Prince Charles who expressed the view that feeding sheep offal to herbivores was the ultimate unnatural practice, an inexcusable contravention of nature's laws. In 1997 Bristol University students' union debated the motion 'this house would not eat a square strawberry', while a London market-stall owner interviewed on television asserted that genetically engineered tomatoes were simply 'not natural'.

Natural foods, by contrast, are defined as those without additives in the form of artificial colourings, flavourings, sweeteners or preservatives. Nature becomes a byword for authenticity, and advertising relies heavily on the association between nature, purity, simplicity and goodness. Notwithstanding the recent conspicuous wave of corporate 'green advertising', this deployment of imagery drawn from nature has been a standard sales device since the 1920s. At that time, images of nature were used for purposes of reassurance, to smooth the way for modernity and to soften its shock.[15] Nowadays, they are deployed to seduce customers disenchanted with modernity. Nature can sell cigarettes, cars and shampoo as effectively as can sex.

Up to a point, nature exists only as a mental and linguistic construct. As C. S. Lewis has mused:

> If ants had a language they would, no doubt, call their anthill an artifact and describe the brick wall in its neighbourhood as a *natural* object. Nature in fact would be for them all that was not 'ant-made'. Just so, for us, *nature* is all that is not man-made; the natural state of anything is its state when not modified by man.[16]

Yet an autonomous physical reality that we can directly encounter – and on which we can observe our impact empirically – undeniably exists 'out there', transcending cognitive and linguistic processes. '*We can never perceive the world directly*', explains Ty Cashman, '*but our actions always affect the world directly*. The actions of our bodies *directly* move, disturb, change, refashion parts of the world.'[17]

We have not made the natural world but we have, in a sense, created nature. Not even the most slavish of postmodernists would deny the existence of an apple, a frog or a snowdrop. But what they signify is indisputably a function of culture, which converts the raw materials of the physical environment into nature. Thus it is more accurate to talk about representations of nature rather than reflections. 'Reflections' suggests direct transmission of meaning, whereas culture, speaking through language, defines reality rather than reporting what already exists. A frog may be real, but can we describe one without interpreting it? Is it possible to look at a daffodil without thinking of Wordsworth's famous poem? Or to contemplate a redwood without summoning John Muir's paeans to nature's cathedrals? Neil Evernden argues that a 'forest may be a mythical realm or a stock of unused lumber, but either way, it is able to serve a social function. It is, in that sense, never *itself* but always *ours*.' As Marjorie Hope Nicolson reflects, 'we see in Nature what we have been taught to look for, we feel what we have been prepared to feel'.[18]

Moreover, apparently universalist notions are provisional and contingent in that they can invariably be grounded in particular circumstances and traced to specific sources. You do not need to speak the postmodernist language of mediation, negotiation, construction and contestation to appreciate that nature's meaning is not inherent but varies according to context and derives from convention. 'What is touted as universal', explains a feminist geographer, 'is really, to borrow [Thomas] Nagel's phrase, a view from nowhere (and of nowhere).'[19] Universally applicable and measurable, non-ethnocentric definitions of the qualities of wild and tame in nature, for instance, cannot be provided. As the nineteenth-century Oglala Sioux, Chief Luther Standing Bear, explained: 'We did not think of the great open plains, the beautiful rolling hills, and winding streams with tangled growth, as "wild". Only to the white man was nature a "wilderness" and only to him was the land "infested" with "wild" animals and "savage" people. To us it was tame. Not until the hairy man from the east came . . . was it "wild" for us.'[20]

Western attitudes to nature and the natural world may depend on a range of variables, but some largely timeless verities stick out. Since classical times, nature has been a source of wealth and amusement for aristocrats and royalty (particularly through hunting), and a fount of joy, beauty, solace and inspiration for poets, while for the majority of people (especially pre-industrial) it has been a challenge to surmount and a set of raw materials out of which to wrest a living.

Diagnoses of the intellectual roots of misconduct

The search for those fateful junctures at which people removed themselves from nature, formulated anthropocentric views, became aware of humanity's authority over nature and started to abuse their power has absorbed scholars in various disciplines over the past quarter-century. Anthropologists have traditionally thought of gathering communities as nature-bound, with hunting – involving the use of tools – leading to greater control and environmental impact. The beginnings of

plant cultivation and domestication of animals in the so-called
Neolithic Revolution (the changes actually unfolded over thousands of
years) are conventionally identified as the first major step in human
separation from the rest of nature. Commentators with a more overtly
environmentalist agenda, who talk of 'alienation' from nature rather
than simply our separation from it, have characterized this evolutionary stage as a disastrous estrangement and colossal fall from ecological
grace. Clive Ponting's *A Green History of the World* (1991) typifies the
anguished view of our tenure on earth as a remorseless, intensifying
saga of environmental woe and waste as human numbers have spi-
ralled out of control and successive societies have refused to accept
nature's carrying capacity.

Other scholars downplay the significance of the agricultural revolution as a seminal divide. Agriculture is usually considered an exclusively human activity, yet other creatures also manipulate nature to
their advantage. African termites 'farm' fungus in a loose sense of the
word, while other ants enter into reciprocal 'agreements' with certain
flowering plants to disperse their fruits and seeds, gaining food and
nesting sites in return. Accordingly, some have identified the invention
of fire as humankind's great leap forwards (or backwards), for it facilitated cooking, habitat manipulation for hunting, land clearance and the
working of clay and metal.[21]

Ponting's highly materialistic account, focusing on relationships between population, food and energy resources, and the problems of
disease, overcrowding and poverty, leaves little room for intellectual
history. In so far as he engages with attitudes to nature, Ponting views
the course of Western thought as a largely unmitigated disaster. Many
analysts opt for this linear, declensionist approach. The American
ecophilosopher George Sessions traces the anthropocentric hegemony
back to Socrates, who believed that philosophy should concern itself
mainly with people. After Socrates, according to this model of incremental decline, came Aristotle, who taught that everything in nature
existed for people. This thrust was extended by Judaeo-Christianity,
consolidated by Renaissance humanism and intensified by the scientific and technological revolutions, which marked the culmination of
the reduction of all natural phenomena to quantifiable, inert entities.[22]

Others prefer to single out a particular phenomenon as the primary
root of all evil. Some insist that ecological abuse began in earnest with
the advent of capitalism in Europe, spreading outwards to taint the rest
of the world (see chapter 5). The scientific revolution has been advanced as the critical stage in the emergence of Western confidence in
the human ability to actualize the control over nature to which people

aspired (see chapter 4). Those looking for the original source of this
desire rather than its materialization have pinpointed the Judaeo-
Christian God's injunction to man (Genesis) to 'fill the earth and subdue it; and have dominion over the fish of the sea and over the birds
of the air and over every living thing that moves upon the earth'.
The sheer weight of citations in environmentalist literature suggests
that White's thesis is the most influential of all diagnoses (see chapter
3).[23]

Anna Bramwell goes too far in dismissing these efforts to assign
responsibility (and blame) as the 'varied conspiracy theories' of the
'manichaean ecologist'.[24] Nevertheless, we are hard pressed to find a
single doctrine of man–nature relations in any era, let alone a straight-
forward descent over time from unity and harmony with nature. The
modernist who assumes that greater conceptual unity prevailed in
apparently less complex, more religious, times will be disappointed. A
number of attitudes, notions and orientations invariably coexist in
often messy contradiction. The prominence of different ideas and
trends has of course varied according to historical circumstances. To
indicate a series of shifts with a cumulative net effect is certainly less
dramatic and perhaps also less satisfying than to home in on one
particularly marked watershed. However, it is more serious history.
One thing at least is certain: no human society has ever lived completely inside nature or outside of environmental change.

The role of ideas

Do ideas, ethics and values derive from how we make a living or do our
ideological constructions shape the way we live? For most historians of
the ideas and ethics of nature, their status is normative, providing a
general context for how we behave rather than dictating our actual
behaviour. Actual behaviour is more often a direct function of population pressure, a given level of technology, or a particular economic
mode of production. The reaction of Soviet theorists in the 1970s to
White's thesis that the modern environmental crisis is rooted in
Western religion provides a taste of the debate between idealists and
materialists. These communist ideologues rejected cultural explanations because, as Marxist structuralists, they believed that underlying
economic structures (the base) explain the surface phenomena of ideas
and beliefs (the superstructure). In their view, culture is an epiphenom-
enon or secondary symptom that simply expresses ideas shaped by
economic forces.[25]

Ideas are certainly materially determined in that they do not arise in a vacuum (at least not those that become influential). It was not the sheer brilliance of Bacon's and Newton's ideas that ensured their acceptance (see chapter 4); there has to be a societal predisposition and correspondence between the dominant economic system and the ideas that a society endorses. Recognition of the interplay between idealist and material factors renders bluntly phrased, 'chicken and egg'-style questions such as whether medieval peasants feared nature out of respect or because they lacked the hardware to impose their authority rather redundant. Nevertheless, beyond stating the obvious – that both levels of explanation must be taken into account – the nature of their interaction remains enigmatic. All we can safely say, perhaps – and this is not a cowardly shirking of the issue – is that ideas and material factors are intertwined in a dialectical relationship from which neither can be extracted or defined in isolation. In this relationship, there is no 'other'.

Because figuring out the relationship between idealism and materialism is so confounding, environmental historians have tended to focus on one aspect to the exclusion of the other. 'We have either had studies of ecology and economy, or studies of ideas of nature', William Cronon explains; 'too rarely have we had the three together.'[26]

The emergence of a feeling for nature

Tender feelings for nature can readily be located in most Western societies from ancient times: witness the quantity of books whose titles start with the phrase *The Love of Nature among the* . . . or *The Development of the Feeling for Nature among the* . . . However, these usually turn out to be literary histories and, in many instances, nature and natural phenomena simply served imaginative writers as convenient metaphors. Besides, the approach of literary historians is often indiscriminate. Writing at the turn of the century when a 'cult of nature' was sweeping Germany (see chapter 8), Alfred Biese dwelt on Christopher Columbus's deep 'love for Nature'. He quotes Fernandez de Navarrete's paraphrase of Columbus's utilitarian reaction (in his so-called diary) to the majestic pines he encountered on Caribbean islands in 1492 ('he perceived that here there was material for great store of planks and masts for the largest ships of Spain'), and various other passages expressing wonder and astonishment. '[A]ll this shews a naive and spontaneous delight in Nature', concludes Biese, a remark bound to astonish contemporary environmentalists, for many of whom Columbus is a peerless 'eco-villain'.[27]

What I mean by the development of a feeling for nature is the shaping and expression of preferences for particular aspects of the natural world. We continually evaluate nature, prioritizing some species and places over others (the perceptual geographer Yi-Fu Tuan has coined the term 'topophilia' to describe how we are drawn to certain features).[28] Once identified, these animals and sites may become favoured species and reserved spaces, ranging from ancient sacred groves and medieval hunting chases to twentieth-century national parks and wildlife preserves.

Chapters 7 and 8 address aspects of this history: namely, the contribution of Romanticism and evolutionary theory to ecology and environmentalism, and 'non-elite' interest in nature and 'the outdoors'. The reader will need to look elsewhere, however, for a proper account of the evolution of the conservation and environmental movements since the late nineteenth and mid-twentieth centuries respectively. The related histories of natural history, ecological science and environmental ethics also lie beyond my scope. Bear in mind too that there is no necessary overlap between 'environment'/'ecology' and 'nature'.[29]

'Conservation', 'preservation' and 'environmentalism', though often used interchangeably, are far from monolithic categories. To attach the terms 'environmentalism' and 'environmental protection' to the pre-1945 era is, strictly speaking, anachronistic. Besides, how nature's various defenders conceptualize nature depends on whether their approach is pragmatic, sentimental, aesthetic, recreational or ecological. So-called 'utilitarian conservation' does not query the treatment of nature as natural resource: it still looks at a mountain and sees ore and lumber. Focusing on the consequences of shortages for economic health and state security, it seeks prudent use and efficient management over the long term. The Romantic poet and nature preservationist might reject the conceptualization of nature as a set of extractable commodities, but continue to regard it as a resource, if one of aesthetic and/or spiritual and recreational as opposed to monetary value. By contrast, the biocentric ecologist or ecophilosopher will view a mountain as a community of life, especially valuable as habitat for species that have intrinsic, non-resource value – even rights – simply because they exist.[30]

I may not be addressing the history of nature's defence and defenders directly, but I cannot write about nature without reference to Anglo–American 'green' thinking, especially since a good deal of commentary on nature over the past thirty years has a green complexion and advocatory tone. Just as women's history was sparked by feminist ideology and the feminist movement in the 1960s, environmental history was launched by ecological sentiments and the environmental movement during the same decade. In their formative periods, both these new branches of historical study have been heavily engaged in the construction of explanations for oppression and mistreatment.[31]

The often inquisitional search for the roots of disharmony in our relationship with nature has been complemented by an earnest quest for the sources of enlightenment. The appeal of this eminently Whiggish enterprise (which shares the view of the nineteenth-century Whig/liberal school of history, interpreting the past as the triumphant and uplifting story of improvement and progress, worthy of study as a guide to the present) has been articulated by a literary historian: 'The pleasure of the biologist in the lower forms of life is paralleled by the delight of the student of literature in tracing out the first vague, ineffective attempts to express ideas that are afterward regnant.'[32]

While acknowledging forgotten forebears and notable antecedents of modern thinking, I have tried not to succumb to the temptation to try to discover 'firsts' (as in the first person to climb a mountain for the view rather than to get to the other side) nor attempted to unearth the deepest, most gnarled of taproots. This kind of exercise can quickly degenerate into a desultory string of quotations. The search for a past relevant to the present can also distort the past to the extent that it would prove unrecognizable to its inhabitants. Many figures from the past have been forced to work overtime for current causes, however worthy. Many activists and theorists regard historical material primarily as a means of empowerment, approaching past ideas of nature in terms of their enhancement value in today's marketplace of competing ideas about the appropriate relation of people to nature.

The objectives and pitfalls of these historical forays should be noted. Recognizing that in various religious traditions can be found the wellsprings of hope as well as the sources of trouble, Roger Gottlieb dedicates his collection of readings, *This Sacred Earth* (1996), to 'all beings who have suffered needlessly because of human folly and injustice: May we remember their pain and change our ways'. Yet it is essential to bear in mind a vital distinction between concern *with* nature in its capacity as the phenomena of the universe, which has been a central feature of all religions since they first appeared (not least in terms of their doctrines of creation), and concern *over* nature as a fragile entity in a late twentieth-century, ecological sense.[33]

Scholars who owe their main allegiance to a particular historical period will frown on these excursions into the past to gather ammunition for contemporary debates and raise the self-esteem of today's activists. While recognizing the need to study what was important *then* as well as what is thought to be important *now*, those interested in exploring a big theme across a broad expanse of time (and for whom activist scholarship is something worthy of study in its own right) will be intrigued by this ransacking and annexation. Anyone who doubts the potency of tales from the past as a recruitment device and source of inspiration should ponder the fortunes of the now famous story by the pioneering US environmentalist Aldo Leopold, about his conversion to ecological thinking in the 1920s. The trigger-happy young Leopold had a Pauline experience as he watched the 'fierce green fire' die in a wolf's eyes. This episode, described in his essay, 'Thinking Like a Mountain', formed the basis in the early 1980s for Earth First! 'green fire' roadshows that, according to Bron Taylor, amounted to 'biocentric revival meetings' ('ecovangelism'): 'the personified wolf of the green fire narrative calls humans to repent their destructive ways and defend the Earth'.[34]

Over the past twenty years, radical groups such as Earth First! (founded in 1980) have expanded the meaning of environmentalism far beyond resource conservation, wildlife protection, the creation of national parks and pollution control. But instead of approaching deep ecology, ecofeminism and ecosocialism as facets of environmentalism in a separate chapter on developments within environmentalist thought during the last quarter-century, I shall deal with them as and when their singular explanations for environmental ills (human chauvinism, patriarchy and capitalism respectively) and proposed solutions have been brought to bear on the study of attitudes to nature. The ideology of deep ecology features, for instance, in the context of Fritjof Capra's views on the seventeenth-century scientific revolution. Similarly, I am only concerned with the direct-action group Earth First! to the extent that anti-modernism has shaped their view of the conceptions of nature held by pre-industrial peoples.[35]

Readers should also look elsewhere for a history of environmental change in the West since ancient times. I can do no more here than point to the various agencies and mechanisms of natural resource exploitation and human-induced (anthropogenic) transformation.[36] However, since many intellectual histories of nature are rather disembodied and overly cerebral, largely divorced from material changes in the physical environment – just as many ecological histories neglect the role of ideas – I will try to offer more than token reference. Nature is far more than an assembly of organic and inorganic compounds, but it also cannot be dismissed as an elaborate human artifice. 'To say that nature is a construct does not reduce it to a version of [Jean] Baudrillard's hyperreality', explains Michael Zimmerman, 'but emphasizes that nature is an ongoing coproduction, generated by humans as well as by organic, material, linguistic and technical nonhumans.'[37]

We also need reminding that change and damage are as old as humanity and that no region has enjoyed immunity. Easter Island was virtually treeless when first visited by Europeans in 1722 but pollen analysis shows it was once thickly wooded. Large trees were needed to transport the island's characteristic huge monoliths from quarries to ceremonial sites.[38] I devote most attention to pre-industrial transformation and problems because their range and severity is rarely appreciated. Those whose images of urban filth have been shaped by the writings of Friedrich Engels and Charles Dickens might assume that pollution is a nineteenth-century invention. But *industrial* consumption of fuel is not a precondition of dirty and hazardous air and water. Any concentration of people burning wood as domestic fuel will contaminate the atmosphere. London's air-quality problems, already considerable, were aggravated in the late thirteenth century as wood, increasingly scarce, was replaced by sea coal, which had a high sulphur content and produced heavy soot and clouds of acrid smoke.

Parliament banned coal fires but the prohibition only applied while it was in session.[39] Parliamentarians' indifference to London's air quality when they were resident at their rural estates offers an early example of 'nimbyism' (the 'not in my backyard' approach to environmental problems). London's dependence on sea coal intensified over the centuries. John Evelyn's *Fumifugium* tract (1661) recorded how this caused premature birth, high infant mortality, barren fruit trees and various health problems, not to mention visual impairment (the sun, when it shone, could barely penetrate the pall).[40] 'Even if it is true that humans became more and more prone to alter the surface of the Earth', argues the microbiologist, René Dubos, 'this was not because they ceased to regard themselves as part of Nature, but simply because the world population constantly increased and the means of destruction became more powerful.'[41]

The study of nature: enter environmental history

Since the beginning of the century, a range of geographers (historical, perceptual and regional) and various literary and landscape historians, historical ecologists, ethnohistorians, ecological anthropologists and practitioners of 'total' history have been addressing attitudes to nature, the impact of natural phenomena such as climate on human processes and events and the human role in shaping the natural world. Then in the 1960s environmental history appeared in the United States as a self-conscious specialism, in large part as an adjunct to the environmental movement.[42] What Peter Burke calls the 'youthful and ambitious enterprise' of 'eco-history' is arguably the newest strand of the so-called 'new history'.[43] For despite their mission to liberate the voices of 'the other' that have been muted by the paradigm of modernity, postmodern theorists have rarely extended Michel Foucault's notion of the 'circuitry of power' to what we might fashionably call the colonial metanarrative of human hegemony over nature.[44] Yet animals and plants, rivers and forests – like non-whites, non-elites, women, gays and other 'marginalized' groups of people – have a history that should be restored to them.

Though there are increasing overlaps and parallel developments as the field becomes internationalized, certain national traditions can be detected during environmental history's formative years. The history of ideas of conservation and environmentalism, attitudes to nature (particularly wilderness) and nature preservation (especially of wild places), constituted much of the pioneering work in the United States; so did the story of the public movements springing from these impulses and their legislative achievements (not least the establishment of national parks).[45]

British scholars have made a more furtive contribution in the field of landscape (topographical) history since the 1950s.[46] Often closely allied to local history and landscape archaeology, the focus has frequently been pre-industrial if not prehistorical.[47] Landscape history, however, has concentrated on the visual – the literally superficial. It has not been much informed by an understanding of the workings of the natural world or of how human activity has affected them. Historical ecology, while more scientifically stout than landscape studies, also differs from much environmental history in being less censorious, less driven by the values of environmentalism. (Many environmental historians have taken Edward Gibbon's famous reference to history as the record of the crimes, follies and misfortunes of mankind as a perfect description of human relations with the natural world.)

To the British social historian, R. H. Tawney, is attributed the aphorism: 'History needs not more books but more boots.'[48] But Tawney was no latent historical ecologist; he was admonishing sedentary historians of the built environment. Much more clearly directed at library-ensconced historians of the natural world is the critique of the botanical historian Oliver Rackham. Rackham, who has no doubts about the existence of a real world to be read and listened to beyond 'the text', demands a rectification of the shallow and often misleading versions of the physical environment served up by historians wedded to conventional documentation: 'Unfortunately, many historians confine themselves to the written word or, worse still, to the literary word; they are reluctant to put on their boots and to see what the land itself, and the things that grow on it, have to say.'[49] Instead of poring exclusively over maps and deeds to date a hedge, for example, Rackham's historical ecologist scrutinizes its flora. Certain species, such as the wood anemone, are very slow colonizers: as a rule, the more floral types, the older the hedge.

Sceptics may suspect that environmental historians do their work simply by gazing out of the window (or by trading the dust of archives for the dust of the fields). The contribution of historical ecology and the tensions between field and documentary sources are explored in this book largely within the context of ancient and medieval Britain, with specific reference to the rate and character of the process whereby the physical environment was transformed into a cultural landscape (chapter 3).

In other areas, however, British scholarship on Britain has lagged far behind American study of the US national experience.[50] Even in the late 1970s, environmental history was a term used in British academia (and the rest of Europe) mainly by archaeologists and physical geographers investigating topics such as prehistoric climate change, erosion and tectonic shifts.[51] The great exception to date, as chapter 5 demonstrates, has been British study of Britain's colonial possessions.

The most powerful non-American influence on environmental history has been the 'total' history associated with the *Annales* journal founded in 1929 by the French geographer–historian Lucien Febvre, and the medieval historian Marc Bloch. In his classic exposition of the *Annales* school's approach, *The Mediterranean and the Mediterranean World in the Age of Philip II* (1949), Febvre's protégé Fernand Braudel popularized the history of 'the very long term' (*la longue durée*): the slow and deep-seated, if unspectacular, rhythms of 'submerged' natural history underlying the frenetic and dramatic surface events of 'conspicuous' history.[52] Inverting standard assumptions, Braudel regarded physical entities such as mountains as 'conspicuous actors' and treated biological entities such as the soil as historical protagonists.[53] Such was his dedication to what he called 'geohistory' that he devoted over 300 pages to setting the natural scene in the Mediterranean ('The Role of the Environment') before introducing human agents.

Those interested in the reconstruction of anthropogenic changes in the natural world rather than the exploration of thought about nature would agree with Karl Marx and Friedrich Engels's assertion (with regard to historians' neglect of the material basis of history, specifically economic modes of production) that 'the relation of man to nature is excluded from history and hence the antithesis of nature and history is created', and endorse their call for explanations rooted in the 'real *ground* of history'.[54] Some critics accuse this brand of environmental historian of displacing people from their rightful place at the core of historical study, either by presenting them as prisoners of the physical world or by reducing them to the status of 'human insects'.[55] To reassure those who feel it is beneath a humanist's dignity to engage with natural phenomena, it is worth quoting Emmanuel Le Roy Ladurie's reply to Bloch's reminder in 1949 that 'behind the tangible features of landscape . . . it is human beings that the historian is trying to discern':

> It is mutilating the historian to make him into no more than a specialist in humanity. The historian is the man of time and archives, a man to whom nothing which is documentary and chronological is alien . . . He may . . . in certain cases be interested in nature for its own sake, and make known by his own irreplaceable methods nature's own special Time.

Le Roy Ladurie's own work (he calls it 'climate history with a human face') reveals the subtle interplay of social, economic and environmental factors to explain the impact of harvests on great public events and the problems of viticulture.[56] This is a far cry from the inflexible determinism of Ellsworth Huntington, the turn-of-the century US geographer and meteorologist who was bent on erecting a monocausal interpretation of human history. In *The Pulse of Asia* (1907), he correlated Mongol migrations westward with rainfall levels on the central Asian steppes. This is environmentalism as it was generally understood before the term was appropriated by the green movement, and early this century it was often allied to a racist view of history. This blend of environmentalism with Nordic supremacism permeates *Civilization and Climate* (1915), in which Huntington matched centres of civilization with 'invigorating climates', alleging that 'the climate of many countries seems to be one of the great reasons why idleness, dishonesty, immorality, stupidity, and weakness of will prevail'.[57]

We take for granted our capacity for environmental damage, but people have not always appreciated their ability to compromise the natural world. There is no mention of deforestation, for example, in Braudel's grand saga of the Mediterranean: Braudel was no environmentalist in the recent sense. The first environmental history coloured by conservationist sentiment was in fact published as early as the 1860s by the US scholar and pioneer conservationist, George Perkins Marsh. His *Man and Nature* (1864) contains the prototype of the now standard environmentalist discourse identifying man as a powerful destructive force. Marsh's book grappled with profound assumptions about man's role in nature and about nature itself, and was designed to show that, whereas some maintained that 'the earth made man, man in fact made the earth'. David Lowenthal reports the following exchange of views in 1863 between Marsh and his publisher:

> 'Man the Disturber of Nature's Harmonies' was the title Marsh first proposed for the book. 'Is it True?' objected his publisher. 'Does not man act in harmony with nature? and with her laws? Is he not a part of nature?' And Marsh replied: 'No, nothing is further from my belief, that man is a 'part of nature' or that his action is controlled by the laws of nature; in fact a leading spirit of the book is to enforce the opposite opinion, and to illustrate the fact that man, so far from being . . . a soulless, will-less automaton, is a free moral agent working independently of nature.[58]

Marsh's view of relations between man and nature emphasized damage and disruption: 'Wherever he plants his foot, the harmonies of nature are turned to discords.' By contrast, 'Nature, left undisturbed, so fashions her territory as to give it almost unchanging permanence of form, outline, and proportion, except when shattered by geologic convulsions.'[59] This outlook remains central to the assumptions of many environmentalists.

Much environmental history (taking its cue from Marsh) has been written in terms of the monolithic categories of 'man' and 'nature'. Considerations of class and gender were absent, for instance, from Roderick Nash's seminal intellectual history of American attitudes to wilderness. Yet, as Raymond Williams has pointed out, 'If we talk only of a singular Man and a singular Nature we can compose a general history, but at the cost of excluding the real and altering social relations.' For 'what was being moved about and rearranged was not only earth and water but men'.[60] Influenced by Williams, scholarship is moving towards a keener appreciation of how class, gender, race and ethnicity influence dealings with the natural world.

William Cronon blends social and environmental history in his account of a copper mine and its associated communities in early twentieth-century Alaska. He examines how a middle-class mother and wife living in the company mining town of Kennecott experienced nature and place differently from both a prostitute in nearby McCarthy and an unmarried 'ethnic' male miner living on the ridgetop at the mines. Whereas, for the miners, nature represented a forbidding place of work, for the professionals running the mine and their families, who visited a nearby lakeside tent resort in summer, it was a place of recreation. Cronon ponders the difference between two girls engaged in the same activity – berry-picking – one a Scandinavian immigrant and the other her immediate predecessor, an Ahtna Indian.[61] In this book, however, the social specificity of nature and its role as an instrument of power will be largely organized around the aforementioned eighteenth-century English case-study: the rearrangement of nature and people through enclosure and the creation of parkland (imparkation) (chapter 6).

Notwithstanding these efforts to produce a more historical nature and a more natural history, the scale of the remaining challenge can be illustrated by trends in global history. Alfred Crosby has remarked of Arnold Toynbee's ten-volume *A Study of History* (1951–4) that 'anyone who scans the indexes ... for such items as soil, rainfall, cattle, fish, disease, or extinction will be disappointed'.[62] But not much has changed. Despite its effort to wheel the common folk into the limelight and its studied avoidance of Eurocentrism, Felipe Fernandez-Armesto's 710-page *Millennium* has as many index entries for Canada as for Nature.

2

Ancient Greece and Rome

Since ancient Greek thought provides the bedrock for the Western intellectual experience, the ancient world is the natural starting-point for our investigations.[1] Indeed, forty-four of the sixty-six meanings of nature listed by Arthur Lovejoy and George Boas were already current in classical times.[2] Greek thinking about nature was inseparable from scientific, philosophical and religious speculation – themselves thoroughly intertwined. Aristotle (384–322 BC), from his premise that nature (*physis*) is everything outside culture (*nomos*), characterized nature in his *Metaphysics* variously as the origin of living things ('nature' comes from the Latin verb *nascere*, to be born); the 'immanent' part of a growing thing; the principle of life; and the source, constituent material or essence of something.[3] As Frederick Woodbridge comments on Aristotle's efforts to conceptualize the sum total of natural phenomena in his *Physics*: 'It is a theory of nature, that system of things which allows a plant to grow, an animal to graze, and a man to think, fully as much as it allows the sun to be eclipsed or bodies to be in motion or at rest.'[4]

Nature, in short, was an internal property rather than a physical territory, a principle and process rather than a material entity. From Greek investigations of the active principle or source of matter, for instance, derives the discipline of physics.[5] Greek ideas of nature also included deliberations over the properties of the human body and the relationship between matter and spirit/soul. That Woodbridge's book, *Aristotle's Vision of Nature*, includes a chapter entitled 'The History of the Soul' warns against too contemporary an approach to ideas about nature – one that reduces its coverage to those meanings and representations recognizable today.[6] At the same time, we should not overlook the convergence between ancient and modern approaches. Nor should we neglect the common ground between our worlds in terms of what has been done to the earth.

Ancient processes of environmental change

'Any ancient historian . . . not immersed . . . fully in the problems of ecology', Robert Sallares cautions, 'can have, at best, only a very limited comprehension of the course of history in antiquity.'[7] In his six-volume *Decline and Fall of the Roman Empire* (1776–88), Edward Gibbon concentrated on moral corruption and military, political, economic and financial problems. He discussed the difficulties of raising revenue to support massive standing armies, but without reference to declining soil fertility. Nor did he look into the problems of feeding the troops. The ecological challenges confronting the territories of the Roman empire – as well as ancient Greece and the urban civilizations of the Near East – were first highlighted by George Perkins Marsh in *Man and Nature* (1864). Marsh's reputation for classical scholarship, and his long periods of residence and frequent travels in the Mediterranean basin while serving as US ambassador in Constantinople, Turin, Florence and Rome, lent particular authority to his sombre findings.

In the opening pages of this pathbreaking study (subtitled *Physical Geography as Modified by Human Action*), Marsh examined how irresponsible tree-felling, grazing and farming had rendered one of the world's best-endowed regions barren and depopulated. From our vantage-point in an age of fossil fuels and nuclear power, it is easily forgotten how dependent ancient civilizations were on wood for cooking and heating (think of all the trees consumed by the furnaces in the ubiquitous Roman public bath!). 'Vast forests have disappeared from mountain spurs and ridges', Marsh remarked, adding that 'the vegetable earth accumulated beneath the trees by decay of leaves and fallen trunks, the soil of alpine pastures which skirted and indented the woods, and the mould of upland fields, are washed away'. By the fourth century, substantial tracts of Mediterranean woodland were confined to the less accessible upland regions of Macedonia, Corsica, Cyprus, Lebanon and North Africa.

The earth's moisture-retaining properties having been stripped away, 'rivers famous in history and song have shrunk to humble brooklets . . . rivulets have ceased to exist as perennial currents, because the water that finds its way into their old channels is evaporated by the droughts of summer'. Then, during the rainy season, 'sealike torrents' boomed down watercourses, literally transporting hillsides to the sea.[8] Silt made once thriving harbours high and dry while coastal cities the size of Leptis Magna in Libya (population 100,000) were stranded inland. At the height of imperial Rome's power, as demands on the land intensified, North Africa and Syria functioned as the metropolitan breadbasket. By the first century AD, North Africa was exporting half a million tons of wheat annually to the city of Rome, which was dependent on the region for two-thirds of its grain. Soon, however, this area was too barren even for olives.

Marsh went beyond a chronicle of environmental decay to develop a critique that attributed a powerful role to such factors in explanations of the collapse of ancient societies. Though he failed to exert any immediate or short-term influence, research has since confirmed that these civilizations overreached their natural resource bases. In the 1920s, Marsh was partly vindicated by the economic historian Mikhail Rostovtzeff, who attributed the food shortages, inflation and declining birth rate of the late Roman empire to an agricultural crisis, as land passed from an independent yeomanry to absentee owners of vast estates.[9]

The notion that environmental problems are largely a modern phenomenon is also belied by pollution in ancient cities from Babylon to Athens. Human waste and household garbage were discharged onto narrow streets and into rivers. With 1.2 million residents in the middle of the second century, Rome was the world's biggest city. Traffic congestion was already so acute under Julius Caesar's dictatorship (60–44 BC) that he banned wheeled traffic from sunrise to two hours before sundown. Moreover, mining affected many parts of the Mediterranean, contaminating watercourses with mercury, lead and arsenic.[10]

André Piganiol contended in the 1940s that 'Roman civilization did not die a natural death. It was murdered.'[11] He had external enemies in mind, not poisoning, but Jerome Nriagu, a geochemist, has argued that Romans unwittingly committed mass suicide through lead poisoning. Lethal compounds leached out from lead water-pipes and tableware while the popular dish *garum*, a highly acidic fish sauce, corroded lead utensils. Lead was also an ingredient in medications and cosmetics, and was added to wine for colour and bouquet. While all social sectors were affected, Nriagu holds lead poisoning particularly responsible for the withering away of the ruling oligarchy, afflicted with an inordinately high dose of stillbirths, sterility and mental degeneracy during the first two centuries AD.[12]

Though the reorganization and intensive management of the natural world is not readily associated with antiquity, environmental historians often cite the urban-agrarian civilizations of the ancient Near East as the original ecological cautionary tale. The Neolithic revolution, which replaced largely nomadic gathering and hunting cultures with mainly settled, agrarian lifeways, was inaugurated in the Near East. In the valleys of the Tigris, Euphrates and Indus, prehistoric agriculture evolved to its most elaborate stage. Around the fourth millennium BC, so-called 'hydraulic civilizations' (the phrase was coined by Karl Wittfogel in *Oriental Despotism and Hydraulic Society* (1956)) began to convert marshland and desert into farmland through extensive, centrally directed water control and redistribution. Salinization – the rising concentration of toxic salt in the soil due to evaporation, a problem often compounded by poor drainage and low humidity and rainfall – is an ecological backlash that usually springs to mind in connection with the latest version of hydraulic society in regions like southern California. In the Imperial Valley, irrigation has 'greened' the desert for agribusiness, but rapid soil ruination there has given fresh meaning to the old practice of shifting cultivation. Ancient Sumerian society disintegrated by using its soil no less remorselessly. The decentralization of settlements, fall in the number of occupied sites and the abandonment of land testified to the full-blown crisis that had taken hold by 1700 BC.[13]

Classical attitudes to nature and the natural world

This was not a case of land abuse in the modern sense. The forgotten majority who shaped the land with axe, plough and spade, but who left no formal record of their beliefs, were not acting in defiance of antiquity's sense of proper human comportment with the land. Lynn White argued that 'by destroying pagan animism, Christianity made it possible to exploit nature in a mood of indifference to the feelings of natural objects'. Because Christianity replaced the pantheistic outlook of societies such as those of ancient Greece and Rome with a monotheistic creed, removed God from the material world, taught that man was made in God's image and that all creation existed for human benefit, White lambasted it as 'the most anthropocentric religion the world has seen'.[14] Yet all agrarian and urban societies, whether ancient or modern, pre-Christian or Christian, are imbued with the imperative to domesticate the physical environment. Ancient thought was pervaded by the idea that civilization advances in stages, with humans progressing beyond an original condition in which they lived in a rude and savage state of nature, via pastoralism, into a more productive and pleasing state of cultivation. The environmental impacts of antiquity are those typically associated with a burgeoning population and an expanding empire. From 800 BC onwards, Greek colonization opened lands from the Crimea to the Iberian Peninsula to grain fields, olive plantations and vineyards. As early as the sixth and fifth centuries BC, in a bid to feed growing urban populations, Roman colonists busied themselves draining first the swamps around the Tiber estuary, then marshlands throughout central Italy.[15]

The fashioning of what the Roman orator Marcus Tullius Cicero (106–43 BC), referred to as 'a second world within the world of nature' was conceived of as a duty dictated by providential design that accorded with nature's own plan for its enhancement.[16] This conviction that the state of nature was just a starting-point – an idea inherent in the ward *nascere* – was eloquently expressed by Lucretius (99–55 BC):

> And day by day [men] would constrain the woods more and more to retire up the mountains, and to give up the land beneath to tilth, that on hills and plains they might have meadows, pools, streams, crops and glad vineyards . . . even as now you see all the land clear marked with diverse beauties, where men make it bright by planting it here and there with sweet fruit-trees, and fence it by planting it all round with fruitful shrubs.[17]

This teleological Graeco-Roman world-view located in nature a creator–artisan who wrought order out of chaos and instilled a common purpose in all creatures. Man was part of a great chain of being, but each link served the interests of the next highest stage, with man perched at the apex of the worldly realm (just beneath the gods). The earth was designed as a comfortable abode for man, and it is hard to identify the biblical injunction to subdue the earth as the root of anthropocentrism when the Greek Stoic Chrysippus (c.280–207 BC) had this to say about the purpose of creation:

> Here somebody will ask, for whose sake was all this vast system contrived? For the sake of the trees and plants, for these, though without sensation have their sustenance from nature? But this at any rate is absurd. Then for the sake of the animals? It is no more likely that the gods took all this trouble for the sake of dumb, irrational creatures. For whose sake then shall one pronounce the world to have been created? Doubtless for the sake of those living beings which have the use of reason; these are the gods and mankind, who assuredly surpass all other things in excellence, since the most excellent of all things is reason. Thus we are led to believe that the world and all the things that it contains were made for the sake of gods and men.[18]

All the great Greek and Roman thinkers endorsed the righteousness of human control: for example, Pliny the Elder (AD 23–79), who wrote extensively on agricultural matters, celebrated nature as a storehouse in his *Natural History* (AD 77). They assumed a sharp dichotomy between nature and culture. Man, set apart by his intellect, proceeds to mould nature through the practical arts of agriculture, forest clearance, fishing, domestication of animals, construction and mining.

Nevertheless, Greek and Roman confidence in the legitimacy of human interventions in the natural world and awareness of their transformative capacities were complemented by an appreciation of their ability to inflict damage. Eratosthenes attributed the retreat of forests on the coastal plains of Cyprus in the third century BC to pressures caused by copper and silver smelting. Lucretius's approving chronicles of human dominion over nature are tempered by chastening tales of the destructiveness of goats. ('The goat', René Dubos has commented, 'has probably contributed even more than modern bulldozers to the destruction of the land and the creation of deserts.'[19]) By far the best-known critique of environmental malpractice, however, is the account by Plato (c.429–347 BC), in *Critias*, of the consequences of excessive logging and grazing in the mountainous region of Attica, near Athens. Anticipating Marsh, Plato explained how heavy rainfall eroded bare slopes and adversely affected the hydrological cycle. Plato's metaphor of an emaciated person ('what now remains compared with what then existed is like the skeleton of a sick man, all the fat and the soft earth having wasted away, and only the bare framework of the land being left') might be dismissed as a vivid figure of speech. But recent authorities confirm that Attica used to be one of the most intensively farmed and thickly settled parts of the Greek world, and that it constitutes an exceptionally degraded environment.[20]

Though his observations have often been invoked by twentieth-century conservationists, Plato did not regard erosion as evidence of any fundamental malfunctioning. Clarence Glacken emphasizes that Plato's comments were uninfluential at the time, and Eugene Hargrove has insisted that not only was the prevailing intellectual climate inauspicious for the emergence of ecological thinking, aesthetic appreciation of nature and nature preservation; it was positively hostile.[21] Adopting a deliberately anachronistic approach, however, the leading environmental historian of antiquity, J. Donald Hughes, has been engaged in an overt search for a usable past since the 1970s. Eager to construct as long a historical pedigree as possible for contemporary 'green' ideas, Hughes explores alternative views such as the holistic ideas of Heraclitus (c.500 BC), who believed the cosmos was regulated by an unchanging law (*logos*), the nature poetry of the female lyricist, Sappho (*c.*630–580 BC), and the mystic vegetarianism of the mathematician, Pythagoras (*c.*530–500 BC): 'Were these . . . the early environmentalists we are looking for?' Three decades earlier, R. G. Collingwood had written about Pythagoras without mentioning vegetarianism.[22]

Pythagoreans, in accordance with their belief in the universal possession of a soul, thought all living creatures were rational and that they experienced the same range of emotions as humans. They devised a complicated series of dietary rules that permitted the consumption of fruits like apples and grapes, which did not involve the destruction of the plant itself, but proscribed vegetables such as beans. But we should not be over eager in our attempt to identify elements of today's ecological thinking in embryonic form. Pythagorean vegetarianism was nourished by a hierarchical theory of evolution according to which meat-eating by any life form reeked of lowly savagery. Pythagoras's own status as a vegetarian remains unclear despite his hagiographers' enthusiastic claims (none of his original writings survive). But the speech on behalf of vegetarianism attributed to him by his Roman admirer Ovid (43 BC–AD 17) expressed distaste for untamed beasts that 'delight in butchered food'.[23] Pythagoreans certainly wasted no love on predators such as tigers and wolves. Avoiding meat was ultimately a way to purify the human soul, on which Pythagoreans placed such a premium. And the belief in the separation of soul (*psyche*) and body (*soma*) came to dominate Pythagorean thinking.

Today's green thinkers often interpret Greek and other ancient European religious beliefs as being especially conducive to earth care. In 1972 the British chemist James Lovelock advanced the hypothesis that the earth operates as a single living organism with a self-regulating feedback system that maintains critical factors such as temperature, gases and ocean salinity at exactly the levels needed to ensure the healthy functioning of all life forms. At the suggestion of British novelist William Golding, Lovelock named his thesis after Gaia, the Greek goddess of the earth. Symbol of fertility, healing and renewal, Gaia rapidly became a green icon.[24]

Ecofeminists also find inspiration in antiquity, though they alight on an earlier epoch. Their case is built on wall art, vase decorations and engravings on seals and jewellery. This archaeological evidence includes numerous images of goddesses and life-affirming pictures drawn from nature; there is a marked absence of spears, swords and other symbols of authority and aggression. On this basis, ecofeminists argue (some more tentatively than others) for the existence, notably in early Bronze Age Crete, of a matriarchal society rooted in a belief system that revolved around ecocentric female deities.

According to Charlene Spretnak, the westward migration of Indo-European barbarians (Ionians, Achaeans and Dorians) in the later Bronze Age (*c.*2500–1000 BC) ruined this harmony by introducing a patriarchal mythology that worshipped a distant male sky god or gods, displacing the pre-Hellenistic earth-goddess religion and ushering in a male-dominated social system and warrior culture. Some ecofeminist theorists have interpreted the overthrow of female deities as the fateful moment when 'humankind' gave way to 'mankind', which began to isolate itself from the rest of nature.[25] 'Father-rule', argues Andrée Collard, 'destroys the moral relationship with nature characteristic of mother-rule by changing the concept of *nature* into one of *nation*.'[26] Since then, many ecofeminists contend, women have been systematically marginalized through a process of ideological dehumanization and derationalization (to adapt a phrase of Janet Biehl) that defines them in terms of their proximity to nature and stresses the attributes of irrationality, emotionalism and chaos that they supposedly share with nature – a tendency reinforced rather than initiated by the scientific revolution.[27]

Regardless of their sex (and many female deities were actually retained), Greek deities were overwhelmingly nature-based. They either represented elements of nature such as the sky (Zeus), the sea (Poseidon) or plants (Demeter), or they included parts of nature in their constituencies: wolves, lions and bears were devoted to Aphrodite while the creatures of the forest warmed to Apollo's musical skills. The correspondence between the domain of the gods and the world of nature encouraged the belief that the natural world was ordered and that parts were sanctified. To intervene in the natural world was to encounter these deities and run the risk of offending them, especially Zeus. The deterrence value of such beliefs is suggested by an incident that Hughes cites. When the people of Cnidus started to dig a canal through a strip of land connecting them to Asia Minor, some workers were hurt by falling rocks. The Delphic oracle was dutifully consulted, and replied: 'Do not fence off the isthmus; do not dig. Zeus would have made an island, had he willed it.' On hearing this, the labourers apparently downed their tools.[28]

Like Pan, the universal god of nature, most gods and goddesses dwelled in wooded and mountainous areas (notably Mount Olympus). So places of outstanding natural beauty were invariably selected for shrines and temples. Groves were favourite sites, protected from fire, grazing, ploughing, felling, horses and dogs. Particular trees were sacred to specific gods: the oak to Zeus, the black poplar to Persephone, the white poplar to Heracles, the laurel to Apollo and the vine to Dionysus. Wildlife in sacred groves was also technically off-limits to hunting, and sometimes even fishing was banned. Mountain tops were set aside too, though embellished with a summit throne or shrine honouring the local deity. Anyone who wielded an axe or weapon in the sacred grove might incur not only the wrath of a resident dryad (tree-dwelling spirit) but also that of the priest–guards who lived on site and, Hughes would have us believe, behaved rather like today's park and forest rangers. In some instances, protection was even formalized by legal ordinance.[29]

We should be aware, however, of the relatively modest areas involved. A grove at Daphne was 10 miles in circumference but most were much smaller.[30] The vast majority of Greek (and Roman) trees and animals enjoyed no divine association so could be chopped down or killed with impunity. Hughes finds the analogy with categories of land in today's United States irresistible. Sacred groves were 'the classical "national parks", small "wilderness areas" surrounded by vast tracts of "clearcutting"'.[31] Besides, protection within sacred groves was rarely absolute. Whereas some trees were never felled (they eventually toppled and rotted *in situ*), others (the spirit having been placated) were actually used to build the temples themselves, while additional structures such as hospitals and schools were sometimes allowed within the hallowed precincts. And when it came to a direct confrontation between a man-made image of a deity and a tree, the former usually prevailed, especially in Roman times. Hughes recounts a story from Pliny's *Natural History*: 'A tree growing in front of the temple of Saturn in Rome began to upset a statue. After appropriate sacrifices, the tree was cut down; the statue was not moved. It was a statue of Sylvanus.'[32]

The current debate over the rights of animals and our duties to them can fruitfully be located within the framework of ancient controversies over the relationship between matter and spirit; specifically, whether animals possess souls, intelligence, a sense of purpose, and the ability to reason and experience emotion. The Platonic/atomist tradition, building on the concept of the atom as the smallest indivisible unit of matter, demarcated sharply between spirit and matter. The material world was inert and inferior and the spiritual world alone, notably the soul, was seen as the proper object of the philosopher's attention – a *Weltanschauung* many environmentalists feel has dominated Western thought ever since, and which the better-known Cartesian dualism (see chapter 4) simply amplified.[33] Platonists insisted that the soul was an exclusively human commodity, uncreated and eternal, its aim being to free itself from bodily encumbrance. Though Plato characterized the living world of matter as a tomb, representations of his views in the early centuries of Christianity were more extreme, regarding all matter as imperfect at best, evil at worst. For Philo Judaeus (30 BC–AD 45), the body was the 'polluted prison' of the soul.[34] This Manichaean view of nature, which places the next world above the debilitating present, has been examined especially among the Greek Christian Fathers of the first four centuries AD by D. S. Wallace-Hadrill, partly in defence of Christianity against the charge that it devalued the natural world.[35]

Aristotle, Plato's most distinguished pupil at his Academy near Athens, stood apart from strict Platonists in maintaining that every form of life had a soul. He believed that people shared nutritional and procreational functions with plants and animals, and a sensitive soul with animals. This did not mean, however, that a dog's soul was comparable to a human's. Man enjoyed the greatest amount of soul quantitatively and qualitatively for he alone possessed the rational or intellectual soul. According to the criterion of rationality, Aristotle equated an animal with a human slave as an 'animate' tool and 'living piece of property', condemned by inferior intelligence to serve free men blessed with superior powers of reason.[36]

Other Greek philosophers were uncomfortable with this exclusive focus on soul and spirit, insisting that the body was also part of God's creation. Origen, an early Greek Christian thinker (AD c.185–252), pointed out how seasickness and fever turned the mind dull, drawing the larger conclusion that 'we human beings are animals composed of a union of body and soul, and in this way alone is it possible for us to live on earth'. In *On the Nature of Man*, Nemesius of Emesa, another early Church Father, promulgated a view of the world marked by gradations between inanimate forms of life, plant life, irrational animal life, animal life, mankind and spiritual beings. He mused over man's importance as a mediator between the lower echelons and the higher realms. While occupying the top slot in the phenomenal order, man is also a navigator, writer and thinker who contemplates the future and converses with God. The centre ground, straddling both worlds, was the right spot for man in Nemesius's view.[37]

On the question of intelligence, the Greek thinker Plutarch (AD c.50–120) disputed with the Stoics whether it was intelligence or simply instinct that prompted ants to store grain for the winter (biting each one to prevent germination), and goats and tortoises to eat certain plants to heal arrow wounds and snake bites. Intelligence was not the main criterion for Pythagoras, whose school became the most conspicuous rival to that of the Platonists. The crux of the matter was sentience – the capacity to feel pain – and in this respect he refused to distinguish between people and animals. Indeed, Hughes embraces him as an early 'defender of animal rights' (however ineffectual). The Greek Pythagorean Empedocles (*c*.492–432 BC) argued for vegetarianism in *Purifications* on the grounds of the universality of the soul and transmigration, explaining that 'in the past I have been a boy and a girl, a bush, a bird, and a silent water-dwelling fish'.[38]

Educated Greeks entertained some bizarre zoological notions by our standards, among them the belief that the bear gives birth to a formless lump and proceeds to lick it into bear shape, that bees breathe with their whole bodies, and that the hyena undergoes an annual sex change. Moreover, by being measured according to human standards, animals were defined as moral rather than biological creatures, characterized variously as lazy, brave, cowardly and industrious. According to Phocylides, the female character derived from four sources: beautiful women were descended from the horse, industrious housewives from the bee, dirty but essentially decent women from the sow, and violent, mean women from the bitch dog. These ideas attained their highest form in the animal fable – a short, cautionary tale featuring animals that serve as stock characters representing various traits – the best known being those associated with Aesop, a sixth-century BC Greek slave.

Though moral ordering preceded scientific classification, Greek natural history was fairly sophisticated in other respects. Roger French denies that any of this activity was scientific in the current sense of the word (a sense distinct from the general pursuit of knowledge, and which has only prevailed since the mid-nineteenth century). But others have detected traces of proto-ecological thinking, especially in the work of Aristotle and his pupil and successor Theophrastus (*c*.373–*c*.275 BC). The term 'ecology' is of fairly recent vintage (1866) but was foreshadowed in the notion of an 'economy of nature', widespread among natural scientists since the eighteenth century. Both 'ecology' and 'economy' stem from the ancient Greek *oikos*, meaning household. So while our understanding of ecological science may have lacked conceptual currency among the Greeks, Aristotle and Theophrastus endeavoured to understand the substances and processes of nature and the relationships between its constituent parts. Aristotle's *History of Animals* and *Parts of Animals* classified animals into vertebrates and invertebrates on the basis of direct observation and dissection, while Theophrastus's botanical investigations even extended to ruminations on the climatic changes resulting from deforestation.[39] (Aristotle, however, could still describe the attributes of a particular animal in great detail without thinking about how the animal interacted as a member of a species within a larger system.)

These are delicate matters, for there is no necessary correlation between ecology and ecological consciousness. The science of ecology need not reject a hierarchical model of nature and question mankind's status as supreme earthly being. Donald Worster, a leading historian of ecology, distinguishes between an imperial tradition, which regards understanding of the workings of nature as power over nature, and an arcadian/natural history tradition that tends towards the egalitarian/kinship model.[40] Though the former tradition has been historically dominant, for many today the litmus test of ecological credentials is denial that everything in nature exists for people and a democratic conviction that everything, including humans, is connected in a mutual support system. This 'Gaian' orientation was exemplified in the ancient world by Orpheus and the Orphic tradition stemming from the sixth century BC. Some of its features would even receive the seal of approval from today's deep ecologists and animal liberationists – specifically the belief that all forms of life are intelligent and possess souls and vital interests.[41]

In an effort to establish the distance between ancient and modern approaches, Matt Cartmill stresses that 'when ancient Romans spoke of *natura*, they were talking not about wild landscapes or the unspoiled countryside, but about something more like what we call natural law'.[42] On the other hand, the evidence of ceramic art, floor tiles, wall paintings (not least the frescos of Pompeii and Herculaneum preserved under lava following the eruption of Vesuvius in AD 79), sculpture and architectural motifs, as well as drama and poetry (whether epic, lyrical or pastoral), suggests that the ancient Greeks and Romans enjoyed and appreciated aspects of the natural world.

These sensibilities are most strikingly displayed in the perception of the countryside as a cure for urban ills. The origins of the myth of the countryside – the countryside being the most powerful symbolic landscape in Britain today – can be traced back to the growth of ancient cities. The distinction between urban and rural also became associated with the poles of culture and nature. As Varro, the Roman agricultural prose-writer (116–27 BC), expressed it, 'divine nature made the country, but man's skills the towns'.[43] Nor was this representation of nature as 'other' merely a literary affectation. It catered to societal cravings and served to shape a cultural mood. Archibald Geikie believed that the Roman pastoral genre powerfully influenced public taste and habit. Romans flocked into the countryside on public holidays, often by boat up the Tiber. Meanwhile, the patricians periodically retreated to their rural villas and estates.[44] The persisting Western tradition of the week-end cottage or lakeside cabin echoes the Roman search for respite from the stresses of city life, personal troubles and public office.

The first school of pastoral poetry coalesced around the Greek poet Theocritus (c.300–260 BC) in Alexandria, whose population was at least 300,000 in 60 BC, making it the largest city in the world after Rome.[45] Theocritus, who had substantial experience of country living (and arid lands) in Sicily and Egypt, vented his dismay at urban encroachment. The image of a cool shady grove through which flows a translucent stream dominates pastoral poetry from Theocritus's *Idylls* to Ovid. The most celebrated Roman pastoral poems, however, are Virgil's *Eclogues* (or *Bucolics*), which trumpet the virtues of the simple life, close to a serene earth, far removed from the corruption, vexation, excess and decadence of an urban existence increasingly designated as unnatural. Government policies of dispossession, whereby existing occupants of the countryside (including Virgil himself) were displaced to provide land for military veterans, provides the impetus for the events of the first poem. Yet the most enthusiastic exponent of the belief that a retreat from humanity brought deeper understanding of life's verities was Virgil's contemporary, Horace. 'Is the grass poorer in fragrance or beauty than Libyan mosaics?' he enquired in *Epistles* (20–17 BC), and contrasted the lead-piped urban water supply with that which 'dances and purls down the sloping brook'.[46] Appreciation of the countryside combined with affection for the countryman. In an arcadian tone akin to that of Thomas Jefferson's late eighteenth-century physiocratic paeans to agrarianism, poems such as Virgil's *Georgics* (composed between 37 and 30 BC in Naples) extolled the husbandman's self-reliance, celebrating honest, open-air toil as man's original pursuit.[47]

Yet were these sentiments anything more than literary posturing? In many instances, nature is deployed essentially as a foil for human activity, its alleged qualities of calm and permanence highlighting the tribulations and flux of city life. More hatred of the city is betrayed than love of nature. The presence of people (especially in the bloom of youth) accentuates nature's attractions. In their absence, nature can be intimidating. In Theocritus's *Idyll*, Daphnis exclaims: 'Spring is every-where, and everywhere the udders swell with milk and the young are nourished, where fair Nais wanders; ah, if she depart, more parched and thin are herdsman and herds!'[48] The pathetic fallacy – the conceit that nature reflects human moods, sharing humanity's joys and sorrows – is rife in ancient poetry. In his recitation *Lament for Adonis*, the Greek bucolic poet Bion (2nd–1st century BC), wrote that 'the wells of the mountains shed tears for Adonis; the flowerets flush red for grief, and Cythera's isle over every foothill and every glen of it sings pitifully'.[49]

Instances of nature observation and appreciation among the Greek Church Fathers qualifies the view that their elevation of mind over matter made them indifferent to or scornful of earthly things. Yet their tastes in nature were entirely consistent with the ideology of control. The earth might be animate (literally 'with soul', *anima* being Latin for soul), but it still existed to serve humankind. And though the bucolic poets may have boasted about living close to nature, the nature they worshipped was just as much the product of cultural intervention as the urban landscape. It is hard to superimpose nineteenth-century Romanticism onto classical Greek poetry, despite Homer's lavish descriptions of natural scenes such as the island of Ogygia to which Zeus sends Hermes in the fifth book of his eighth-century BC epic, *The Odyssey*. These poets were no latent Romantics leaping across torrents and swooning over the fragrance of wild flowers. Their typical 'outdoor manner' was that of the Greek Christian Clement of Alexandria (*c.* AD 150–215), whom D. S. Wallace-Hadrill praises for knowing 'what it is like jumping a ditch or smelling the dung in a farmyard'.[50] Small wonder that each Roman crop was protected by a resident deity. With reference to Odysseus's search for a decent harbour on the island of Aeolus, George Soutar remarks that 'the practical Greek liked a rock when there was a convenient cave in it'.[51] For the Roman bucolics, the happiest of men was the shepherd sprawled under a shady tree playing his flute. They sought what Leo Marx calls a middle ground between the two extremes, equally undesirable, of city and wilderness.[52]

A Scotsman who loved his native hills, Soutar was especially keen to locate evidence of Romantic feelings towards mountains. Yet he came away disappointed. He excluded opinions that mountains were fair because they furnished grazing for livestock. He also rejected respect for solitary heights because they were Pan's abode. Mountains 'did not move in them the sublime transports of Wordsworth but compelled thoughts of deity'.[53] Virgil came closest to an appreciation of wild country and wildlife. Yet even his approving references were brief and highly occasional. Whereas doves and nightingales were approved poetic material, hawks and other predators were illegitimate. The wolf threatened the poet's pastoral idyll as much as it frightened the farmer's flock. In *Georgics*, Virgil complimented Mother Nature for keeping lions and tigers out of Italy.[54] Romulus and Remus, the twin boys who, according to legend, founded Rome, may have been nurtured by a she-wolf but we have it on Plutarch's good authority that wolves were vigorously persecuted throughout the Roman epoch. Clement of

Alexandria articulated the classical consensus when he compared heresy to 'good land gone back to nature, bearing a crop of weeds, thorns and wild trees'.[55]

Current sensibilities may shudder, but the greatest expressions of awe and affection for wild places were connected with hunting. Alexander the Great's thrust into Asia acquainted the Greek world with parks and hunting reserves (*temenos* in Greek, *templum* in Latin). Greek fondness for the chase is suggested by its prominence in mythology. Though Greek women did not hunt (nor did Roman women), the most famous deity connected with the hunt was Apollo's sister Artemis (the Roman Diana).[56] The grove of Artemis, where Agamemnon poached one of her stags (a transgression for which she demanded his daughter's life), has been identified as 'perhaps the earliest example of a game preserve'.[57] The ethical hunter featured in Greek mythology as someone who was respectful of game sanctuaries and who was linked to his prey by a sacred bond.[58]

Any Greek tenderness towards wildlife was largely lost among the Romans, whose mass entertainments revolved around violence. These games (*ludi*) were initially dominated by gladiatorial contests. But according to the leading nineteenth-century historian of morality in premodern Europe, William E. H. Lecky, 'the single combat [of human gladiators] became at last insipid, and every variety of atrocity was devised to stimulate the flagging interest'.[59] Sometimes creatures were pitted against each other. Elephants versus bulls and bulls versus rhinoceroses were standard matches, though Nero (emperor, AD 54–68) once flooded an arena with salt water and set polar bears to devour seals. On other occasions, the spectacle took the form of staged hunts (*venationes*), during which animals were savaged by professional killers (not all of whom were male). The *venatio*, initially a morning prelude to the afternoon's main event – a confrontation between two gladiators – eventually became the main billing. These bloody encounters became a regular form of free entertainment. Under Trajan, emperor between AD 98 and 117, they apparently continued unbroken for 123 days.

The first *venatio* held in Rome has been traced back to 186 BC, from where they spread across the empire. They became so popular that in fourth-century Syria spectators would queue up overnight to guarantee a place. The number of animals involved grew and the brutality intensified as the Roman republic advanced in age. Tremendous body counts were recorded under the first emperor, Augustus (31 BC–AD 14): 3,500 animals were killed in twenty-six bouts. And to mark Titus's dedication of the Colosseum (seating capacity 87,000) in AD 80, 9,000 were massacred in 100 days – 5,000 in one day.[60]

Patricians enjoyed these spectacles, but the main constituency was the masses. Bankrolled by prominent public figures to curry favour with the plebeians, these games were an integral part of the strategy of social control that the satirist Juvenal (*c.* AD 55–128), famously called *panem et circenses* (bread and circuses).[61] The Roman establishment surmised correctly that gory extravaganzas would satisfy the emotions of the populace, rendering it more tractable. Lecky appreciated that spectacle was more important than bread: 'So intense was the craving for blood, that a prince was less unpopular if he neglected the distribution of corn than if he neglected the games.'[62]

To feed the appetite for staged massacres, suppliers scoured the Roman imperium. Units of the regular army were sometimes excused from customary duties to procure animals, which were also paid as tribute. Not surprisingly, the 'purveyors to the carnage' (Roland Auguet's phrase) have been blamed for the disappearance of the rhinoceros, zebra, hippopotamus, elephant and lion from North Africa, and the lion and tiger from the Near East.[63] However, the incremental elimination of habitat as agriculture spread, while far less dramatic, must not be overlooked. European lions were confined to northern Greece as early as the fifth century BC. In the case of the elephant's demise, their use as beasts of war and the ivory trade also need to be taken into account.[64]

In his Whiggish 'natural history' of European ethical advance, written at a time (the 1860s) when humanitarian sentiments were welling up in western Europe, Lecky expressed particular disgust over these Roman practices. J. M. C. Toynbee, an authority on Romans and animals (from elephants to tortoises), found it paradoxical that the Romans, whose art, sculpture and other creative media display such a strong interest in and appreciation of animal beauty, could delight in such cruelty. He was particularly puzzled and dismayed by the silence of the intellectuals. One of the few recorded protests is that of Cicero, who expressed his feelings about one of Pompey's *venationes* in a letter to a friend in 55 BC: 'what pleasure can it give to a civilized man when . . . a noble beast is pierced through and through by a hunting spear?' (The animals in question were African elephants, which had defended themselves heroically. Even the crowd was apparently appalled on this particular occasion.) Moreover, it appears that any elite disquiet usually entailed disapproval of what inflamed the masses rather than condemnation of cruelty as such. And Cicero acknowledged that the hunts were 'magnificent; nobody denies it'.[65]

While Toynbee was perplexed, an earlier commentator, Geikie, offered an explanation anticipating the phenomenon that Hannah

Arendt later identified in 1963 as 'the banality of evil'. Arendt used this to explain, with reference to Nazi extermination of Jews, how people who were not demons, killers or sadists by nature, and who were in many other respects decent and well-balanced individuals, could be conditioned into thinking of such acts as utterly normal.[66] Many Nazis retained a capacity for demonstrating tenderness in other areas of their lives. A concentration camp commandant might well fret over a thorn in the paw of the family dog when he got home from just another day's work. Likewise, in Roman times, as Geikie explained, 'the fashionable matrons who took such keen pleasure in the combats of the arena were often kind-hearted and careful mothers to their children. Many of them who sat as interested spectators through prolonged scenes of carnage and death would shed tears over the illness of some favourite bird or dog.'[67]

The degree to which ancient civilizations were callous in their treatment of animals and the extent to which they transformed and often damaged their physical environments should not be regarded as yet another regrettable deviation from high ideals. Despite all the noble dissenting views that historians like Hughes have resurrected, and regardless of the promising religious traits ecofeminists and environmental historians have drawn to our attention, the prevailing approach to nature in antiquity, which united the majority of intellectuals with the rest of society, was manipulative.

What remains fascinating is how fringe beliefs at variance with the temper of the times have been rediscovered by activist scholars. Lovelock's almost coincidental coupling of his thesis with Gaia not only ensured his book's commercial success. The book fostered a popular cult of Gaia that often fails to appreciate that the Gaia concept, by giving the impression of invincibility, can work against the environmentalist argument that the earth is fragile and threatened. The cult of Gaia has also led to selective interpretation of notions such as the world soul. The concept of the world soul, so prominent in Plato's *Timaeus*, did not promote the idea of nature as a precious and vulnerable earthly place in need of gentle handling. Yet this is how many enthusiastic environmentalists have characterized the idea of a cosmic spirit suffusing the entire physical body of the universe, each individual creature belonging to a collective rationality and sensibility. On the strength of such evidence, the ancients as a whole have been invested with an ecological halo. Jonathon Porritt, a leading British green in the 1980s, has bestowed the ultimate accolade by comparing their world-view to that of the American Indians.[68]

3

The Middle Ages

Environmental transformation is often approached as a function of modernity, largely inconceivable prior to the rise of capitalism and the scientific, agricultural and industrial revolutions. According to this view, the relationship between earlier societies and their physical environments – whether medieval England or pre-Columbian America – was essentially passive. Even if pre-modern dealings were not dictated by an explicit ethic of respect, it is frequently held that the natural world still benefited from benign neglect: pre-capitalist economies, if not stagnant, lacked dynamism, while technological capacity was rudimentary.

Popular treatments of the evolution of the English landscape typify this unsullied picture of pre-Tudor times. In *The English Panorama* (1936), Thomas Sharp remarked that 'a great part of the country was still in an unredeemed primeval state. In the fifteenth century an unbroken series of woods and fens stretched across England between Lincoln and the Mersey . . . Sherwood Forest covered nearly the whole of Nottinghamshire.'[1] The work of many literary and art historians also displays an unsophisticated understanding of material conditions. One pair depict the medieval landscape as 'a wilderness dotted with castles and churches', claiming that, in portraying the forest as a mysterious place of exile and hardship, the writers of high medieval romance were reflecting 'physical reality' for, until the late twelfth century, 'forest still covered most of Western Europe'.[2] But the extent to which woodland had already shrunk back by the tenth century is suggested by Clarence Glacken's story about the 'witty' Heriger, bishop of Mainz (913–27). When informed of 'a false prophet "who with many good reasons had advanced the idea that Hell was completely surrounded by a dense forest", he laughingly replied, "I would like to send my swineherd there with my lean pigs to pasture."[3]

As well as trying to reconstruct medieval environmental conditions, we must address Nature in an abstract sense and consider medieval relationships with the uncapitalized 'nature' that consists of a variety of individual physical entities. Some literary historians might have over-reached themselves in their attempts to construct a grand theory of Nature out of various scattered references and images. As George Economou muses, 'if the role of capital N *nature* in works of art cannot be concretely depicted or articulated, can we be certain it is there? In effect, I am asking when is a raven a raven, and when is it a symbol of a larger unit of meaning? When is the sea the sea, and when is it *nature*?'[4] Nevertheless, trying to figure out what people thought about nature is no less important than establishing how old a tree was and what its uses were. We should rejoice as well as fret over the adulterations of subjectivity. Images, myths and perceptions are worth studying, regardless of their accuracy as representations of the physical world.

Yet the environmental historian of the Middle Ages faces difficulties the modernist does not share. There was no group of medieval English landscape painters comparable to those of Italy or the Low Countries, so it is difficult to know what medieval England looked like.[5] Reconstructing the views of the great mass of people who left no written records is also daunting for the medievalist. The problem is compounded because most work on nature has been undertaken by historians of philosophy, theology and literature. A student may go beyond the secondary literature to the primary sources in the hope of achieving greater insight, only to find that medieval writers themselves were equally preoccupied with philosophical and theological matters!

The foreignness of many medieval understandings of nature to the late twentieth-century mind makes matters even more complex. When he refers to 'the discovery of nature' in *Nature, Man, and Society in the Twelfth Century* (1957), Marie-Dominique Chenu does not mean the arrival of a poetic appreciation for flowers and animals. He means an awareness of the universe as an external entity to be confronted intellectually. Chenu informs us about the idea of a world soul and the relationship between man as microcosm and the universe as macrocosm – specifically the parallelism between the cosmic elements of earth, fire, wind and water, and the human elements of flesh, blood, breath and warmth.

Though we learn nothing about flora and fauna or the lie of the land from Chenu, we do discover that Christianity is deeply implicated in every aspect of the life of the medieval mind. I include a discussion of Christian theology in this chapter because I am just as interested in recent 'green' reinventions of medieval Christian theology as I am in medieval attitudes in their own right.

The stages of the English natural world's recession

Despite its title, Charles Young's book *The Royal Forests Of Medieval England* (1979) actually tells us nothing about the appearance or com-position of a medieval forest. (Today's tree trunks are mostly bare due to air pollution. In the Middle Ages they were thickly encrusted with lichens.) There is not even a picture of a remnant medieval forest. Young was interested in the administration of forest law. But thanks to gleanings from conventional sources such as the Domesday survey (1086), and the endeavours of historical ecologists, historical geogra-phers and climate historians not afraid to get mud on their boots, we know a surprising amount about England's physical environment, cli-mate and natural resources during this largely pre-literate era. The main tools with which these earth-bound historians work are aerial photography, non-excavatory archaeology (including field observa-tion), pre-enclosure maps, the derivation of place-names and, increas-ingly since the turn of the century, the pollen analysis of stratified plant debris through core samples. The most useful source of evidence for animals and food plants – available since the 1970s – is archaeo-zoological and archaeo-botanical. Bones and pits in refuse piles tell us about the kind of fruit people put in their pies and the fish they ate. We can also find out about the relative numbers of sheep, cattle and pigs and what the state of a sheep's teeth reveals about the condition of the pastures (overgrazing caused gum disease).[6] Belying the conventional picture of stasis, nature's ascendancy and human impotence, what emerges is a vibrant picture of human intervention on land and inland waters.

The debate over the rate at which primeval England receded has dominated British historical ecology. The founding father of English landscape history in the 1950s, W. G. Hoskins, also subscribed to a pristine pre-industrial nature. He romanticized pre-Norman times, when 'vast areas' survived 'in their natural state, awaiting the sound of a human voice ... there still remained in the far west and north millions of acres of stony moorland haunted only by the cries of the animal creation, where the eagle and the raven circled undisturbed.'[7]

Yet the Norman conquest was no more a confrontation with 'virgin soil' than was the European invasion of North America launched by Columbus. Large-scale environmental transformation can be pushed back even beyond the arrival of cultivation with Neolithic peoples *c.*3500 BC. Thirty years ago, the standard view (consistent with prevailing attitudes to hunting and gathering peoples across the world prior to European contact) was that English hunters left few marks. England's physical environment was self-evidently nature's creation. It is still commonly thought that moorland and heath invariably signify land with soil too poor or wet for trees. Yet many heaths revert to woodland when the pressures of burning and grazing are relieved. Pollen analysis and charcoal remains indicate that *c.*7500 BC, at the onset of the so-called Mesolithic era (Britain's final hunter-gatherer cultures), today's heathlands were tree-covered.[8]

Well-preserved trees dating back 4,000–6,000 years, dug out of Pennine, North Yorkshire, and Dartmoor peat, supply further evidence that these areas were thickly wooded in the early Mesolithic era. Forest clearance through fire was a key Mesolithic hunting mechanism. It allowed browse plants to flourish, thus encouraging scattered animals to cluster, to the advantage of hunters.[9] Neolithic stone circles, whose construction required large cleared areas, are particularly telling evidence that many areas were treeless by the middle of the Bronze Age (a conclusion confirmed by analysis of molluscan fauna in the underlying soil profile). Oliver Rackham claims that half of England was no longer 'wildwood' by the early Iron Age (500 BC).[10] Just as population estimates for pre-Columbian America are being revised upwards, so are levels for prehistoric England as field archaeologists expose hitherto unappreciated numbers of settlements, fields and tracks. Emphasis on the active role of ancient Britons has serious implications for the traditional characterization of pre-Roman England as a largely unmodified 'frontier' environment and for the view that the Roman occupation in AD 43 triggered deep-seated changes.

Most British megafauna (such as the lion, leopard, bear and elk) vanished through pre-modern over-hunting and habitat loss. Bears and most beavers were probably gone when the Romans arrived. Wolves survived longer in areas such as the Forest of Dean, where the authorities recommended severe coppicing to expose 'wolves and malefactors'. But England and Wales had been cleansed of the wolf by the fourteenth century, though it hung on in Scotland a few more centuries.[11]

Substantially more land had been reclaimed by the time the Romans departed *c.*410. While some fenland returned to swamp as elaborate

Roman drainage systems collapsed, Hoskins overestimated the extent to which wildness was regained. According to Christopher Taylor, who in 1988 judiciously updated Hoskins's pioneering study, *The Making of the English Landscape* (1955), the Saxons encountered 'a crowded, totally exploited country, covered in fields, roads, towns, villages and farmsteads'.[12] Place-names offer additional insight. If many trees were cleared during a given period, one might expect this to be reflected in the names of places founded then. But the comparative dearth of names ending in 'ley' (a clearing in the wood) or 'hurst' (a settlement in a clearing) from the Saxon era suggests clearance was not an especially striking feature.[13]

Cistercian monks, arriving from France in 1128, have been credited with a pivotal role in deforestation during the twelfth and thirteenth centuries, which Hoskins identified as the period of most intensive clearance. Challenging the Benedictine establishment which they believed had strayed too far from hard work and the simple life that had characterized the original apostolic existence, their order encouraged them to farm in remote places (an impulse that scattered them from north-east Scotland's Moray Firth to Hungary). By the end of the twelfth century, some 230 Cistercian abbeys and priories had sprouted in Britain.[14] Many surviving ruins lie near open moorland, notably Fountains and Rievaulx abbeys in Yorkshire and Kelso and Melrose in southern Scotland. Some accounts refer to these farmer-monks as pioneers and accord them a frontier-busting role, in 'virgin area . . . never before subjugated by the axe and the plow', that is akin to the activities of Puritan settlers in seventeenth-century New England.[15] Comparisons of this nature are tempting but may fail to account for Cistercian allusions to 'wilderness' being ideological statements regarding religious identity rather than references to the actual condition of their physical environments. Bearing this in mind, it is still useful to compare the human and environmental impact of thirteenth-century Cistercians with that of seventeenth-century settlers in the New World. Both sometimes directly displaced local peoples. Walter Map complained how the Cistercians in England and Wales 'raze villages and churches . . . and level everything before the ploughshare' (c.1182–92), while Guiot de Provins, writing in 1206, protested that they 'frightened the poor and drove them from their land'. Archaeology corroborates these observations. Cryfield hamlet in Warwickshire was removed to build Stoneleigh Abbey and the foundations of the abbey at Pipewell, Northamptonshire, are intermingled with the earthworks of an earlier hamlet.[16]

Moreover, Rackham cautions against over-interpreting the mass of records which are available for the Norman period thanks to a Norman administrative revolution which multiplied the number of sources detailing land clearance, reclamation and settlement. Information from Domesday underscores that Britain was already well on the way to achieving its current status as the least forested country in Europe with the exception of Ireland. The paucity of wild boar bones unearthed in midden heaps confirms these findings. Even in the early Middle Ages, the boar's head on the banquet platter was likely to be that of the domestic male.[17] In 1086 only 15 per cent of England constituted woodland and wood-pasture, with only a further 5 per cent decline in woodland cover by 1350.[18] Any subsequent tree loss is statistically insignificant. Rackham's scrutiny of Sherwood Forest highlights these figures, puncturing its legendary mystique. At Sherwood's core today is a wildwood of late medieval oak trees with the characteristic 'stag head' of dead boughs. Already by the late thirteenth century, however, most of the forest had been converted to heath, with the percentage under trees probably less than a quarter of what forest law (see below) designated as Sherwood Forest.[19]

Climatic conditions have been assigned an influential and sometimes decisive role in the explanation of the economic and demographic trends reflected in these changes in the land. In a period characterized by temperatures a few degrees centigrade warmer than they would be in later periods, England's population escalated from 1.5 to 4 million between 1086 and 1300, during which period vast tracts of increasingly marginal fenland, forest and hillside were cultivated. By 1300, few valleys were unsettled, even in peripheral regions such as Cumbria.[20] Vestiges of ridge and furrow cultivation at 300–400 metres above sea-level and of vineyards in spots that now constitute frost hollows have been detected.[21] And pollen analysis of moorland in Devon and Derbyshire indicates that there was cereal cultivation at higher levels than is possible today.

Farming on marginal lands was proving unsustainable by the second half of the thirteenth century. With colder and wetter conditions after 1300, the incidence of cattle disease and poor harvests rose across western Europe. The resulting malnutrition, exacerbated by population growth and dwindling fuelwood supplies, aggravated susceptibility to the fourteenth-century epidemics of bubonic plague known collectively as the Black Death. 'The greatest biological-environmental event in history', as one historian hails the disease (another compares it to a nuclear holocaust), claimed 20 million lives across Europe. The death toll in England (1–1.5 million people over thirty years) represented 25–40 per cent of the population. Environmental repercussions were enormous as fields and villages were abandoned, marginal lands surrendered to brush and trees, and crops gave way to less labour-intensive pastoralism. In this way, many of today's downlands acquired their essential appearance.[22]

The medieval woods: from historical ecology to social history

What was left of marsh, moor and woodland by 1300 supplied local inhabitants with pasture for common grazing, thatching and flooring materials, timber, fuel in the shape of peat, gorse, heather and bracken, and livestock feed, not to mention fish and fowl. Given this intensity of use, conflict between users was frequent. Closer scrutiny shows that the so-called 'landscape of power' is a prominent feature of medieval history – 'landscape of power' being a term that human geographers have coined recently for a place that shows how the reconfiguration and appropriation of nature as property can be interlinked with human dispossession. As C. S. Lewis observed almost half a century before the 'landscape of power' concept became fashionable, 'what we call Man's power over Nature turns out to be a power exercised by some men over other men with Nature as its instrument'.[23]

Seeking to grab remaining areas of wetland and moor for their exclusive use, abbots, lords of the manor and the wealthier farmers denied their rich subsistence value and undercut their communal status, reinventing them as underdeveloped, unreclaimed 'waste'. Yet it is hard to surpass the forest as a contested terrain. Ordericus Vitalis's twelfth-century *Historia Ecclesiastica* (*Ecclesiastical History of England and Normandy*) records, if with excessive zeal, how William the Conqueror carved out the New Forest in the eleventh century by ransacking villages. Up to 2,000 people were displaced, according to a reliable account.[24] By the mid-thirteenth century, most remaining woodland was privately owned and heavily managed through pollarding and coppicing to provide items such as hurdles and fences. Many woods were protected from grazers with ditch, bank, hedge or pallisade. If the enclosure was also a hunting preserve governed by forest law, it would probably be marked off by an imposing wooden pale of cleft oak stakes – some of which survive – set upon a bank with the extra protection of an internal ditch (deer can jump 3 metres vertically and 6 metres horizontally).

We should not leap to the conclusion that medieval England was densely wooded because so much land was designated as 'forest'. 'Forest' was a legal, not a botanical, definition, meaning a place where deer were protected. Forest law was an effective royal device for maintaining tight control over land use by nobility and peasantry alike, with royal forest and forest law covering an estimated third of England at the height of the Norman era. The legal boundary of Waltham Forest in Essex encompassed 60,000 acres, but three-quarters was ordinary countryside.[25]

Not all royal forests doubled as game preserves, but the desire to arrogate hunting rights was often the overriding objective of forest law, which spawned a bureaucratic apparatus as regimentative as any in Western history. Norman forest law entailed fines for unauthorized cutting, grazing and building, as well as penalties for poaching (introduced by Richard I in the late twelfth century), such as blinding or castration.[26] The image of the heartless forest court meting out cruel and unusual punishment to hapless poachers, bound up with tales of the heroic exploits of those that defied them, remains one of the strongest popular visions of the Middle Ages.

William's seizure of forest resources was a major complaint in the *Anglo-Saxon Chronicle* (1087) and a prime source of grievance in the baronial confrontation with King John in 1215. The forest was the most hated aspect of royal authority throughout western Europe, with forest law especially oppressive in France. French courts dealt brutally with peasants who shot pigeons that fed on their newly planted fields or killed boar and deer that ate grain ready for harvest. Game wardens prohibited weeding and mowing before 24 June so as not to disturb nesting game birds. Peasants were also forbidden to remove stubble before 1 October as this provided vital cover for quail and partridge.[27]

When forest law was finally abolished, those who had been excluded plundered forest resources with glee. Jules Michelet cites an incident in the French Pyrenees from the early nineteenth century: 'whole trees were sacrificed for the most insignificant purposes; the peasants would cut down two firs to make a single pair of wooden shoes'.[28] At no point, however, did the excluded identify with deer as fellow victims. 'Disputes about the game laws', Keith Thomas explains, 'did not lead on to doubts about man's rights to hunt birds and animals, because the lower classes were as committed to the idea of human domination as anyone else.'[29] But Europe's underprivileged would not be able to enjoy access to what they considered the common property of fish, fur and fowl until the seventeenth century, when they were able to emigrate to Britain's and France's North American colonies.

Norman kings were so passionate about hunting that they introduced the fallow deer, now considered the characteristic English deer. As William of Newburgh remarked on Henry I's death in 1135: 'He

cared for the wild animals more than was right, and in public punishment he made too little distinction between a person who killed a deer
and one who killed a man.' Henry II's favourite resting-places as he
travelled the country were hunting lodges in royal forests. Gerald of
Wales even alleged that hunting was the primary occupation of a
wayward ruler. Hunting's importance to the elite and its status as the
only substantial recreational use of the natural world in the Middle
Ages is suggested by its choice as the representative activity for October by an eleventh-century English manuscript painter, whose work is
preserved as part of the Tiberius manuscripts in the Cotton Collection
at the British Museum.[30]

Through the vehicle of forests and hunting reserves, we have moved
from a discussion of historial ecology to questions of social control and
the pleasures of hunting. We now shift to the issue of the hierarchy of
life forms. When William of Newburgh castigated Henry I for his
excessive love of deer (hunting), he implied that the king had subverted
Christian doctrine regarding the rank of animals. It was clear enough to
William that to kill a man was a far graver offence than to slay a deer
illegally. For though the medieval Church officially disavowed hunting
as barbaric, endeavouring, if in vain, to get clerics to refrain from it, it
did not doubt the inferior status of the quarry.[31]

A Sunday newspaper report of an incident in 1963 illustrates the
tenacity in some quarters of this belief in the subordinate position of
animals. Two otters belonging to the naturalist and author Gavin
Maxwell (best known for his *Ring of Bright Water*) had been shot while
playing on a Scottish beach by a minister of the Church of Scotland.
Defending his action, the clergyman reminded a journalist that 'the
Lord gave man control over the beasts of the field'.[32]

The contribution of Christianity

Prior to the 1960s, theological works addressing the subject of nature
were innocent of ecological overtones. William Temple's *Nature, Man
and God* (1934) dealt with the distinctions between natural and revealed
religion (the latter based on the Bible and ecclesiastical authority, the
former on ideas derived from other sources); Eric Rust's *Man and
Nature in Biblical Thought* (1953) was an intricate disquisition on truth,
beauty, freedom and determinism. But during the turbulence of the
1960s, Christian beliefs began to be discussed in an unsettling new
context of nuclear fission, genetic engineering, soil exhaustion and
battery farming. Widespread public fears about the environmental con-

sequences of human interventions in the natural world were being voiced in Western society. Lynn White's thesis that the Judaeo-Christian tradition bore 'a huge burden of guilt' for the modern environmental dilemma was by no means unprecedented, but no critique enjoyed a comparable impact in scholarly and lay circles.[33] After 1967, no work of theology dealing with nature overlooked the role of religion in shaping our dealings with the natural world or ignored problems of pollution, wildlife preservation and natural resource scarcity. Rust's next book, which appeared in 1971, was *Nature – Garden or Desert? An Essay in Environmental Theology.*

The controversy focuses on whether Christian doctrine is hostile to or in sympathy with the recent upsurge in environmental consciousness, a debate often turning on the novelty of the Christian perspective.[34] The case for Christianity as a revolutionary development contends that its triumph over paganism stripped nature of its divinity. 'Desacralization', 'demystification' and, on occasion, the German *Entgötterung* are the key terms employed by critics. In depicting God as transcendent rather than immanent, Christianity, it is alleged, relegated nature to a position far below the divine. This divorce was deepened by the teaching that humans, created in God's image, are also separate from and superior to other creatures. The result was the unleashing of what world historian Arnold Toynbee has described as 'man's greedy impulse to exploit nature', which, in classical times, was 'held in check by his pious worship of nature'. From the perspective of 1971, Toynbee declared, Genesis 'reads like a licence for the population-explosion, and like both a licence and an incentive for mechanization and pollution'.[35] This explanation, which overlooks the possibility that Genesis might be a rationalization of processes already under way, accords a powerful role to the idealistic realm in that man's beliefs are treated as an antidote to his urges. It is often supplemented by the thesis that this new orientation laid the foundations for the eventual emergence of the ruthless modern Western scientific-technological world-view.

Trying to say anything definitive about Christian views on nature, based on the Bible, is as dodgy an exercise as trying to establish an early Christian attitude to women, alcohol, homosexuality or slavery.[36] Needless to say, the temptation has proved irresistible. We can find numerous warnings that to admire or worship nature itself – closely identified with the evil of material phenomena – is idolatrous. The millennial belief in Armageddon (the imminent destruction of the world as a prelude to the creation of a new heaven and a new earth, and the conviction that salvation involves liberation from the material world) also tends to be inimical to earth care.[37]

Those seeking to rebut these arguments stress that part of Genesis where God looks down on his material creation and pronounces it good. They insist that God (distinguished by love rather than authority) is present in his creation, cares about it, and is affected by its use. They reason that, since he has gone to so much trouble making the earth, humans are not free to disregard it. Modern green theologians explain that the glory, order, beauty and utility of nature have traditionally been regarded as a powerful argument – perhaps the most convincing one – for the existence of God. They have recruited the thirteenth-century St Thomas Aquinas to their side because this physico-theological argument for God's existence was the fifth of the five proofs for the existence of God that Aquinas identified. But it was by no means the most important proof for Aquinas. He made it quite clear that the 'book of nature' (natural theology) was subordinate and essentially supplementary to the the the 'book of God' (revealed theology).

The green gloss put on many medieval religious ideas by theologians conducting a damage limitation exercise is part of a denial that wanton exploitation of nature is man's prerogative within the Christian tradition. For Christianity's rehabilitators, 'rule over' need not translate into 'exploitation' or 'abuse'.[38] They explain that man's authority over nature, derived from his special status as God's earthly representative (vice-regent), is tempered by his special responsibilities and accountability. In the same spirit, ecotheologians have taken the metaphor of shepherd and flock that Augustine (354–430) used to characterize God's relationship to creation and given it a green 'spin' that transforms it into a 'source of ecological spirituality'.[39]

The view that man is higher than other creatures but does not possess absolute sovereignty over them (this is God's prerogative) is often referred to as the 'stewardship tradition'.[40] According to this way of thinking (a form of enlightened despotism?), abuse of nature is attributable to human sin, not divine purpose. Noah's ark provides these green Christians with a fitting metaphor for biodiversity because all animals regardless of utility were taken aboard. Likewise, passages such as that in Deuteronomy instructing us to spare the mother bird when taking eggs from a nest have been held up as evidence of biblical conservationist consciousness.

The arguments advanced by those appointed as advocates for the offending parties in the notorious animal trials of late medieval/early modern France and Germany highlight the malleability of Genesis. Early this century, E. P. Evans wrote a startling book about the conviction and public hanging of animals following secular legal proceedings that (short of public appearance in court) almost exactly mimicked human trials. Infanticide was the most common offence and the culprits were usually pigs.[41] In the fifteenth century another kind of trial appeared, an ecclesiastical affair, in which entire groups of animals – often insects – were accused of being a public nuisance. A few specimens were hauled into court to hear their sentence of excommunication pronounced. (One suspects that the disappearance of insects following excommunication was largely coincidental; they were simply moving to greener pastures having consumed every leaf and blade of grass locally.)

In the case of weevils accused of devastating vineyards in St Julien, France, in 1587, the defence lawyer's argument hinged on his interpretation of Genesis. Pierre Rembaud (who, like a number of lawyers at this time, made his reputation through such cases) argued that God had blessed and commanded all creatures to be fruitful and multiply. Evans paraphrases Rembaud's case thus:

> The Creator would not have given this command had he not intended that these creatures should have suitable and sufficient means of support; indeed, he has expressly stated that to every thing that creepeth upon the earth every green herb has been given for meat. It is therefore evident that the accused, in taking up their abode in the vines of the plaintiffs, are only exercising a legitimate right conferred upon them at the time of their creation.

The advocate for the plaintiffs (the local commune) insisted that, although insects may have been created prior to man, they were none the less intended to be subordinate and had no independent *raison d'être*. The prosecution suggested a compromise: allocation to the weevils of a desirable area outside the vineyards wherein people retained certain rights (to mine and extract water, to pass through and take refuge in time of war), provided that the insects' interests were not violated. The defence rejected this proposal because the earmarked area was too barren. The outcome of this case is unknown: vermin destroyed the last page of the official record. Evans comments wryly: 'Perhaps the prosecuted weevils, not being satisfied with the results of the trial, sent a sharp-toothed delegation into the archives to obliterate and annul the judgment of the court.'[42]

Notwithstanding the imagination and resourcefulness that early modern animal defence lawyers and recent ecotheologians have demonstrated in their efforts to reinterpret Genesis and to identify and resurrect marginal and forgotten aspects of the Christian tradition, the most influential interpretation has been despotic.[43] In this respect, early Christian theologians reinforced the existing logic of a dualism that downgraded the physical environment and enshrined the spiritual. The division of mankind into mind and matter, the removal of God from the earth, the elevation of humanity above the rest of creation, the fixation on heaven, and the admonition to the ascetic not to love this corrupt and inferior world also built on solid classical foundations, namely, the division of the world into 'us' (those with souls) and 'them' (those without). The biblical injunction that man should multiply, subdue the earth and have dominion over its creatures, often associated with Aquinas's notion of the the hierarchy of nature, was also essentially a reaffirmation of the arrangements in the ancient notion of a great chain of being. The idea that mankind is completing a divine task through his interventions in the natural world has also been served up as a telling point of convergence between the classical and Christian traditions.

To assert that one set of ideas parallels or echoes an earlier group of notions is one thing. Determining whether one influences another in any meaningful way is a different matter. Whereas Glacken emphasizes the independent foundations of Christian conceptions ('they were not Greek and Roman ideas in Christian dress'), John Passmore is so persuaded of the tenacity of Greek ideas that he refers to a 'Graeco-Christian tradition'.[44]

Regardless of the common ground that has since been identified, in some respects the early Christians presented the classical heritage as an obstacle to be overcome. Alert not least to the idea of nature as the creative principle at work in the universe, some early Christian theologians believed that the classical heritage attributed too much power to an autonomous nature. They were keen to establish that nature served God and had no independent moral force.

The Franciscan alternative

It is often assumed that Lynn White was completely estranged from Christianity. Yet he saw glimmers of hope in St Francis (1182–1226), whom he celebrated as the great exception to the arrogant anthropocentrism of the dominant Christian tradition:

> Francis tried to depose man from this monarchy over creation and set up a democracy of all creatures. With him the ant is no longer simply a homily for the lazy, flames a sign of the thrust of the soul towards union with God; now they are Brother Ant and Sister Fire, praising the Creator in their own way.[45]

In his essay, White nominated Francis as the patron saint of ecologists. In 1980 Pope John Paul II issued a papal bull from Assisi; in 1989 he concluded an unprecedented environmental address ('The Ecological Crisis: A Common Responsibility'), which reflected on the hole in the ozone layer and tropical deforestation, with a reference to his action in 1980. He praised the inspirational example of St Francis for keeping 'ever alive a sense of "fraternity" with all those good and beautiful things which Almighty God has created. And may he remind us of our serious obligation to respect and watch over them with care.'[46]

Francis is a striking example of our proclivity for making figures from the past over in our own image. Some moderns expect so much 'relevance' that they have expressed disappointment that he was not even more advanced – a vegetarian, for instance. Recent interpretations typify the distorting consequences of an unrealistic present-day expectation that Francis should conform to our own standards. The price is the neglect of those ordinary and typical aspects of thought that figures from the past shared with others of their era. Nineteenth-century Romanticism (especially in its German form) launched the modern process of reinvention by casting Francis as a nature mystic who spurned a go-getting society and ecclesiastical convention to roam the Umbrian countryside marvelling at nature's wonders and lavishing affection on birds and wolves – a medieval Wordsworth. More recent commentators (none of them medievalists) have polished this green image. Ralph Metzner even claims him as a near-pagan. Meanwhile, an incident during his Lenten fast of 1211 on Isola Maggiore in Lake Trasimeno has caught the imagination of modern animal liberationists; Francis encountered a rabbit in a trap and released it.[47]

Those focusing more directly on Francis have downplayed the novelty of his views. G. K. Chesterton's strong interest in egalitarian creeds and alternatives to industrial capitalism attracted him to Francis. In the biography of his hero (1932), Chesterton argued that Francis had no conception of 'nature' distinct from the specific items making up the natural world: 'He did not call nature his mother; he called a particular donkey his brother or a particular sparrow his sister.' Since Francis never bestowed an independent divinity on the cosmos itself (and never even used the word 'nature'), Chesterton finds it hard to see how he could be idolized as a Byronian lover of nature who adhered to 'sentimental pantheism'.[48] It was largely on the basis of his exuberant vernacular poem, *The Canticle of Brother Sun*, which contains the famous references to 'brother' and 'sister', that nineteenth-century Romantics claimed Francis as a kindred spirit. But the poem's view of creation is utterly conventional: external nature is good, a sign of God's providence and how God reveals himself to men. Nature's whole purpose is to make men more appreciative and respectful of God.[49]

That Francis firmly believed in a hierarchy of creation is indicated by his miracle-working shows. He granted birds permission to leave and commanded them to start and stop singing gestures that, according to Roger Sorrell, belong more to 'an abbot or priest than anything resembling a senator in a democracy'. His first biographer, Thomas of Celano, relates the story of how, while boating on the Lake of Rieta, Francis is given a live fish, presumably to eat. Instead, he calls it brother, releases it into the water and starts praising God. The fish, entranced, swims around the boat until Francis allows it to leave. In so far as it revolved around the natural world, Francis's evangelism differed from that of his contemporaries most conspicuously in the enormity of its zeal. Humans and the rest of nature were on an equal footing only in terms of their universal ability and duty to praise their maker. Nothing was exempt, according to Celano, not flowers and trees nor even stones. Sorrell is prepared to concede considerable originality to Francis, not least 'his extraordinarily sustained emphasis on things in the environment as beneficent instead of ambivalent'. Yet he is steadfast that even if Francis thought and did recognizably modern things, his motivations were profoundly medieval.[50]

In so far as a cardinal tenet of ecological consciousness today is a tender feeling towards once reviled wild carnivores, evident in the reintroduction of the wolf in the American Rockies (while some hope to restore it to the Scottish Highlands), Francis falls well short. His much-admired non-aggression pact with the hitherto incorrigible wolf that apparently terrorized the Umbrian village of Gubbio hardly evinces an appreciation for the natural lives of wolves. In full accordance with the saintly tradition of transforming wildness with a view to restoring the prelapsarian vision of the perfect kingdom promulgated by Isaiah, where the lion lies down with the lamb, Francis tames and pardons the old rogue. In the words of another thirteenth-century biographer, St Bonaventure, he 'subdued ferocious beasts, tamed the wild, trained the tame and bent to his obedience the brute beasts that had rebelled against fallen mankind'.[51] Francis wanted animals to be more civilized, condemning the reformed wolf of Gubbio to a meek life of penance as he crept from door to door begging for food. (We are not told what the townsfolk of Gubbio gave him to eat. Let's hope it wasn't straw.)

Sorrell's denunciation of the great exceptionalist approach to Francis is part of two larger agendas. While deploring the excesses of recent green reappraisals, he believes that the firmer rooting of Francis within the mainstream Christian tradition demonstrates its potential for internal change. His denial of Francis's radicalism also belongs to a broad attack on what he sees as the wholesale misrepresentation of medieval attitudes to nature. Inseparable from his contention that Francis speaks just as much, if not more, to his own age as to ours is a far more favourable assessment of medieval conceptions of nature. Sorrell claims that most historians have drawn unfair general conclusions largely on the basis of a single strand of interaction with nature of which they heartily disapprove: the ascetic tradition whereby monks withdrew to wild places, which they allegedly detested because of their fear of demonic temptation via the sensory world. This approach to nature as cursed and threatening, he argues, has been taken as *the* medieval view.[52]

Medieval approaches to nature

A closer look suggests that the ascetic tradition in particular and the wider monastic tradition in general were actually associated with many positive trends of thinking about nature according to the standards that have become increasingly accepted over the past 150 years. Monks were identified as a special breed of nature-lover by the Count de Montalembert in *The Monks of the West, from St. Benedict to St. Bernard* (1861). Noting their choice of majestic sites for monasteries, Montalembert explained how the splendours of external nature were seen to reflect God's beauty.[53] The eremetic tradition has now been so dramatically reassessed that our picture of monks (so annoying to Sorrell) has been largely transformed. The shock troops of agrarian and Christian colonization, merrily chopping down sacred groves, have metamorphosed into rapturous nature-worshippers. Green scholars are especially enamoured of ascetics and anchorites who forsook society to imitate the biblical experiences of Jesus's forty days and the Israelites' forty years in the wilderness (described in Exodus). Their role model is the 'desert father', Anthony (born *c*.251), who withdrew to do penance in the wilderness of the 'interior desert' between the Nile and the Red Sea, where he and other hermits enjoyed gentle and co-operative relations with wild creatures such as lions, leopards, wolves and wild asses.[54]

But retreat into the wilderness as a spiritual proving-ground did not automatically bestow independent value on wilderness or signify approval of it. English Puritans who migrated to New England in the early seventeenth century also situated themselves within the Exodus tradition. Their quest for the promised land of Canaan did not promote fondness for the wilderness condition itself. Once again, delight in wild places is most clearly expressed in connection with hunting (and even this is highly tangential). Note how St Basil (aka Basil the Great, *c*.330–79) explained the attractions of his newly established hermitage above the River Iris in Pontus (north-east Asia Minor, near the Black Sea). After describing the hills, forest, river and fields to his close friend Gregory of Nazianzus, he added:

> the highest praise, however, which I can give to the place is that, although it is well adapted by its admirable situation to producing fruits of every kind, for me the most pleasing fruit it nourishes is tranquillity, not only because it is far removed from the disturbances of the city, but also because it attracts not even a wayfarer, except the guests who join me in hunting.[55]

Hermits and Franciscans are not the only promising objects brought back by those who have scoured the Middle Ages in search of a usable green past. René Dubos has proposed St Benedict of Nursia as a far more appropriate patron saint of ecology than St Francis. The debate over the relative merits of Franciscans and Benedictines is a telling example of a reductionism that approaches medieval thought in terms of its applicability to contemporary discussion of conservation and ecology.

Shaping his assessment of the Benedictines was Dubos's basic conviction that, since change in nature is natural and biological systems are dynamic with no end state in mind, the natural world can be transformed without qualitative losses. He also believes that true conservation is all about fashioning human attitudes and activities that foster a working relationship with nature.[56] He rejects the 'leave nature alone' mentality, which he associates with the Franciscan approach, for its limited relevance to a densely populated planet in which people have no choice but to impose on the natural world, virtually none of which remains in an unmodified state anyhow.

The Benedictines established their major monastery at Monte Cassino (midway between Rome and Naples) in the early sixth century (where St Benedict (*c*.480–*c*.544) is reputed personally to have hacked down the pagan sacred grove). The Order's relationship with nature (as distinct from its members' lives in a more general sense, which revolved around prayer and worship) was organized around work (mainly gardening and farming) rather than following a contemplative or recreational pattern. 'Saint Benedict believed that it was the duty of the monks to work as partners of God in improving his creation or at least in giving it a more human expression', comments Dubos approvingly. 'Implicit in his writings is the thought that labor is like a prayer which helps in recreating paradise out of chaotic wilderness.'[57] The Order's Cistercian offshoot won Dubos's particular approval. The most direct inheritors of the bucolic tradition of antiquity, Cistercian monks equated a beautiful landscape with a productive one. This is clearly seen in the images of pastoral bliss that saturate St Bernard's twelfth-century *Description of Clairvaux*. (Clairvaux, of which Bernard was abbot, was a cloister located in a valley at the base of the French Alps.)

The number of hermits and monks was tiny, however, in comparison with the size of the peasantry. 'The parasitic members of the church hierarchy were shut off from nature', argues a Marxist scholar, 'whereas the common people were forced to make a living by dealing directly with both domestic and wild animals.'[58] Closer to nature they may have been in a technical sense, but this left little room for an aesthetic 'feeling for nature' to develop. The instrumentality of their relationship is suggested by the medieval manuscript-painters, who depicted calendar months in terms of seasonal outdoor activities. September showed peasants cutting corn and swine feeding on acorns. Pruning was the chosen activity for February, ploughing for March and the tending of sheep represented May. The medieval peasant believed that the changing of the seasons, and the suffering involved in winter, were directly attributable to God's curse on the land, where eternal spring and summer had once reigned. Special saints were 'charged' with ensuring the right kind of weather: the sixteenth-century stained glass window in a church in Côte d'Or, France, depicts St Médard, a rain mediator, and St Barbara, guardian against thunder and lightning.[59]

The tenuous human hold over nature and concentration on its capricious and dangerous qualities may help explain why the townsfolk of Falaise, Normandy, sent a pig to the gallows dressed in human attire in 1386. Too much time and effort were devoted to these trials for us to dismiss them as mere foibles of a cruel and irrational medieval mind. Nicholas Humphreys argues that the perception of the world as a chaotic, lawless place offers the best insight into these trials. He sees the treatment of damage and death caused by animals as crimes in a human sense (with the offending animals assumed to be fully cognizant of what they had done and aware that they must pay the penalty) as part of an effort to impose order and meaning on an unpredictable world.[60]

The medieval peasant's apprehension hardened into fear and loathing where nature in its wilder forms was concerned. Unmodifed nature in one of the finest examples of Irish illumination, the early eighth-century Book of Kells, is a place of spiritual anxiety.[61] In his *Life of St. Guthlac*, the eighth-century monk Felix recounted how Guthlac was confronted in his search for a suitable retreat in the watery fens of East Anglia by the 'manifold horrors and fears, and the loneliness of the wide wilderness'.[62] (Such terrors were not entirely metaphysical. Ague and malaria thrived in the damp conditions.) The image of wilderness as terrestrial hell also coloured the depiction of the monstrous Grendel's lair in the epic poem *Beowulf* (eighth-century?), which is a vivid written embodiment of what was surely a venerable oral tradition. To reach the mere at the heart of forest darkness where Grendel and his mother dwell, the intrepid hero Beowulf must penetrate 'a land unknown, wolf-haunted slopes, wind-swept headlands, perilous marsh paths'.[63] White claims that Christianity drained nature of its vitality, but during the early Christian centuries (witness *Beowulf*) it still teemed with spirits. *Beowulf* may have been more pagan than Christian in this respect, but this does not signify that people in the eighth century had a sense of affinity with the enchanted mountains and forests. Animistic beliefs do not necessarily promote reverence for nature.

By the standards of Old English poetry, the evocation of the bewildering haunts of the sinister fiends in *Beowulf* amounts to a sharp portrayal of the physical environment. But even these memorable scenes will impress today's reader as inchoate and fuzzy. *Beowulf* typifies the allegorical approach to nature and landscape that pervades much medieval fiction and visual art. While we cannot claim that an interest in nature for its own sake is entirely absent, you rarely feel that the artist or poet is concerned to recreate a particular scene.[64] Natural scenes are usually invoked for their heavenly or hellish qualities.

If rugged places were bracketed with hell, gardens were invested with heavenly qualities. Medieval conceptions of paradise, both earthly and celestial, fed off various established traditions of affection not only for gardens, shady groves and other pastoral locales but also for hunting reserves: the term 'paradise' (*pairidaëza*), whose literal meaning is 'walled enclosure', was originally used for the Persian nobility's hunting parks. Representative medieval ideas of terrestrial Eden inform *Paradiso* and *Purgatorio* by Dante Alighieri (1265–1321) (part of his *Divine Comedy*), in which paradise features as a fruitful plain encircled by ravines and gorges representing a place of exile.[65]

Whereas Dante viewed gardens in allegorical terms, they served the aristocracy as potent status symbols. A rage for enclosure gripped the western European elite by the twelfth century, and the appeal of this new landscape distinct from city and countryside was mirrored in literature, particularly the poetry of Geoffrey Chaucer, who visited many royal gardens. Privacy and intimacy were key features of these pleasure gardens (not to be confused with plots for raising medicinal and culinary herbs).[66] The characteristics admired in Jean Froissart's *Le Joli Mois de May* (late fourteenth/early fifteenth century) were refinement, organization, order and regularity. The gardens receiving the highest approval were those that looked almost as if they had been sculpted. One garden, as described by Froissart, 'was exactly marked out, and bounded by a thick, firm hedge, evenly cut; the shrubs looked as if they had been trimmed to a precise pattern'.[67] Groves were painstakingly planned and planted to mimic outdoor rooms, sporting grassy floors, leafy ceilings and wooden pillars (and preferably bursting with deer).

Other depictions of the garden were openly hedonistic. Nature in its springtime garb supplied an appropriate stage for the sensual pleasures of human courtship. The description of a lawn in Guillaume de Lorris's thirteenth-century French poem, *Roman de la Rose* (*The Romance of the Rose*), as translated by Chaucer, is strongly suggestive:

> Sprang up the grass, as thicke yset
> And softe as any veluet,
> On which men myght his lemman [lover/mistress] leye,
> As on a fetherbed, to pleye.[68]

In a passage memorable for its analogy with the sexual geography of American youth in the 1950s and 1960s, Laura Howes emphasizes the medieval garden's function as vehicle for 'courtly dalliance':

> Manuscript illustrations show numerous couples engaged in the medieval equivalent of 'heavy petting', especially when seated, and it seems to me likely that the ubiquitous turf bench – well hidden within walled gardens from the prying eyes of curious onlookers – was the medieval equivalent of the backseat of a Chevrolet.[69]

Gardens aside, there are fewer signs in medieval literature of the urbane pleasures widely extracted from the natural world by the elite of ancient society. The collapse of urban culture during the Dark Ages and the distance this had imposed between people and the natural world provides a large part of the explanation. Christian disapproval of the sensory world also played a role in the submergence of nature's good qualities. The natural world's positive appearances are mostly confined to a personified Natura, who operates as a secondary creative force (the 'vicar of God') to give form to what Thomas Aquinas called 'the wax of things'.[70] According to this way of thinking, the fashioning of a garden out of chaotic waste did not amount to the conquest of an original nature. Nature, having no previous identity, came into being through the garden.

The allegorical approach created more than just hellish wildernesses and heavenly gardens. It taught that nature as a whole was a book of lessons through which God instructed people how to behave – the natural world having the inestimable advantage of being a 'book' accessible to all in a largely unlettered and illiterate society. This so-called emblematic tradition (or natural theology), was first clearly articulated by the Greek Stoics, one of whom argued that fleas had a role in the larger scheme of things because they awakened the lazy by biting them, while mice were a warning against untidiness. 'Nature study' in the Middle Ages meant a search for sources of morality. The busy ant was 'a sermon to sluggards', from whose activities one could learn the virtues of industry.[71]

The Book of King Mode and Queen Reason, published in France in 1486, distinguished between two types of creature – 'sweet beasts' (*bestes doulces*) and 'stenchy beasts' (*bestes puantes*). The book gave the deer pride of place as the sweetest animal. The deer drinking at a stream symbolized the soul's quest for God and stood for religious devotion and striving. One further example will suffice to illustrate the function of what Joyce Salisbury dubs 'illusory' animals.[72] The pelican was reputed to feed its young on its own blood, a trait taken to be symbolic of Christ giving life to mankind through his blood. 'In such a world', remarks White, 'there was no thought of hiding behind a clump of reeds actually to observe the habits of a pelican. There would have been no point in it. Once one had grasped the spiritual meaning of the pelican, one lost interest in individual pelicans.'[73]

As a result of the intellectual changes in western Europe associated with the so-called twelfth-century renaissance, the received wisdom runs, the allegorical tradition was eventually superseded by a more naturalistic mode of understanding. Descriptions of animals were increasingly derived from the methodology of what we now understand by natural history.[74] Such assertions have been stimulated by a reappraisal of a popular genre, the bestiary (a generic term for a popular book containing information about real and imaginary animals, usually thought to exemplify the allegorical, moralizing tradition).[75] The most scientifically astute work of this kind is the zoological treatise of Emperor Frederick II of Hohenstaufen on birds associated with hunting, *De Arte Venandi cum Avibus* (*c*.1250). As it marked the culmination of a tendency to use falconry as a springboard for probing the role of birds in the wider community of nature, grandiose claims have been made for its status as the antecedent of modern experimental science.[76]

At the same time, Frederick's work remains alive with allegory. As nature acquires new meanings it does not necessarily shed old ones. Intellectual change, like change of any kind, is rarely swift, neat or complete. Tradition and innovation usually coexist during an extended transitional period distinguished at most by a gradual movement away from the past. In the specific instance of the medieval artist's representation of animals, this took the form of a slow but conspicuous shift towards an anatomical authenticity grounded in direct experience – a phenomenon exemplified for one commentator by the appearance of the flexible knee joint in pictures of elephants! A similar impulse, described by Otto Pächt as 'the courage . . . to look nature straight in the face', was affecting the depiction of plants. Fourteenth-century seeds came to fruition in early fifteenth-century Italy, when herbal illustrators such as an anonymous Paduan ditched the tendency to draw an entire plant, as hitherto required by the 'abstract conception of the botanical specimen'. That the anonymous Paduan (anticipating Leonardo) might just draw a flower, leaf or single branch indicates to Pächt that he was more interested in 'the empirical truth of the one-sided view' than 'the lifeless completeness of an abstract image'.[77]

Moreover, the impetus for change often emanates from the old. Instead of seeing the symbolic tradition as the epitome of a naïve, pre-scientific view of nature, Salisbury discerns elements of modernism within it. Under the pressures of the twelfth-century renaissance, the symbolic tradition proved itself to be far from monolithic and static. Collections of morally instructive animal fables (exempla) became extremely popular in the thirteenth century, being widely drawn on for sermons. Salisbury contends that

> early Christians established a view of the world that posited a chasm of difference between humans and animals; the use of animals as human exemplars suggested, however, that the two species were sufficiently similar that animals could be imagined to act like people, to possess personalities like people, and thus to offer models for human behavior.[78]

Leaving aside questions of the subversive tendencies of the allegorical approach, traces of emblemism persisted into the seventeenth century, when the mole represented the papist who was too blind to see the error of his ways, and the caterpillar symbolized the Resurrection.[79]

The impact of the twelfth-century renaissance was not restricted to attitudes to animals and plants and their portrayal. Whereas earlier medieval writings give the impression that people are barely coping with the natural world, we can now begin to detect more confidence in the human capacity to understand, use and regulate nature and natural forces in all their forms through analytical enquiry. This new sense of authority (and of the legitimacy of such enquiry) was born of an increasingly complex society marked by the rise of the professions and the founding of universities.[80]

It also emerged against a background of economic expansion, urbanization and technological innovation that resulted in substantial environmental modification, not least of fresh waters. The quality of aquatic ecosystems deteriorated through soil erosion, the discharge of human and animal waste, and the effluent of tanneries. The proliferation of water-mills impeded migratory fish. The increase in population also placed heavier demands on fish as a food source, encouraging the spread of artificial ponds. These pressures were reflected in changing dietary patterns. By the 1400s, wealthy Parisians were eating carp rather than trout and salmon. Carp, once rare in western European waters, now flourished in the warmer, reedier and quieter waters that were replacing the cold, clear, gravelly conditions preferred by trout and salmon.[81]

Some scholars have established a special relationship between changes in technology and attitudes to nature. Lynn White, whose speciality is the socio-economic impact of medieval technology and who leans towards technological determinism in his book *Medieval Technology and Social Change* (1962), zeroed in on a single dramatic invention as the crucial divide between the old nurturing and the new rapacious attitude to nature in Europe. The so-called 'scratch' plough, entirely adequate for the lighter, drier soils of southern Europe, barely made an impression on wetter and heavier northern soils. But in northern Europe in the late seventh century appeared the iron ploughshare, a heavy-duty device that, to quote White, 'attacked the land with such violence' that cross-ploughing was made redundant. But it needed eight rather than two oxen to pull it, which had major repercussions for patterns of land distribution, now dictated not by 'the needs of a family' but by the capacities of 'a power machine'. In this way, asserts White gravely, 'man's relation to the soil was profoundly changed. Formerly man had been part of nature; now he was the exploiter of nature.'[82]

A less idiosyncratic case can be made for a technologically associated shift in perceptions during the twelfth century. Whereas White erected his hypothesis on a solitary item, those arguing for the twelfth century as the crucial divide can cite the mill-wheel, the windmill, the fulling mill, the clock, the three-crop rotation and the hard collar for draught animals as evidence that some Europeans were progressing from fear of change to active pursuit of better means of transformation. The fulling mill deserves special mention because it marked the first extension of water-power to an industrial procedure. (E. M. Carus-Wilson was so impressed by the fulling mill and windmill that she invented a thirteenth-century industrial revolution, while the amount of inventiveness between the tenth and fourteenth centuries prompted Jean Gimpel to refer to a medieval industrial revolution.)[83]

At the core of what was in some ways the rediscovery of a classical ambition was the desire to explain the rhyme and reason of the universe that dwelled on the complementary roles of God, man and nature: God creates basic raw materials, after which it is nature's responsibility to keep things going and man's role to fashion them into products in an open-ended creative process. David Herlihy calls this 'ecological triumphalism', defined as 'a belief that man the maker can shape the world according to his needs and multiply his own numbers with impunity'.[84] For Charles Bowlus, the Gothic cathedrals of the twelfth and thirteenth centuries symbolize technological derring-do. Indeed, these awesome structures resonate with a sense of human mastery over nature no less potently than do the skyscrapers of early twentieth-century New York City and Chicago. Symbolism aside, the environmental impact of cathedral construction was enormous. One hundred square metres of timber were needed for every square metre of stained glass. And think of how many large timbers the frames of cathedrals such as Ely in Cambridgeshire consumed, not to mention the quantity of stone gouged from the earth.[85]

Chenu argues that it is during the twelfth century that nature becomes something predictable and dissectable, and that the seminal triumph of mechanism and secularity over animism and divinity occurs.[86] Though sharing Chenu's and Herlihy's sense of the greater importance of the later Middle Ages for subsequent developments than the earlier advent of Christianity – or the later emergence of Renaissance humanism or capitalism for that matter – Karen Jolly is far more judgemental of the modernism ushered in during the twelfth century. Though in agreement with Carolyn Merchant regarding the causes of the 'death of nature' (see chapter 4), Jolly dates nature's demise to about five centuries earlier, isolating the twelfth century as the key stage in the victory of the rationalistic, patriarchal view of nature over the mystical/supernatural one. In the earlier Middle Ages, she claims, the natural world bristled with messages from God, and its workings were inexplicable without recourse to an elaborate cosmology of angels, spirits and demons. The new rational empiricism despiritualized nature by introducing the privileged category of supernature. Whereas supernature was immutable and transcendent, nature was material, observable and transitory. As Ian Wei has explained:

> The separation of natural and supernatural made it possible to define a realm (the natural) within which human reason could seek explanation without undermining beliefs about God. God could be recognized as the primary cause of everything, but secondary causes could legitimately be sought within his creation.[87]

Jolly identifies a transitional period between the seventh and eleventh centuries during which Christianity progressively ousted paganism, introducing a distinction between early Christianity and its later, mature, form. Unlike White, she highlights the similarities between early Christianity and paganism, seeing the change as one of degree rather than kind. Belief in an animate nature was retained, though nature was increasingly inhabited by a monotheistic God instead of a variety of pagan spirits.

Against Jolly's conclusions and Chenu's and Herlihy's identification of a later medieval ecological triumphalism more frequently associated with the Renaissance (see chapter 4) must be set a growing appreciation of nature, evident in its more detailed and credible portrayal through various media in addition to herbal illustrations. From the late thirteenth century onwards, manuscript illustrations grew more naturalistic.[88] And as the ancient forests shrank, the hostile sentiments of *Beowulf* were challenged by odes to the beauty and soothing purity of the wildwood, such as the Irish poem 'The Frenzy of Mad Sweeney'. In Gottfried von Strassburg's *Romance of Tristan and Iseult*, the unruly forest's role as a sanctuary for social outcasts – in this instance illicit lovers – might be thought to modify its reputation as a place where people lapse into barbarism (though another reading might feel that a barbaric place was the perfect resort for two people who had already lapsed into barbarism). With the waning of the Middle Ages and the wildwood, the growth of the benign image of the greenwood threatened to overshadow the forest's gloomy and savage reputation.[89]

This fresh view of nature reached its apogee across western Europe during the fourteenth and fifteenth centuries in the shape of a new realism that Kenneth Clark dubs a 'landscape of fact'.[90] Emanating from the great urban industrial centres of Flanders and northern Italy, this mode attained its highest expression in the style of the Sienese painter Ambrogio Lorenzetti and the sixteenth-century Flemish artist, Pieter Brueghel, whose paintings were based on direct observation as well as on tradition, memory and imagination, while their philosophical and aesthetic meaning derived from actual form rather than symbolism.

According to Clark, the single most important intellectual influence was the Italian humanist Francesco Petrarca (Petrarch). In 1336, when in his early thirties, Petrarch apparently climbed Mont Ventoux, one of the highest peaks in the Provence Alps. This ascent has acquired a hallowed status in accounts of the emergence of appreciation for the wilder aspects of the natural world ('he was, as everyone knows', asserts Clark, 'the first to climb a mountain for its own sake, and to enjoy the view from the top').[91] The majority of his peers certainly considered mountains more or less coeval with the Fall and the Flood, the devil's hideous abode. The folk view was no more sympathetic. As Chaucer's country squire shudders in *The Canterbury Tales*:

> *But, Lord, thise grisly, feendly rokkes blake,*
> *That semen rather a foul confusion*
> *Of werk than any fair creacion*
> *Of swich a parfit wys God and a stable,*
> *Why han ye wroght this werk unresonable?*[92]

The pleasure Petrarch took in the view, and how it inspired him to reflect on creation, as described in a letter to a friend, is usually hailed as a revolutionary ejaculation (witness Clark's assessment). True, he did not shudder with horror when he reached the top after climbing all day ('The great sweep of view spread out before me, I stood like one dazed'). Nor did the feeling that he was obeying the biblical injunction to lord over nature well up within his breast. But whether he was smitten with a proto-Romantic sense of awe and sublimity – the impression given by Jacob Burckhardt – is less certain. To assert that Petrarch was enjoying the scenery pure and simple – and to leave it at that – lumps his experience together with the uncomplicated response of today's thousands who go weekend walking in the Alps. But before quitting the summit, Petrarch delved into St Augustine's *Confessions*, which he invariably carried. Though Augustine did not teach that the earth was to be detested on account of its patent inferiority to God, he constantly warned against confusing the created with the creator (for him the fundamental sin of paganism).

Petrarch apparently opened *Confessions* at random and – as if admonished by higher authority – came across the passage warning men to concentrate on their salvation instead of being seduced by scenery: 'I was abashed, and . . . I closed the book, angry with myself that I should still be admiring earthly things who might long ago have learned . . . that nothing is wonderful but the soul.'[93] Overcome with shame, he recovered a traditional sense of perspective on the way down to his hostelry: 'I gazed back, and the lofty summit of the mountain seemed to me scarcely a cubit high, compared with the sublime dignity of man.'[94] Petrarch had redeemed himself and man was reinstated. The mountain had been put back in its proper place. Conceptions of nature's sublime dignity were still a few centuries away.

4

The Advent of Modernity

The German philosopher Martin Heidegger liked to use the metaphor of a gigantic petrol station to suggest how humanity has reduced the natural world to a resource to fuel its bottomless tank.[1] We have already encountered various attempts to locate the origins of this exploitative mentality in antiquity, Judaeo–Christian doctrine and the twelfth century. Other efforts to discover its taproot have isolated more recent 'paradigm shifts'.[2]

Theodore Roszak, a prominent figure in the American counter-culture of the late 1960s and early 1970s, argued in *Where the Wasteland Ends* that the pulsating green world of the pre-industrial era turned grey and bleak as mankind experienced a decisive alienation from nature between the Renaissance and the scientific revolution. Snared in a 'technocratic trap', people desacralized nature, a process furthered during the Enlightenment. Roszak's perspective on the Renaissance and his approach to humanism as a synonym for anthropocentrism – the belief that meaning stems from human sources and that nothing has value independent of the human valuer – has been emphatically restated by the environmental historian, John Opie: 'Nowhere, not even in today's world of technological dominance, has absolute human autonomy been more radically set forth than in the Renaissance.' Identifying 'humanity's solitary self-affirmation as a unique creative force in the cosmos' (a monstrous presumption to medieval thinkers) as the Renaissance's crowning achievement, he announces that people 'no longer believed that they "belonged" to the natural world'.[3]

The ecofeminist historian Carolyn Merchant places her emphasis on a later period. In *The Death of Nature*, she identifies the seventeenth-century scientific revolution as the handmaiden of capitalist modes of production that 'accentuated human impact . . . over and above effects attributable solely to population pressure'. By transforming nature from a living organism into a machine – simple, unfeeling, inert matter with no intelligence, soul or purpose – the new mechanistic philosophy assisted the commodification of nature and fuelled the cancerous ethic of 'growthism'.[4] Another favourite whipping-boy is the eighteenth-century Enlightenment. With its stress on man as master of his destiny and the supreme explanatory power of reason, the 'Enlighten-ment project' is pinpointed as the locomotive of 'modernity', that which separates our rationalist, capitalist, science- and technology-worshipping world from its predecessor. According to John Gray, who has launched the most strident attack on the humanist ethos, 'the real legacy of the Enlightenment Project to humankind' has been the subju-gation of nature.[5]

   The role of the Industrial Revolution in translating this world-view into highly visible environmental change has led others to pronounce it *the* watershed between today's impoverished world and the nature we have lost. Instead of trying to substantiate or undermine the claims made for a particular epoch or phenomenon, however, it is more helpful to treat their influence as cumulative, not least because they overlap considerably chronologically rather than being, as the various labels suggest, sequential. Though generally associated with the seven-teenth century, the so-called scientific revolution is frequently dated from Nicolaus Copernicus's *On the Revolutions of the Heavenly Orbs* (1543). Meanwhile, flexible conceptions of the Renaissance as a way of thinking and an age rather than a particular period in time ('the age of the Renaissance' versus 'the Renaissance') extend the epoch well into the seventeenth century and far beyond Italy to include both Francis Bacon and René Descartes.[6]

The repercussions of Renaissance humanism

For all its disruptive impact in other respects, the Reformation added little to Christian thinking about nature. Protestantism questioned vir-tually every existing source of authority save that of humans over the natural world. The Lutheran view that nature was cursed, and the Calvinistic notion that it was man's duty to God to subdue the earth, reinforced existing beliefs. However, the 'scholastic' or Aristotelian view (based on the medieval reading of Aristotle) that the investigation of the material world was subordinate to the exploration of the spiritual realm and the contemplation of God's perfection, with its accompanying ways of thinking about the natural world that were primarily religious and symbolic, was challenged by intellectual developments associated with the Renaissance.

In his classic work *The Civilization of the Renaissance in Italy* (1860), the Swiss historian Jacob Burckhardt argued for a new spirit of rational, secular humanism based on 'the development of the individual' nurtured by the the revival of classical learning and hospitable political institutions. Burckhardt portrayed the product of these forces, 'Renaissance Man', as a proud and confident colossus with a 'can-do' mentality. Liberated from theocracy and other restraints, his feet and mind anchored firmly in the secular world, this Promethean being thrust out across the globe.[7]

Though many of Burckhardt's central tenets have been squarely challenged (what precisely was meant by the 'dignity of man', and was the 'march of reason' really so inexorable?), his view of the Renaissance remains the most influential one (at least among generalists). But Renaissance man (and woman) might not have been quite so self-assured and assertive as Burckhardt would have us believe, and whatever individualism did exist within the consciousness of a highly restricted social elite may have been encouraged by forces that Burckhardt neglected, notably the spread of urbanization and the emergence of capitalism, whose origins are often traced to the market economies that developed in the fourteenth- and fifteenth-century mercantile city-states of northern Italy.[8] Nevertheless, in so far as a distinct humanistic ethos can be identified, from it flowed the modern scientific study of the natural world informed by theory and experimentation. Many medieval minds explained both natural disasters such as the plague and social calamities as God's revenge for human pride and sin.[9] Nature's ways and forces were largely unpredictable and uncontrollable – strictly God's realm, on which humans did not trespass. Various Renaissance thinkers confronted this mood of resignation with the desire to figure out how things worked and the conviction that humans can make the world in which they live. The full range of natural phenomena were now considered legitimate for study, entirely knowable and at man's disposal. These convictions redeemed nature in that they questioned the medieval suspicion of earthly things as sinful. They are evident over the next few centuries in a range of investigations, from Michelangelo's dissection of human cadavers as part of the anatomical studies that helped him paint, carve and sculpt images of the body, to Leonardo's studies of the effect of dew on gourds and Newton's gravitational theories. The more naturalistic, secular, detailed and direct recordings and representations of nature that had been emerging since the twelfth century thereby attained wider currency.

We may be inclined to approach what Ernst Cassirer called a 'new lay knowledge' of the world, one based on immediate experience of nature (thanks to which the pelican becomes a bird rather than a symbol of Christ), as a huge step forward in the appreciation of nature. R. G. Collingwood argues hopefully that the Renaissance belief that meaning in nature was indwelling rather than imposed 'lent a new dignity to the natural world itself. From an early date in the history of the Movement [the Renaissance] it led people to think of nature as self-creative and in that sense divine, and therefore induced them to look at natural phenomena with a respectful, attentive and observant eye.' Burckhardt had also devoted a subsection of his seminal book to the 'discovery of the beauty of landscape' by poets and artists. For Burckhardt, nature had medicinal properties: when the artist–architect Leon Battista Alberti (1404–72?) was unwell, 'the sight of a beautiful landscape cured him'.[10]

But the secularization of the pelican was slow and uneven. Perhaps the best-known example of the pious pelican is to be found on the reverse of Pisanello's medallion of an acclaimed early Renaissance educator at Mantua, Vittorino da Feltre. As Michael Levey explains, 'Vittorino's devotion to his pupils is allegorized on the reverse of the medal in a crisply compact design of a pelican in its piety, feeding its young by pecking at its own breast.'[11] Moreover, creatures may have lost more than they gained through the divorce from piety. The display of weird and wonderful animals from Africa and Asia in menageries was a favourite Renaissance means of showing off both monetary wealth and human mental capital. The message was that 'animals might be strong, but man, because of his superior intellect, was stronger'.[12] There is little to suggest a humble attitude towards nature at this time. The new Copernican astronomy (publicized in 1543, after Copernicus's death, since he was too afraid to go public during his lifetime) was shocking because it demoted earth to a minor position within the grand cosmic scheme. Nevertheless, its erosive implications were largely restricted to ecclesiastical authority. Heliocentrism did not threaten human power over nature on earth.

The scientific revolution

Those who prefer a historical approach that stresses continuities and the intensification of existing impulses rather than radical shifts in outlook might interpret intellectual developments between the Renaissance and the Industrial Revolution as the secularization of the dominant thrust of the Western religious tradition. White tied an umbilical cord between the formative years of Judaeo-Christianity and the modern 'Baconian creed that scientific knowledge means technological power over nature' (a view inserted into the mainstream of economic history shortly afterwards by David Landes's notion of 'Faustian mastery' over man and nature).[13] The most White does to counter the strains on credibility posed by the identification of a direct connection between such widely separated eras is to emphasize the scale of early medieval advances in science and technology.[14] This scarcely enhances his case, however. If the impetus that Christianity supplied to the evolution of science and technology was really so powerful, White must still account for a gap of many centuries (quite apart from explaining ancient Graeco-Roman and Islamic science and why they were far closer to modern science than were medieval manifestations). White's view that Judaeo-Christianity was pregnant with implications for the development of science and technology stretches the umbilical cord to snapping point, while the notion of latency is stripped of any real meaning.

The case for the scientific revolution as the crucial divide has proved more popular. The unholy trinity of Francis Bacon, René Descartes and Isaac Newton – Lewis Mumford dubbed them 'Lords of Nature' – has joined Christopher Columbus at the forefront of the Western evironmentalist's rogue's gallery of what I like to call DDWEMs (Dead but still Dangerous White European Males – a variation on the better-known DWEMs). These three leading theoreticians of the scientific revolution vie for the status of supreme bogeyman in many environmentalist accounts.[15] Astronomers Johannes Kepler (1571–1630) and Galileo Galilei (1564–1642) are usually left out of green searches for the evil midwives of modernity – perhaps because they left fewer quotable epigrams. But their insights were fundamental to Bacon, Descartes and Newton. Kepler was by no means the first to use the image of a clock to describe the workings of the universe (the French mathematician and bishop Nicole Oresme had done so in 1370), but its association with the mechanistic outlook is often attributed to him. In 1605 Kepler characterized the sun as a machine-like force dictating planetary movements: 'My aim is to show that the celestial machine is to be likened not to a divine organism but rather to a clockwork.'[16]

The image of Galileo with his telescope serves the ecophilosopher, Max Oelschlaeger, as a springboard for a profound point about the scientific revolution's alienating effect. Galileo thought in terms of primary and secondary qualities, introducing a distinction between objective knowledge and subjective understanding/feeling. Whereas the former was real and measurable (mathematical), the latter was merely human and intuitive: 'Through the telescope Galileo confirmed the Copernican hypothesis. What he lost was the sweeping field of view of naked eye astronomy, the relation of the Milky Way to the starry sky, and the movement of the wandering stars across the ecliptic plane.' Oelschlaeger speculates further:

> And perhaps, in his intense concentration, he lost also the sounds and smells of the night and the awareness of himself as a conscious man beholding a grand and mysterious stellar spectacle. Galileo was standing no longer within nature, but outside it. He became a scientific observer apart from nature, for it had been replaced with a theoretical object of inquiry.[17]

Galileo gave nature an abstract existence apart from humanity, but its meanings and values remained to be found and bestowed by the human mind.

It is not primarily on account of their innovative ideas, or because they directly or indirectly inspired great masses of people, that I single out Bacon, Descartes and Newton for special attention. These luminaries feature here mainly in their capacity as spokesmen who articulated most effectively those areas of shared thought that sprang from the needs of particular groups. Since the early modern construing of the relationship between humankind and nature presupposed the existence of all previous stages of thinking on this matter, Bacon, Descartes and Newton are best approached in terms of their collective impact. There is an argument, however, based on convenience, for taking them in chronological order.

Many commentators over the past two decades have found no ambiguity in the beliefs or purpose of the man who inherited the Renaissance idea of mastery over nature through knowledge and expressed it with peerless aplomb. In the writings of Bacon (1561–1626), nature is forever being moulded, enslaved and penetrated. Goodies and secrets are wrested or coaxed from her. For Bacon, knowing nature was not an end in itself. His aphorism, 'human knowledge and human power meet in one' (usually abbreviated to 'knowledge itself is power'), was no mere rhetorical flourish.[18] The goal of what Max Scheler in the 1920s dubbed *Herrschaftswissen* ('knowledge for the sake of dominion') was manipulation and mastery. With Bacon, the question 'what is nature?' became inseparable from 'what can we do with nature?'[19]

Bacon wrote most expansively about the social implications of science, and in terms far more accessible to the layperson than Descartes. The most complete and eloquent expression of Bacon's views is found in his utopian tale, *The New Atlantis* (published posthumously in 1627). On the fictitious island of Bensalem, an enlightened, technocratic despotism of paternalistic scientists labours selflessly for the public good. From their power-base in Salomon's House, a prototypical scientific research institute (generously state-supported yet autonomous!), this apolitical scientific priesthood conceptualizes its activities directly in terms of the eminently modern idea of progress as improvement in the material condition of humanity through ever deeper control over nature:

> We make (by art) in the same orchards and gardens, trees and flowers to come earlier or later than their seasons, and to come up and bear more speedily than by their natural course they do. We make them also by art greater much than their nature, and their fruit greater and sweeter and of differing taste, smell, colour, and figure, from their nature.[20]

What previous generations might have seen merely as harmless horticultural dabblings and ambitions have been given a sinister spin by recent green commentators. Those who dwell on human contempt for natural processes focus on those aspects of Bacon's thought and writing that approach nature as a set of measurable, rearrangeable, infinitely malleable components. The only recognized limits on interference with natural processes are those of human ingenuity and contrivance. Detractors are fond of quoting the 'reductionist' sentiments of a prominent neo-Baconian, Joseph Glanvill of the Royal Society of London. Through chemical techniques, explained Glanvill in 1668, 'nature is unwound and resolved into the minute rudiments of its composition'. Working with the telescope, microscope, thermometer and barometer, the professed aim of chemistry, mathematics and anatomy was to enlarge what Bacon liked to call 'the bounds of Human Empire'.[21]

For Carolyn Merchant, the harnessing of the atom epitomizes the dangers of the prevailing 'unnatural/non-natural' world-view derived from Bacon. (Her *Death of Nature* closes with a reference to the near-disaster at the nuclear power plant at Three Mile Island, Pennsylvania, in 1979.) It is certainly hard to read passages about improving fruit such as that quoted from *New Atlantis* without thinking of irradiated strawberries and genetically engineered tomatoes.[22] If we follow Merchant's reasoning, today's biotechnology becomes the logical outcome of the Baconian imperative: Bacon rendered the square, unbruisable tomato thinkable.

Merchant's argument was partly anticipated by Marjorie Hope Nicolson, who wrote in the 1950s of the 'death of a/the world'. She advanced this thesis with reference to the demise, through the mechanistic ideology of seventeenth-century science, of the idea of an organic, animate and female Earth and world soul, one predicated on a bodily correspondence between man (microcosm) and the natural world (macrocosm). In Nicolson's view, men and women alike rued the passing of the old living world (encapsulated in the Elizabethan metaphor of 'the circle of perfection'). But Merchant introduced an environmentalist's perspective – Nicolson was mainly interested in seventeenth-century lyrical poetry – and distinguished between men and women, asserting that the new outlook 'sanctioned the domination of both nature and women'. While it couched itself in the rhetoric of universalist, value-free and disinterested service to humankind, she argues that the new science was a white, middle-class male product calculated to serve this constituency's interests.[23] Merchant draws attention to Bacon's penchant for sexually aggressive metaphors and fondness for the language of torture and inquisition. She and other commentators also view the spate of witch trials during the reign of James I as symptomatic of this climactic stage of human dissociation from nature, arguing that the patriarchal enterprise of modern science debased women by strengthening their association with lust, animalism and diabolism.[24]

Though the new world-view retained the femininity of nature, Merchant contends that this nature was transformed into a woman who can be freely violated. This assertion requires a positive view of Renaissance conceptions of nature. This Renaissance outlook, in her mind, was derived from Greek ideas of the universe as an intelligent being, a living unit of interconnected and interdependent parts. Its central feature was the hierarchical chain of being, within which man straddled the animal world and the celestial realms, while God was immanent throughout. To illustrate how these cultural constraints worked to curb behaviour prior to the scientific revolution, she cites ancient strictures against mining as a violation of the earth's living body, a rude rifling of her bowels, rupturing of her veins and revealing of her inner secrets.

In Roman times, earthquakes were interpreted as nature's revenge for such transgressions. However, when mining began to take hold in areas like Saxony in the late fifteenth century, allegorical tales sympathetic to mining begin to appear. One of these cast nature as a mean stepmother 'who wickedly conceals her bounty from the deserving and needy children'.[25] Merchant also discusses changes in artistic depiction with reference to former protests against the unconsented probings of metallurgists, alluding especially to an image in a poem by Alain of Lille (1160), in which humans unlawfully take advantage of Natura, ripping her undergarments:

> The constraints against penetration associated with the earth-mother image were transformed into sanctions for denudation. After the Scientific Revolution, *Natura* no longer complains that her garments of modesty are being torn by the wrongful thrusts of man. She is portrayed in statues by the French sculptor Louis-Ernest Barrias (1841–1905) coyly removing her own veil and exposing herself to science. From an active teacher and parent, she had become a mindless, submissive body.[26]

A host of ecofeminist treatises contending that women and nature share a common stigmatization as 'other' lean on these arguments for historical validity.[27] Contrasting with Merchant's flattering assessment of the Renaissance mind is John Opie's view that its hallmark was the belief that everything in the universe revolved around man as a unique, all-powerful entity who no longer cowers in God's shadow: Bacon's 'Promethean' ethic was not so much a novelty as an embodiment of what Opie calls the 'man-intoxicated' spirit of the Renaissance.[28]

Others will remain unconvinced by the argument that impulses toward a more ruthless exploitation of the earth were bottled up until they were uncorked by the arrival of startling new ideas. For this implies schizophrenia or repression. New ideas may inaugurate fresh practices but they also serve to formalize and rationalize existing practices.

René Descartes (1596–1650) supplied the steeliest intellectual reinforcements for the concrete of modernism in terms of its attitude to living creatures. What is remarkable about Descartes's thinking is not the apartheid between spirit, mind and culture on the one hand and matter, body and nature on the other, but the confidence in our ability to enforce this segregation. This so-called Cartesian dualism, most famously expressed in his *Discours de la méthode* (*Discourse on Method*) (1637), acknowledged the Graeco-Christian division of the world into the separate and unequal realms of mind (*res cogitans*) and matter (*res extensa*), the former irreducible, impenetrable and disembodied, the latter entirely knowable and manipulable. For Descartes, the act of thinking was the criterion of existence (*cogito ergo sum*) and the status of humans as thinking beings ultimate proof of their separation from the rest of creation. Leaning heavily on Baconian method, the Cartesian reduction of everything into its simplest constituent parts left nothing larger than the sum of these parts – substances required 'nothing but themselves in order to exist'.[29] The workings of nature likewise became mere movements stripped of any larger purpose or connections.

The ramifications of Cartesian dualism are generally thought to have been gravest where animals were concerned. Since the greatest potential common bonds between people and the natural world were with animals, they offered the stiffest challenge to the attempt to sever humans from nature. Accordingly, animals had to be dealt with most harshly of all. This required considerable ingenuity, not least the re-interpretation of mental activities related to the body, namely the experience of sensation and sense perception as 'thought' and their annexation to the human side.[30]

Animals, Descartes insisted, were mere automata regulated by the same principles as the clock and with no more capacity for pain or pleasure. Vivisection was practised by Bacon's fictitious scientists at Salomon's House, but Cartesian convictions allowed experimentation without anaesthetic for anatomical investigation (in which Descartes was personally involved) to proceed without serious pangs of conscience.[31] A society increasingly governed by clocks was predisposed to the Cartesian approach.[32] In a footnote to the section of *Capital* (1867) dealing with machinery and modern industrial forms, Karl Marx remarked that Descartes 'saw' animals 'with eyes of the manufacturing period'. It was Descartes, rather than Bacon, in John Passmore's view, who supplied the philosophical 'charter of the Industrial Revolution'.[33] Descartes, *persona non grata* with the humanitarians of the animal welfare movement since the mid-nineteenth century, became the chief ogre of the animal rights movement in the 1970s. For the decade's leading animal rights theorist, Peter Singer, the advent of Cartesian philosophy marked the 'absolute nadir' for non-humans.[34] These detractors invariably target Descartes's assertion that the modern spirit's overriding aim, through a practical rather than a speculative philosophy, was to become 'masters and possessors of nature'.[35]

The charges against Isaac Newton (1642–1727) are equally damning. With characteristic boldness, Merchant announces that 'the world in which we live today was bequeathed to us by Newton', while Jonathon Porritt blames him for 'a complete shift . . . in our relationship with the rest of creation'. Thanks largely to Newton and Galileo, argues Maurice Berman in a passionate polemic excoriating the modern Western mindset, literate Europeans held a radically different view of the world in 1727 (when Newton died) than they did in 1626 (when Bacon died): the idea of the cosmos as 'a place of *belonging*' had been nullified.[36]

But the most influential assault on Newtonianism has issued from the California-based ecomystic-cum-environmentalist, Fritjof Capra.

The Austrian-born theoretical physicist, who is drawn to Gaian theory, ecofeminism, Buddhism and deep ecology ('when I see people cutting down forests I feel real pain'), was steeped in counter-culturalism at the University of California, Santa Cruz, in the late 1960s. His bestsellers, *The Tao of Physics* and *The Turning Point*, which identify convergences between modern physics and Eastern spirituality, are peppered with attacks on Bacon, Descartes and Newton.[37] Capra promotes the quantum mechanics pioneered by Werner Heisenberg, which replaced the Newtonian conception of solid independent atoms with a sub-atomic view of particles that denies their solidity and existence as independent identities. 'The new physics', Capra explains, 'was a radical break with Cartesian, deterministic, mechanistic philosophy. It uncovered the fundamental interconnectedness of nature at the subatomic level. The reality of subatomic physics is that not only are objects tightly interconnected but that there are no objects, just inter-connections. This is close to the eastern mystical way of thinking.'[38]

These various assessments of the Renaissance and scientific revolu-tion are fraught with implications for our view of pre-modern times. The argument that scientific innovation banished the idea of nature as an organism full of vitality, intelligence, inner logic and motivation assumes it was previously very much alive. Merchant's thesis soft-pedals the scale and intensity of environmental interventions before the scientific revolution, painting a thoroughly benign and one-dimensional picture of ancient, medieval and Renaissance ideas of nature. For instance, she dates the widespread drainage of Dutch and East Anglian fens to the late sixteenth and early seventeenth centuries, when the technology of windmills, drainage and sluices – underwritten by big capital – geared up and was applied on a large scale. This downplays Roman ventures and medieval achievements. Between 950 and 1350, settlers in the Rijnland region of Holland acted to combat flooding, subsidence and the destruction of peat bogs, a process of reclamation that converted a frontier wilderness into a controlled agrar-ian landscape.[39] This suggests that substantial environmental modifica-tions do not require the legitimation of a mechanistic world-view.

Skating over the more domineering features of pre-modern ideo-logies, Merchant virtually succumbs to the conceit of a scrupulous golden age. Beside dwelling on the cultural taboos that bolstered a supportive, feminine conception of the earth, she highlights the classi-cal view of the cosmos as 'nurturing mother', and emphasizes lingering pantheistic urges among the medieval peasantry. The environmental historian's critique of capitalism leaves its deepest impression on the study of the lands and peoples invaded by Europeans after 1492 (see chapter 5). Yet its application to pre-modern Europe also stresses the ecological sustainability of subsistence based on communal access to the fruits of nature informed by indigenous knowledge, a system that operated smoothly for centuries before the indigenes were displaced or marginalized by outsiders armed with alien views and technology. Merchant compares the Native American view of nature with representations of the earth in popular Renaissance literature. And the relatively undisturbed East Anglian fen-dwellers she describes might easily be taken for pre-Columbian Native Americans, and the subsequent reclamation drive aligned with the forces of dispossession in North America.[40]

More conservative historians have also idealized pre-industrial relations between people and nature. G. M. Trevelyan, the most influential historian of England during the first half of the twentieth century, grew up reading Wordsworth and Ruskin and roaming the moors surrounding his family's Northumberland estate with rod and gun. In his best-known work, *English Social History*, he romanticized the rural life shared by peasant and lord prior to the seventeenth century: 'There was much hardship, poverty and cold in those pleasant villages and farms; but the simplicity and beauty of life with nature was an historical reality not merely a poet's dream . . . in those days, men were much left alone with nature, with themselves, with God. As Blake has said, "Great things are done when men and mountains meet. These are not done by jostling in the street".'[41]

Oblivious to issues such as conflict over forest and game resources, Trevelyan evoked an arcadian England where agriculture and nature were virtually synonymous, a place blissfully unaware of the imminent industrial invasion and the manufacture of a 'landscape of Hell':[42]

> Indoors and out, it was a lovely land. Man's work still added more than it took away from the beauty of nature. Farm buildings and cottages of local style and material sank into the soft landscape, and harmoniously diversified and adorned it. The fields, enclosed by hedges of bramble and hawthorn set with tall elms, and the new 'plantations' of oak and beech, were a fair exchange for the bare open fields, the heaths and thickets, of an earlier day.[43]

Theological consequences of scientific innovation

Mechanism was allied to naturalism – the attempt to solve philosophical problems with scientific knowledge. Naturalism supposedly eroded supernatural explanation and buttressed the conception of the universe as a machine functioning in accordance with strict laws of material causation. This conflicted with idealism, a philosophical approach privileging the mind and spirit that often venerated religious experience. Given that Newton could detect no trace of divinity in physical phenomena, many theologians have blamed the new scientific cognition for evicting God.[44] The ecological ethic of the 'process' philosopher, Alfred North Whitehead (1861–1947), as expressed in *Science and the Modern World*, accused the new scientific philosophy of reducing Nature to 'a dull affair, soundless, scentless, colourless; merely the hurrying of material, endlessly, meaninglessly'. Whitehead came down with particular force on Cartesian thinking (nature as 'bits of matter, bare of intrinsic value'). He countered with the argument that all things have intrinsic value and are interconnected in a creation in which God is immanent instead of apart from (or identical with).[45]

Yet the new orientation, though anti-supernaturalist, was not inherently antagonistic to all forms of Christian belief. In transferring power to a divine designer, builder and operator – an external agent who supplied the qualitative elements eliminated from nature itself – mechanism restated the venerable idea of transcendence. As the great scientists explained, they were working for God as well as Science. Alfred Crosby acknowledges that a new vision of reality, time and space from which God was extracted emerged between 1400 and 1600. Yet he denies any intentional offence, citing the dictum of Kepler, a deeply religious man, that 'God's counsels are impenetrable, but not his material creation'.[46] And though the Church forced him to recant under torture in 1616, Galileo never sought to oust God.

The Bible also served as Bacon's lodestone. Science – which he defined as the study of God's works – would supplement existing religious efforts to recover man's prelapsarian control over nature, ushering in the kingdom of heaven on earth. What 'sin had shattered', explains John Passmore, 'science could in large part repair'.[47] Bacon was careful to distinguish the kind of knowledge that science pursued from greedy curiosity (1620):

> For it was not that pure and uncorrupted natural knowledge whereby Adam gave names to the creatures according to their propriety, which gave occasion to the fall. It was the ambitious and proud desire of moral knowledge to judge of good and evil, to the end that man may revolt from God and give law to himself which was the form and manner of the temptation.[48]

He insisted that the goal of science was conservative, what he called the 'great instauration' (renewal): 'Only let the human race recover that right over nature which belongs to it by divine bequest, and let power be given it; the exercise thereof will be governed by sound reason and true religion.'[49]

Was Bacon primarily intent on rendering shocking ideas more palatable, as part of a genuine bid to accommodate science and religion? Or did he erect a façade to disguise his real aim? The new science was undeniably a pill that needed to be sugared. The fear that God would be upset if man meddled with the natural order had served as a brake on scientific curiosity in the Middle Ages. Bacon challenged this conception of science as sorcery and black magic, and overturned the belief that nature was fallen. By ridding nature of this stigma, Baconian science promised to recover earthly things for God (and man).

Bacon also sought to disguise how far his enterprise deviated from religious orthodoxy. He sought to reassure people that no amount of scientific knowledge would impinge on God's plan or reveal his image (though we would find out plenty about his skill and power since, as Basil Willey comments, 'the Great Machine presupposed the Divine Mechanic'). However, the new creed was patently giving man a far more proactive role in the divine purpose.[50] The onus might have been placed on nature to reveal religious truth and God might remain in overall charge, but the potential for divine disempowerment was latent in the redefinition of him as an engineer standing outside the system.[51]

Scientists with strong religious convictions dissented robustly from the new science. These so-called physico-theologists were protégés of 'Platonist' Henry More, for whom body and soul were one (monism) and the material corpus of nature was suffused with spirit (the 'animus mundi'). Scientific advances that furthered appreciation of the complexity and interrelatedness of the natural world also reinforced the belief that the material world was the product of divine design – as suggested by the title of a book by physico-theology's leading light, the botanist and pioneering zoologist John Ray (1627–1705): *The Wisdom of God as Manifested in the Works of Creation* (1691).

A strand of eighteenth-century thought that stood apart from the dominant thrust of what Donald Worster dubs 'imperial' science is the brand of natural history associated with Gilbert White. The Baconian trend within natural history was represented by the Swedish naturalist Carl von Linné (Linnaeus) (1707–78). In 1749 Linnaeus attached a popular eighteenth-century expression, 'the economy of nature', to the management of nature's household, by which he meant (in Worster's phrase) 'the grand organization and government of life on earth: the rational ordering of all material resources in an interacting whole'.[52] It was White, an English rural curate-cum-naturalist, who helped resurrect a view of nature as living organism. For Worster, this alternative, 'arcadian', tradition was reborn in the anti-mechanistic ecology represented in the 1960s by the American biologist-cum-environmentalists, Barry Commoner and Rachel Carson.[53]

We may well ask how (if at all) elite re-envisionings of the natural world and of God's role were transmitted to the workshop floor. Instead of trying to reconstruct a process of trickle down, or resort to the dubious argument that new ideas impose themselves through their compelling nature, it is more cogent to attribute the estrangement of industrial workers from nature to the direct daily experience of the brutal factory regime where the hegemony of the machine confronted them at every turn in the form of furnace, forge, crane, pump and water-wheel. Industrial processes were already well advanced in some respects by the sixteenth century. In the 1540s, large-scale mill and foundry production of paper, cannon, copper, sugar and saltpetre began to supplement home-based (domestic) production. One of these outfits sometimes employed over 200 workers. 'The printing-press and the windmill, the lever, the pump, and the pulley, the clock and the wheel-barrow, and a host of machines in use among miners and engineers', explains R. G. Collingwood, 'were established features of daily life.'[54] Reconceptualizations of nature were therefore not difficult to grasp: 'Everyone understood the nature of a machine', continues Collingwood, 'and the experience of making and using such things had become part of the general consciousness of European man. It was an easy step to the proposition: as a clockmaker or millwright is to a clock or mill, so is God to Nature'.[55]

5

The World Beyond Europe

At Pebble Beach, California, a wind-contorted cypress clings to a rocky spit. This tree's symbolic value is so great that a sign reads: 'Lone Cypress is a trademark of quality and the corporate logo of the Pebble Beach Company. As such, the use of the tree's image is regulated by law. It may not be photographed or reproduced for any commercial purpose.'[1] Lone Cypress stands as a peerless monument to capitalism's bid to privatize, incorporate and commodify nature – whether as lumber or designer label. (Will the Pebble Beach Company try to sue Mother Nature for loss of potential earnings if a winter storm topples its tree?)

Mindful of how today's multinational corporations raze the Amazonian rainforest for pasture to raise beef (the so-called 'hamburger connection'), we might identify the expansion of Europe and the corresponding development of a capitalist world economy predicated on metropolitan exploitation of the periphery as the fundamental process of the last 500 years. Since the onset of the modern era, western Europe has operated as an often overwhelming source of cultural, economic and ecological pressure on the remainder of the globe. Many environmentalists and environmental historians insist that the natural world has been subjected to unparalleled abuse in those areas invaded in the wake of Columbus and da Gama.

Capitalism's 'gobble-gobble' mentality, argues Donald Worster, has unleashed global havoc comparable to the environmental upheavals associated with the Neolithic revolution.[2] He feels there is no need to go as far back as Judaeo-Christianity to locate the source of our ecological problems (if anything, Christianity acted as a check on the modernist orientation), or even to the seventh-century invention of the heavy iron plough. Move over Bacon and Descartes to make way for Adam Smith, the eighteenth-century Scottish founder of classical economics. If we want 'to get down to the really important roots of the modern environmental crisis', Worster claims, we must concentrate on Smith, for whom the unfettered pursuit of self-interest was nature's most sacred law.[3]

Often complementing this conviction that capitalism shoulders a unique burden of guilt is the belief that pre-capitalist, non-Western societies have been poorly equipped to inflict environmental damage, even positively hostile to the idea of injuring nature. Though he praises environmental history as 'some of the most original and challenging history now being written', Simon Schama is troubled by the monolithic and gloomy tendencies he believes threaten to suffocate a still young and evolving field: 'it inevitably tells the same dismal tale: of land taken, exploited, exhausted; of traditional cultures said to have lived in a tradition of sacred reverence with the soil displaced by the reckless individualist, the capitalist aggressor'.[4]

Devoting attention to the extra-European world both before and after it was sucked into Europe's orbit allows us to scrutinize these contentions and to develop our analysis through cross-cultural comparison. The debate over Judaeo-Christian responsibility for environmental degradation can be extended by reflecting on non-Western religious systems. This chapter begins by comparing Europe's frontier mentality and the environmental impact of colonization to the outlook of indigenous peoples, and their treatment of nature prior to contact. Discussion will focus on the canonization of American Indians as 'the first ecologists', an accolade which is critically examined in the light of the archaeological and ethnographic record. The consequences for aboriginals and their dealings with nature as they are increasingly drawn into a market-oriented economy are then considered. These related exercises help us determine whether European values and practices were really so distinctive and damaging.

Many will take 'ecological imperialism' to mean an economic system's predilection for 'virgin' lands and largely unappropriated natural resources because they offer the highest levels of output and lowest costs in the short run, yielding the swiftest and biggest profits. But Alfred Crosby has applied the term to the ecological onslaughts and biological mixings, intentional and unintentional, that not only undergirded but, in his view, directly facilitated the conquest of the so-called 'empty lands' of the temperate zone. These upheavals are the focus of the penultimate section of the chapter.

We conclude our coverage of the world beyond Europe with the phenomenon of 'native nature'. When Samuel Johnson visited France in 1775, one of his companions, Henry Thrale, expressed admiration for the quality of the scenery. 'Never heard such nonsense', was Johnson's reply (as recorded by Thrale's wife, Hesther), 'a blade of grass is always a blade of grass, whether in one country or another: Let us, if we *do* talk, talk about something; men and women are my subjects of enquiry; let us see how they differ from those we have left behind.'[5]

The belief that nature is somehow neutral persists. The question as to what images should appear on the new European currency, the euro, arose in 1996. Historical events and figures were considered too divisive, so 'bland' motifs such as landscapes were mooted. But these planners, like Johnson, were sorely mistaken in their presumption that a blade of grass has no country and that nature has no culture. A deeply felt nationalism was inseparable from the opposition of the British historian G. M. Trevelyan to the Forestry Commission's blanketing of Lakeland fells with 'German pine forest' in the 1920s, which he later denounced as a 'crime against Nature's local bye-laws'. Trevelyan reminded readers of *The Times* that Wordsworth had once objected to the importation of conifers, which would eliminate 'the old English forest trees – oak, beech, ash, elm and sycamore'.[6] Yet the adoption of nature for patriotic purposes and the cultivation of a special relationship between nature and nationhood has rarely been more pronounced than in the first modern country formally to renounce the imperial yoke: the United States of America.

American Indians and ecological sainthood

It would be a mistake to assume that the moral and ecological issues raised by European imperialism escaped European attention prior to the multiculturalism of the late twentieth century. Columbus's contemporary, Bartolomé de las Casas, originally came to the Caribbean island of Hispaniola (now Haiti) in 1502, intending to learn from and about native peoples so as to convert them to Christianity more effectively. But having been an eye-witness to Spanish atrocities against the locals, las Casas, now a Dominican priest, went partly native. As indicated by his gory tirade, *A Short Account of the Destruction of the Indies* (1552), he devoted the rest of his life to condemning Spanish behaviour and extolling the virtues and achievements of vanishing indigenous cultures. The concept of the noble savage, born of European guilt and longing, took more definite shape with Michel de Montaigne, a leading sixteenth-century French humanist. Francisco Lopez de Gomara's widely circulated *Historia General de las Indias* (1552), an account entirely sympathetic to the Spanish imperial mission, left Montaigne seething with indignation, and reflecting thus (1585–8) on the nature of Europe's contribution to the world:

> So many goodly citties ransacked and razed; so many nations destroyed and made desolate; so many infinite millions of harmelesse peoples of all sexes, states and ages, massacred, ravaged and put to the sword; and the richest, the fairest and the best part of the world topsiturvied, ruined and defaced for the traffick of Pearles and Pepper.[7]

As late as 1977, however, a revised edition of a standard college textbook on US history (written by a team of historians led by Samuel Eliot Morison and first published in the 1930s) still contained the following statement: 'Never again may mortal man hope to recapture the wonder, the delight of those October days in 1492 when the New World gracefully yielded her virginity to the conquering Castilians.'[8] The sexist language of these traditionalist historians echoed that of the original colonizers. Thomas Morton, promoting New England as a new Canaan in the seventeenth century, compared the land to 'a faire virgin longing to be sped and meete her lover in a Nuptiall bed'. Prior to the colonists's arrival, Morton proclaimed, 'her fruitfull wombe, not being enjoyed is like a glorious tombe'.[9] As the Columbian quinquennial of 1992 approached, however, the views of Montaigne prevailed over those of Morton and Morison.

Accusations of rape and genocide are increasingly reinforced by charges of ecocide. Kirkpatrick Sale's *Conquest of Paradise* (1990) is a merciless attack on an eco-villainous European mentality personified and exported by Columbus. Sale, as Simon Schama notes with only slight exaggeration, 'is ready to convict Columbus for pretty much everything wrong with the planet from then until now, including the extinction of the Great Auk and for all I know the hole in the ozone layer, too'.[10] Sale heaps more blame onto Columbus's shoulders than any one person can realistically be responsible for, but he remains the quintessential Renaissance man in his 'resourcist' view of nature as (in Neil Evernden's phrase) 'matter in search of a use'. Francis Bacon certainly thought highly of Columbus, for in the hall of Salomon House stood his statue in the company of the era's 'principall inventors'.[11] Columbus's mind was empirical, eager to probe nature's secrets and turn them to profit. His obsession with commercial value led to many misperceptions. He brought back what he thought were black pepper, cinnamon and ginger but which turned out not to be those spices at all.[12]

'Back to the Paleolithic' proclaims an Earth First! bumper sticker, taking its cue from Jean-Jacques Rousseau, who located the state of nature, that condition of primal liberty and bliss, among the cavemen. Environmentalists who eulogize the hunter-gatherer believe that it all started going dreadfully wrong at a very early stage: 'Once humans became agriculturalists, the almost paradisiacal character of prehistory was irretrievably lost.'[13] Settled agriculture, they argue, yielded a surplus facilitating the accumulation of wealth, from which flowed the evils of social hierarchy, slavery, patriarchalism and commerce, as well as the disparaging of wilderness.[14] 'We haven't had any progress on this planet in sixteen thousand years', exclaimed Dave Foreman, founder of Earth First!, in 1989.[15]

The environmentalist case for archaic peoples as role models draws on their designation as the original 'affluent' societies, a view popularized by Marshall Sahlins's *Stone Age Economics* (1972).[16] Extrapolating backwards in time from the observation of remnant groups of Kalahari desert foragers (Bushmen or !Kung San), Australian Aborigines and, above all, North American Indians, this ethnographic school refuted the classic Hobbesian stereotype of cruel and ignorant savagery. Instead, they projected an enviable lifestyle characterized by tolerance, leisure, radiant health and longevity, communal ownership, abundant food, consumption based on need and, not least, good earth-keeping skills. J. Donald Hughes is another scholar who has delivered the environmentalist's prototypical paean to the Native American as a 'child of nature' who knew 'the secret of how to live in harmony with Mother Earth'.[17] Hughes quotes from a much-lionized speech ascribed to Chief Seattle (Seeathl) of the Duwamish (1854), in which Seattle talks about every molecule of land being sacred, of all things being interconnected, and of how 'even' rocks are alive.[18]

Dead, inert and despiritualized in the European mind, nature as conceptualized by the Indian pulsated with vitality, enjoyed consciousness and was saturated with the divine principle. Every aspect of nature, from humans to stones, flowed from the same godhead. All belonged to an inclusive community of life, and people had ethical obligations towards their fellow, if non-human, members of this 'Great Society'.[19] Perhaps the first Europeans to propagate this view of the American Indian were those impatient to extract cash value from their colonial possessions. That the export of Western ideas of science and material progress was deemed no less important to the advance of civilization than religious conversion is suggested by Robert Boyle

(1627–91), a chemist, who served as governor of the Corporation for the Spread of the Gospel in New England. Boyle hoped the new scientific ethos would dissolve traditional cultural restraints, for 'the veneration wherewith men are imbued for what they call nature has been a discouraging impediment to the empire of man over the inferior creatures of God: for many have not only looked upon it, as an impossible thing to encompass, but as something impious to attempt'.[20]

Scholarly debate between the 'romantic' position (as ecophilosopher J. Baird Callicott, a leading exponent, freely describes it) and more sceptical interpretations revolves around Indian participation in the European commercial world, Indian technological competence, and the relationship between Indian ideas of nature and the environmental impact of their actions. The ecological Indians' would-be demystifiers seize on their adoption of imported goods and widespread involvement in the fur trade, which drove species such as beaver to the brink of extinction, which indicate to them that Indian 'eco-friendliness' was only skin-deep – a largely negative quality reflecting low technological levels and the absence of incentives for heavier exploitation. For the sceptics, the Indian appetite for European clothing, utensils and foodstuffs gives the lie to the primitive communism and non-consumerism that the ecological Indians' supporters have praised.[21]

The Indians' defenders protest that criticism of the Indian role in the fur trade is a grotesque example of blaming the victim. Far from entering more or less willingly into new economic arrangements, they maintain that Indians were essentially forced to do so. Any regression from the high standards governing their previous dealings with nature is adequately explained by the traumatic cocktail of capitalism, disease, dispossession, relocation and religious conversion served up by Europeans.

Were Native Americans really such innocents? We should also examine the general proposition that all indigenous peoples were thoroughly taken over by outsiders. Were introduced regimes quite so incompatible with them? In some instances, European trade was absorbed into existing inter-tribal networks. Moreover, universalizing models of environmental revolution derived from the North American experience (Carolyn Merchant offers New England's environmental history as 'a mirror on the world') fit less well further south in the Americas. In Latin America, some indigenes saw the European arrival as an opportunity rather than a calamity. Looking at the region between 1519 and 1810, Elinor Melville dismisses the crude notion of imposition of alien ways, pointing to considerable indigenous selectivity and European adaptation to local conditions and customs.[22]

The case for the American Indian that environmental activists usually offer is largely preconceived with blanket application across time, culture and space, often failing to rise much above the sophistication of the portrayal of Indians in Disney's movie *Pocahontas*. Sale, for instance, holds up the 'nonstatified', essentially egalitarian societies of North America as the archetype for the whole continent. He overlooks acutely hierarchical, despotic and brutal examples of existing societies, such as Aztec civilization, which rivalled any horror Europeans committed in the New World.[23] No wonder some of the Aztec subject peoples hailed the conquistador Hernan Cortes as the great emancipator when he landed in Mexico in 1519.

Though some American Indians have assented to and sometimes collaborated in the construction of the 'ecological Indian', others criticize the appropriation and commercialization of Indian spirituality through the sale of books and music. Another group advises Euro-Americans to look for role models in their own pre-Christian heritage. Others dismiss the 'ecological Indian' as yet another Eurocentric stereotype, ostensibly flattering but deeply offensive to the variety of Indian culture and experience in its presumption of an 'Indian view'.[24] Some Native Americans also find the idea that Indians are children of nature who blend innocuously into the natural world profoundly racist and disempowering in that it denies both their identity as humans and also their history, defined as an ability to control and shape their lives by asserting themselves within their physical environments.

The designation of the Indian as pioneer ecologist certainly entails a loose understanding of ecology. Some of the most zealous enthusiasts suggest that Indians were tantamount to modern environmentalists in their conscious pursuit of a lifestyle designed for 'green' ends. Even those who disclaim such anachronistic thinking still come close to implying that the Indian graduated informally in ecological science in the virtual university of the woods and plains. Yet overly strict definitions of ecology are no more useful than indiscriminate ones. In no sense were Indians ecological scientists; but then lots of people today without degrees in ecological science call themselves ecologists. A more subtle argument is that Indians were intuitive proto-ecologists who grasped the interdependence of life forms and appreciated complex interactions within a single system. Nevertheless, white ethnohistorian Calvin Martin dismisses the idea of the ecological Indian as 'a silly and cruel charade' – not because the Indian relationship with nature was bogus, but because it sprang from a cosmology so alien to our Western world-view that we cannot hope to learn from it, let alone adopt it.[25]

Agreement that there were elements in Indian thinking and practice that anticipated later notions of conservation and ecology still leaves open the question of how they fit various Western categories, such as utilitarian conservation, preservationism and deep ecology, as well as the related issue of whether their motivations were largely practical or spiritual. Nor does it address the evidence of environmental damage prior to contact with other cultures.

Granted that Indians identified in some form with flying, swimming, creeping and four-legged 'people', were these arrangements mainly of a socio-legal or moral nature? The Algonkians of the northeastern woodlands developed such elaborate rituals around the taking of animal life that their hunting assumed the dimensions of a 'holy occupation' (in anthropologist Frank Speck's famous phrase (1938)).[26] Yet, as Speck makes clear, the hunting nexus between man and animal was a contractual agreement, based on pragmatism, fear and respect born of self-interest. It is a way of thinking reminiscent of the classical Greek appeasement of guardian spirits residing in sacred groves: if you want to ensure good hunting, do not offend the spiritual wardens of the animals, the so-called 'keepers of the game', lest the animals fail to return.[27]

Sale's diatribe against European imperialism in *Conquest of Paradise* does not mention the role of natural resource depletion in the demise of the Aztec or Mayan empires. By 1519, intensive agriculture in central Mexico had placed soil productivity under such heavy pressure that some demographic experts believe the Aztec structure would have collapsed in due course even if the conquistadores had never shown up.[28] (That Mayan ruins were so hard to locate in the early twentieth century – they were overrun by a riot of vegetation – suggests how thoroughly the jungle had once been cleared.) Nor is there room in Sale's account for research on the 'desert culture'. These agrarian societies flourished in parts of present-day Arizona and New Mexico between the seventh and twelfth centuries. They began to decline shortly before the end of the twelfth century. By 1500, two-thirds of the cultivated area had been abandoned to desert. Spanish conquistadores encountered a relic culture and peoples, whose remains are visible today at places such as Pueblo Bonito in Chaco Canyon, New Mexico, and Mesa Verde, Colorado. The onset of this collapse coincided with an era of particularly severe drought. But that the process of disintegration continued even after the rains returned suggests that climate change was simply one factor, and probably subordinate to longer-term processes of environmental degradation caused by over-cropping and excessive deforestation.[29]

Sale refers to the 'Pleistocene overkill' thesis, but does not take it seriously. First advanced by palaeoecologist Paul Martin in 1973, it challenged the prevailing ethnographic wisdom that all or most Indians for all or most of their pre-contact history hunted in a wise and sustainable fashion. Martin's 'blitzkrieg' model saddled the first American 'pioneers' with responsibility for massive megafaunal extinctions as they entered the Americas across the Bering Land Bridge, perhaps as long as 30,000 years ago. Victims of their rapidly expanding numbers (Martin estimates a 3.4 per cent annual rate of population increase and that it took only 1,200 years to sweep down from Alaska to Tierra del Fuego) included mammoth, mastodon, horse and two types of camel. These large animals were wiped out so fast, speculates Martin (sometimes because their own prey had been depleted rather than because they were killed directly), that the first generations of hunter-gatherers had no chance to memorialize them in cave art.[30] Sale attributes these losses to climate change, and Callicott argues that the 'overkill' thesis contradicts the claim that Indians were relatively powerless technologically speaking. Yet it might not have taken much skill to nail animals unaccustomed to human predation.

Good places to examine the hunting practices of Plains Indians before they acquired the horse from the Spanish between the 1680s and 1720s and became enmeshed in market hunting to satisfy the Euro-American demand for hides, robes and meat are the thick piles of buffalo bones at the base of cliffs, such as Head-Smashed-In Buffalo Jump on the southern Albertan prairie. Archaeo-zoological evidence stretching back 10,000 years, and documentary evidence from eighteenth and nineteenth-century white observers, indicate that driving herds over these cliffs (movement was incited by fires) was hardly a precision enterprise yielding exactly the required amount of meat and other resources.[31] It could result in astonishing waste. How did you stop additional buffalo plunging over when the right number had leapt to their deaths?[32] Given that bone remains at the Hudson Meng site in the Nebraska badlands betray no signs of human use, anthropologist Larry Todd estimates that, of the 600 buffalo stampeded over this cliff during a hunt 10,000 years ago, perhaps only 1 per cent was used.[33]

Callicott recognizes this evidence, but argues that objections to the ecological Indian based on such data involve an odd understanding of the relationship between ideals and actuality. To note a discrepancy is not very revealing, in his view, unless you maintain that ideals dictate behaviour. He draws a parallel between aboriginal over-hunting in the past and murder and adultery in Western society today: just because some people commit these acts does not mean that we treat societal

proscriptions against them as absurd or meaningless. Ethics are normative. Departures from prescribed standards do not invalidate them.
Callicott's argument really hinges on his perception of those piles of
buffalo bones and rotting carcasses as lapses and aberrations.[34] This
raises the vital question of statistically meaningful samples: how many
piles of bones are necessary to counter the charge of anecdotal and
biased white evidence and invalidate the Native American's goodly
reputation? What percentage of tribes must be given the official green
seal of approval before we can legitimately talk of an 'American Indian
land wisdom'?[35]

Even if the revisionist interpretation of evidence from sites like
Head-Smashed-In Buffalo Jump is conceded, surely this tells us more
about the invading Siberian hunter-gatherers who 'discovered'
America, and their immediate descendants, than it does about Native
Americans in 1492. Native Americans, it is easily forgotten, were immigrants too. Confronted with the giddy opportunities presented by an
unexploited continent, of which they had no biological knowledge or
cultural understanding, early generations may well have entertained
notions of natural resource inexhaustibility akin to the far better known
'myth of superabundance' that encouraged profligate white settler use
of resources, as well as being equally devoid of a sense of place. 'Land
wisdom', far from being a genetic microchip implanted in the first
Native Americans, was more likely a cultural acquisition, a response to
experience of resource mismanagement.

Callicott also tries to undercut the argument that Indians lacked the
technology and the numbers to cause damage rather than the will. The
materialist position is that Indians did not choose their ecological virginity; they just did not have much opportunity to lose it. Frankly dismiss-
ive of the role of ethics in promoting careful behaviour, some argue that
economic incentives are the key to environmentally appropriate activities. Judging American Indians according to the yardstick of a
universalized 'economic man', and reacting against what they see as an
unjustified orgy of 'West-bashing', one set of economic historians contends that, when any group gains access to levels of technology higher
than those hitherto enjoyed, their environmental impact increases.[36]

Callicott denies, however, that technology can be divorced from
values in the way the materialists suggest. The Indian world-view, he
argues, produced a technology that we might think of as ineffective but
which was adequate to their needs and reflected their ecological sensi-
tivities. In other words, the Indians of New England were not perched
on Plymouth Rock in a state of frustration before the Pilgrim Fathers
arrived, cursing their inept technology.

Another part of the demythologizing process has been a challenge to the neo-Rousseauian research among remnant hunter-gatherers, notably the !Kung San (sometimes referred to as 'soft' primitivism). White ethnographers such as Lee and Sahlins have been criticized for seeking evidence to corroborate their own belief in aboriginal saintliness. By contrast, the new approach ('hard' primitivism) dwells on incidence of hunger and malnutrition and emphasizes brevity of life-span.[37]

The backlash against the ecological Indian also feeds on the revelation that some of the most famous Indian eco-rhetoric has been embellished (if not fabricated). American Indians were pre-literate so there is no written record of their thinking prior to 1492. Instead, we have the accounts (transcribed by whites) of post-contact Indians (usually nineteenth-century) which ostensibly reconstruct 'traditional' attitudes but are inevitably roseate. Seattle's speech of 1854 has become one of the most hallowed utterances in the environmentalist canon, but it now looks as if an admiring journalist was co-author. Hughes remarked on Seattle's good fortune in having a translator of 'considerable literary skill' in Henry Smith, a white physician and journalist. It is a truism that something usually gets lost in translation. In this case, something mighty was gained when the speech was published in the *Seattle Sunday Star* in 1887. Compounding the embarrassment, it has been revealed that the most celebrated extract comes not from the mouth of Seattle, nor from the official interpreter, or the pen of Smith. ('If we sell you our land, love it as we've loved it. Care for it as we've cared for it . . . How can you buy or sell the sky, the warmth of the land? . . . The idea is strange to us. The earth does not belong to man. Man belongs to the earth.') The author is actually Ted Perry, a scriptwriter for *Home*, a movie by the Southern Baptist Convention's Radio and Television Commission about the ecological crisis of the early 1970s. Perry had heard an updated version of Seattle's speech read at an Earth Day rally in 1970.[38] How quickly these findings will enter the textbooks remains to be seen. Most white environmentalists in the West will probably continue to believe in the authenticity of Seattle's words and insist on the verity of the ecological Indian because a sense of shame demands something better from non-whites.

Aboriginal transformations of the natural world

The notion that human disturbance of nature is something reserved for Europeans has profound implications for environmental management policies in that it can influence definitions of what is a 'natural' environment. The view of many Americans that 'natural' is synonymous with pre-Columbian has been echoed in various policy recommendations of the United States National Park Service, not least the 'Leopold Report' of 1963, which characterized parks as vignettes of 'primitive' America, as it was when the first whites arrived. This is surely too recent. But how far do we need to turn back the clock before we arrive at truly natural environments operating unimpeded by human intervention? Strictly speaking, to the latter stages of the last ice age, to the eve of the first Siberian hunter-gatherers' migration into Alaska.

Attempts to restore past environments may be psychologically soothing and emotionally satisfying but they are vainglorious and fatuous from an ecological standpoint. Elk currently make up over three-quarters of ungulates in Jackson Hole, Wyoming. Recent archaeological investigations, however, suggest that elk were practically non-existent in 1492, when aboriginal hunting and animal predation was part of the ecological equation.[39] We can never know what the natural world of the Americas would be like today had Europeans never appeared, not least because Indian populations would have kept growing.

Geographers aloof from the emotive debate over the American Indian's attitude to nature are accumulating incontrovertible evidence (such as relict field features) for an almost heretical conclusion: that the physical environment of the New World bore heavier human traces in 1492 than it did in the mid-1700s, before mass immigration from Europe. Challenging the declensionist (downward spiral) approach to environmental change in post-contact North America, geographers see a more complex, multi-directional series of movements, with more cumulative change over the thousands of years prior to 1492 than in most areas during the next two-and-a-half centuries.[40]

The intellectual historian looks at the various ideas enshrined in religion and philosophy and is likely to be impressed by the differences between cultures. The geographer studying the record of human action left on the ground will be struck more by their similarities. William Doolittle stresses the commonality between European and Indian farming practices, not least their ecological unsustainability over the longer term. Admittedly on the basis of the observations of early European visitors, Doolittle highlights the extent to which Indian cultivation was extensive and of lengthy duration rather than conforming to the norm of 'slash-and-burn' shifting cultivation whose hallmark is long periods of fallow between short, discrete and intensive bursts of cropping. Whereas present-day slash and burn practices in the tropics tend to leave tree stumps in place, Indian agriculturalists frequently grubbed them up and removed them.

Small seems to have been beautiful (i.e. sustainable) with regard to many New World irrigation systems. Yet it is hard to identify a single, let alone representative, practice. The modest irrigation systems of eastern Sonora (northern Mexico) that allowed double cropping facilitated elaborate social organization. But the Hohokam people of nearby New Mexico dug canals up to 10 metres wide and 4 metres deep. Some up to 30 kilometres long with hundreds of branch canals proved unsustainable.[41] Eric Jones points out that most discussion of aboriginal environmental impact is couched in the euphemistic language of 'manipulation' rather than of 'damage'. However, these manipulations were sometimes deleterious and not always localized and short-lived.

Certainly, in terms of soil erosion, the European role was to accelerate rather than initiate processes.[42] On the evidence of various temple, burial and settlement mounds, one of which, Monk's Mound, Missouri, is almost 100 feet (30.5 metres) high and covers 6.9 hectares, prehistoric American peoples from Ohio to Bolivia demonstrated a 'mania for earth moving, landscape engineering on a grand scale'.[43] Callicott surmises that if Europeans had simply come, deposited piles of knives, guns and other hardware, and then returned home, these items may well have been left to rust.[44] One suspects, however, that the moundbuilders would have quickly found a use for bulldozers.

Indian modifications assisted European colonization. Sudden depopulation of catastrophic proportions through 'virgin soil' epidemics meant that some initial settlers were almost literally in a position to reap what they did not sow. Plymouth Colony, Massachusetts sprouted from soil where Indians had raised corn just four years earlier, on the eve of the smallpox epidemic of 1616. The majority of early settlements were located on abandoned farmland and village sites and the accounts of early European explorers and settlers contain descriptions of villages and fields as well as of the howling, impenetrable wilderness. The Indians were often the pioneers who had hacked down the forest and turned the earth. Moreover, they had done so on a considerable scale. The orthodox wisdom that the native population north of the Rio Grande was a sparse 1–1.5 million on the eve of contact has been dramatically revised over the past few decades, some demographers now setting the figure as high as 10–12 million. They even speculate that in the early seventeenth century the more climatically favoured parts of the east coast hosted population densities comparable to those of western Europe.

In 1600 there were possibly 100,000 Indians in the New England region, 80 per cent living in areas supporting agriculture. Agriculture was even more substantial in Virginia, where a more benevolent climate and more fertile soils permitted cultivation of tobacco, tomatoes and sweet potatoes in addition to the archetypical New World food trio of corn, beans and squash. Ethnohistorians currently emphasize the high productivity, relative to more intensive European farming, of this aboriginal agriculture. That Virginian Indians could supply Jamestown's abject and incompetent English colonists with food to tide them over their first few winters suggests a surplus.

Further inland, settlers did encounter substantial forests, and they were not deceiving themselves by characterizing these places as wilderness. What they failed to appreciate, however, was the human role in shaping this apparently unmanaged environment. Forests may have looked untouched to Europeans, but examination of sedimentary charcoal accumulations confirms the link between Indians and frequent burning, which dictated species composition. Wherever Indians were exterminated (whether by disease or warfare) or evicted, wildness rebounded. The treeless character of the midwestern prairies was maintained, if not exactly created, by indigenous peoples regularly firing the grassland to suppress the process of vegetational succession that replaced grass with trees. In the fallow period between Indian removal and the full onslaught of European farming in the later nineteenth century, trees reclaimed the prairies' eastern margins.[45]

Every culture has the capacity not only to transform but to damage the natural world. It is particularly naïve to assume that a world-view that includes humans within nature precludes the possibility of harm. Human numbers and technological capacities are perhaps the key variables, and Europeans should be rendered less visible while Native profiles are raised. The physical environment is often compared to a palimpsest – a manuscript from which the original writing has been effaced to make way for a second inscription. Instead of being written on a page rubbed blank, the colonial imprint copied over the existing letters in bold print.

Nature and Asian religious traditions

Christians persuaded by Lynn White's attack on their religion's orientation towards nature have three choices. They can seek reform from within by emphasizing the stewardship element. A more radical alternative is to embrace the nature ethics represented by pre-Christian Europeans or pre-contact Native Americans. An option for the seriously disenchanted – whose appeal White appreciated but from which he personally shrank – is to turn to Asian religions in general and to Japanese Zen and Chinese Taoism in particular.[46]

In the United States the quest for Eastern salvation stretches back to the mid-nineteenth-century community of intellectuals that clustered in the small town of Concord, Massachusetts. Henry David Thoreau, the poet, nature writer, social critic and professional nonconformist who is often feted as the great-grandfather of American environmentalism, combed nearby Harvard College library for Oriental philosophy and religion in English translation. Thoreau shocked many of his god-fearing farmer-neighbours with his leisurely and reflective lifestyle. To those who insisted that he honour the work ethic and make a proper contribution to the community, he retorted that he already had an appropriate calling and full-time occupation, that of 'inspector of snowstorms'. Though a skilled inventor (he could have made a fortune in the pencil-making business), he preferred more productive pursuits such as wading joyously through bogs in holy (if muddy) communion with a seething mass of mating toads.

Contemptuous of his brash young nation's plunge into industrialism, and lambasting its vulgar commercial preoccupations and spiritual maldevelopment, Thoreau decamped from Concord to a rustic hut on Walden Pond, a two-year semi-retreat that provided the material for the autobiographical *Walden* (1854), one of the gospels of modern American environmentalism. Thoreau's sentiments and the actions they informed have appealed to intellectual historians as a Western manifestation of the teachings of the Zen masters who preached the virtues of solitude, contemplation and immersion in nature. For this singular Yankee-cum-Hindu ascetic, 'the pure Walden water is mingled with the sacred water of the Ganges'.[47]

In the early 1950s, Daisetz Suzuki, a Japanese authority on Zen Buddhism who was its foremost promoter in the United States during the first half of this century, isolated Genesis as the origin of what he saw as the Western urge to conquer nature.[48] A revival of interest in Oriental spirituality coincided with Suzuki's hypothesis, as did the advent of the beat generation, some of whom Suzuki directly influenced. As White remarked, 'the beatniks, who are the basic revolutionaries of our time, show a sound instinct in their affinity for Zen Buddhism, which conceives of the man–nature relationship as very nearly the mirror image of the Christian view'.[49] Japhy Ryder, the major protagonist in Jack Kerouac's *The Dharma Bums* (1958) brims over with the ecstasies of mountain-climbing, chanting haikus as he bounds across scree slopes in California's Sierra Nevada, destined at the novel's end for a Japanese monastery. Ryder was closely modelled on the young Gary Snyder, whose eco-poem *Turtle Island* would receive the Pulitzer Prize in 1975. The belief in Eastern superiority was strengthened in the 1960s, when Snyder became a counter-cultural guru expounding an exhilarating brand of 'West Coast' Buddhism ('Pop Zen') that fused Zen with Native American cosmology.[50]

For Westerners, the appeal of a generic Orientalism resides in the ostensibly more humble position allocated to people within the larger biological community. The oneness of all life is a central plank in the Zen quest for enlightenment (*satori*). Everything in the universe is imbued with divinity and intrinsic meaning. Also admired are the Buddhist, Hindu and Jain convictions that all beings are caught up in an endless cycle of life and death, spending many lives in the separate spheres of human, animal, ghost, god, demigod and dweller in hell. This belief in the transmigration of souls (metempyschosis) is thought to promote a certain equality of life forms.[51]

'New Age' economists have been equally impressed. The arguments advanced in *Small is Beautiful* (1973) by E. F. Schumacher (1911–73), a former chairman of British Coal turned eco-prophet, were shaped by his experience of Buddhism while serving as a development economist. In Burma, he formulated his concept of 'Buddhist economics' with its stress on low consumption levels. Kenneth Boulding, the pioneering 'green' economist who coined the 'spaceship earth' metaphor to replace the prevailing image of freeloading cowboys roaming inexhaustible plains with one that evoked a closed space and limited resources with nowhere to dump waste, also thought Asian religions had a lot to teach the West: 'The East has never had any illusions about being able to conquer nature, and has always regarded man as living in a somewhat precarious position, as a guest of doubtful welcome, shall we say, in the great household of the natural world.'[52]

Vandana Shiva, a feminist philosopher and ex-nuclear physicist, has promoted the green credentials of Hinduism. With its belief in a unity of life forms arising from a feminine principle (*Prakriti*), she feels that Hinduism offers a radical contrast to the Cartesian dualism that reduces the rich complexity of nature to mere 'environment' – something that is around us but not part of us. Hinduism's profile was boosted in the early 1970s by the Chipko (tree-hugger) movement in the northern Indian provinces of Garwahl and Uttar Pradesh. Reviving the custom of resistance to both commercial timber harvest and state forestry, subsistence users of forest resources for items such as agricultural implements and fuelwood – mostly women – formed human chains to prevent felling by a sporting goods company.[53]

How much of this enthusiasm for Eastern religions is genuinely warranted? In some ways, the Buddhist tradition is just as ambivalent towards nature as its Christian counterpart. Ian White feels that the Buddhist notion that the world is purposeless and flawed, with decay and extinction the inevitable lot of life forms ineluctably trapped in the vicious cycle of *samsara*, runs counter to the notion of a purposeful, enduring ecosystem with elements worthy of preservation: 'There can be no Buddhist justification for the fight to preserve habitats and environments.'[54] Moreover, the doctrine of non-injury (*ahimsa*) – the logic of which is that since we are all fellow sufferers by definition it would be reprehensible to inflict further pain – contains a strong dose of self-interest, specifically fear of retribution: if you are cruel to a dog, you might come back as one next time and get kicked around yourself. Besides, the idea that human and animal states are just 'stations on an eternal circle' is not necessarily complimentary to animals. In early Buddhism (as in ancient Greek thought), animal stations signified terrible punishment. The warning is clear: those who behave badly will sink to the level of animals after death.[55]

Ancient Taoism instructed that loving kindness towards animals (*metta*, which might take the form of buying captured animals and liberating them) built up credit in various ways. It assisted one's spiritual development, improved chances of longevity in this life, and was a passport to immortality. It even held out the possibility that you might be reborn a god. Aldous Huxley, a severe critic of Christian hubris concerning nature, was greatly enamoured of Chinese Taoism, arguing that the poetry of William Wordsworth and Walt Whitman had made it easier for Westerners to absorb its teachings. Having just read Fairfield Osborn's *Our Plundered Planet* (1948), Huxley explained to its author that Taoism offered 'an ethical system comprehensive enough to take in Nature as well as man'. Yet Xinzhong Yao reveals that Taoist approaches to nature were far from disinterested or based on awareness of natural rights: 'the first consideration is to reach immortality or to maintain a long life, and only from this consideration were derived the strong duties of protecting living things or forbidding the eating of meat.'[56]

Nowhere in Buddhist teaching is it claimed that other forms of existence are of even approximately the same (let alone equal) value to human life. The Confucian hierarchy of life, as outlined by Hsun Tzu over 2,000 years ago, would be acceptable to most Christians today: 'Water and fire have essences but not life; herbs and trees have life but not knowledge; birds and beasts have knowledge but no sense of what are rights [*yi*]; man has an essence, life, knowledge and in addition has a sense of rights. Hence he is the highest being on earth.' Hsun Tzu issued instructions not to fell saplings or trees in bloom, and not to take young fish or turtles or fish with young. Xinzhong Yao interprets this as a call for 'the preservation of the forest, animals and ecological environment'.[57] But his injunction smacks more of commonsense than morality or ecological understanding.

It is one thing to scour Buddhist scripture for interdicts against chopping down trees, and to show that Hindu vedic hymns are replete with expressions of human partnership with nature, love of natural beauty, and notions of Mother Earth as an almighty power.[58] But the vast majority of Buddhists and Hindus were (and still are) farmers who were not expected to sit back while tigers harassed their livestock and elephants trampled their crops.

These caveats are reinforced by evidence of environmental damage and insensitivity towards other creatures. Dolphin-unfriendly mist (seine) nets were in use in south-east Asia well before any noteworthy contact with the West, and the Japanese are among the world's last unregenerate whalers. Nor did a Buddhist heritage prevent Japan industrializing at the usual environmental price. In the episode that the BBC's documentary series on twentieth-century history, *The People's Century* (1996), devoted to the state of the environment since 1945, the origins of the global ecological crisis were located not in the public health debate generated in the 1950s and early 1960s in the United States or Britain by nuclear fall-out or pesticides, but in the scare precipitated by consumption of fish from mercury-polluted waters in Japan in the 1950s.

Apologists for Asian religious traditions (both Eastern and Western) seek blanket immunity by attributing all environmental damage in the region over the past 700 years to the corrupting influence of European imperialism and technology.[59] Many environmental histories dealing with the early modern era privilege western Europe and its international market economy as the supreme if not sole source of ecological pressure on other regions – a Eurocentric approach that presents much of the past half-millennium in terms of an active West and a passive 'rest'.

Metropolitan desire for items such as silk stimulated the production of non-food crops, the cost of converting rice paddies into mulberry tree embankments being the reduction of ecological diversity. Yet other major changes predated any significant Western influence. China's forests contracted enormously between the eighth and third centuries BC (the Eastern Chou period), prompting the appointment of forestry officials.[60] A further bout of large-scale deforestation during the Middle

Ages has been exposed by the Chinese-American geographer, Yi-Fu Tuan, whose historically informed approach is rare among those who work on the environmental dimensions of Oriental religions. Distinguishing between intelligentsia and peasants, Tuan chronicles the former's laments during the late Ming dynasty of the sixteenth century over soil erosion and interference with stream flow from clearance. The demands on Chinese forests during the Ming period were much the same as those operating simultaneously in Europe.[61] Among them were industry's need for charcoal, the desire to evict predators, and the sheer weight of expanding human numbers. (Between the fourteenth and nineteenth centuries, China's population swelled by 300 million.)[62]

Other factors were peculiar to the region. Buddhism introduced cremation to China, and between the tenth and fourteenth centuries this placed additional strain on sorely stretched timber resources (as did temple construction), especially those of the south-eastern coastal provinces. Bureaucrats especially, but everyone who wrote on paper (not least poets glorifying nature), were implicated in the denudation of the Shan-tung mountains of northern China during the thirteenth and fourteenth centuries; ink was made from the soot of burnt pine.[63]

For Ramachandra Guha, the Western identification of Eastern traditions as eco-friendly precursors of biocentrism is just another glib, patronizing and highly selective exercise in the Western construction of Oriental 'otherness', which favours an elite mysticism and perpetuates the stereotype of the Eastern mind as non-rational, pre-scientific and non-assertive.[64]

Conservation and colonialism, ecology and empire

That the subjugation of nature and of certain groups of people proceed hand in hand is clearly demonstrated in the various 'new worlds' that Europeans invaded, occupied and annexed. The study of these zones of conflict between existing populations and incursive groups has fostered an environmental perspective because the role of environmental factors and processes of environmental change are more dramatic and palpable in 'frontier' situations where technologically advanced capitalist cultures wrested control from more subsistence-oriented and less technologically potent ones.

Focusing on pre-industrial Europe, the French *Annalistes* presented man–nature relations as a repetitive conversation or dialogue with few remarkable developments ('almost silent and always discreet').[65] Notwithstanding the continuities between pre-colonial and colonial

times that have been highlighted earlier in this chapter, the environmental history of European overseas expansion is often far removed
from what Braudel dubbed *histoire quasi immobile*. Relatively few
colonial interactions between people and environment would merit
description as a conversation or dialogue. Instead, environmental
historians have largely perceived vicious quarrels, with upheaval
being the norm. Not all of the 'conspicuous' events of history which
Braudelians hold in contempt are merely political and superficial. An
event such as the European invasion of the Americas triggered deep
structural changes in some regions, like the capitalist environmental
'revolution' that Merchant identifies in New England between the late
1700s and the 1850s.[66]

Alfred Crosby has provided a provocative explanation of the ease
and speed with which Europeans were able to conquer the world's
temperate zones: the biological superiority of various European organisms. He raises themes unfamiliar to most historians of these regions,
who were preoccupied with European prowess in battle (chiefly superior firepower and horses), cruelty, acquisitiveness and other qualities
of European civilization and technology. Wheeling livestock, crops,
weeds and microbes into the historical foreground as non-human allies
and agents of environmental change, Crosby introduces the idea of
biotic exchange and disruption, as previously unrelated people, plants,
animals and germs collide. He also highlights the notion of displacement, as imported species successfully compete with indigenous ones,
occupying their niches and shaping new ecosystems. Livestock, imported to furnish 'food, fiber, hides, and labor', required extensive
grazing and prevented trees from regenerating. They also reduced soil
fertility by compacting the ground with their hooves.[67]

Crosby bombards his readers with seductive images of plants,
animals and germs marching remorselessly across new worlds, threatening to overwhelm us through sheer force and his argument's compelling simplicity. That pigs were allies (however unwitting) in the
conquest is incontestable. Pigs are similar to people anatomically and
they share our ability to adapt to a wide range of environments and
climates. If a boar and a sow had been deposited on a Caribbean island
in 1066 BC or AD 1066 by Africans or Chinese they would doubtless have
proliferated with the same devastating effect on native flora and fauna
as those planted by Spanish buccaneers in the early sixteenth century.
Nevertheless, while pigs do not require humans to guide their activities, human direction can make a difference.

'Are capitalist pigs intrinsically more destructive than noncapitalist
pigs?' ponders William Cronon. Swine are hard to control at the best of

times but are also extensions of particular human cultures located in specific times and places. On the North American mainland they ruined the crops of colonist and Indian alike. The colonists' solution was to banish them to islands and peninsulas. Here they ran amok in clam-beds and other shellfish colonies on which coastal Indians relied for subsistence. No wonder Indians hated pigs more than any other imported animal.[68]

These vast impersonal forces stressed by Crosby are perhaps best exemplified by viruses. 'The Americas were not conquered', explains James M. Blaut, 'they were infected.' Imagine how different the demographic profile and history of southern Africa would have been if the region's indigenes had been as vulnerable to imported disease as their American counterparts.

The effect, however unintentional, of biocentric explanations is to absolve Europeans of a good deal of direct culpability. For how is it possible to speak of the fate of American Indians in terms of holocaust or genocide when accidental factors such as microbes were so critical? A return to a more human-centred, multifaceted explanation is evident in recent work offering a more nuanced restatement of the original sixteenth-century 'Black Legend' (an Anglo-Dutch, Protestant assault against Spanish imperialism that capitalized on the critique of las Casas), which refocuses attention on European brutality and rapacious cultural and economic values.[69]

As well as coming close to reviving turn-of-the-century environmental determinism, Crosby gives the impression that only in the so-called white settler colonies ('neo-Europes') of North America, southern South America, Australia and New Zealand did European imperialism truly triumph. In Asia, a continent far less isolated from Europe (of which Europe might indeed be described as an appendage), a combination of larger populations, greater immunity to disease and more highly developed technology and socio-political organization equipped its peoples to resist more effectively. However, biological and demographic takeover are not the only mechanisms of conquest. Though Europeans did not settle in the tropics in any great numbers, nor Europeanize these areas in other ways by importing familiar plants and animals, they none the less drastically altered the physical environment. Natives may not have succumbed to disease or been displaced, but they were subdued with other strategies. The methods Europeans employed beyond the temperate zone – predicated on firm political control – included irrigation, deforestation, forestry and the transfer of plants and plantation crops between tropical areas.[70]

Historians of Asia, Africa and the South Pacific have also stressed the role of science and scientists as engines of conquest. Today we often assume that ecological science and criticism of economic development are closely related. But ecology and science have often catered to those for whom knowledge of nature's workings is power over nature. The strongest case for scientists as lackeys of the imperial enterprise has been made by Lucile Brockway, who examines the role of botanists at Britain's Kew Gardens in the development of plantation agriculture.[71] Richard Grove takes issue, if obliquely, with the view that ecology was grounded predominantly in agricultural science. Grove's *Green Imperialism*, whose title deliberately plays on Crosby's *Ecological Imperialism*, aims to provide a foil to the latter's saga of destruction by celebrating the simultaneous emergence of an ecological consciousness in the imperial arena. Grove's evidence for the greening of imperialism are the policies pursued by eighteenth-century British, Dutch and French colonial authorities on tropical islands such as Mauritius, St Helena and St Vincent, where ecosystems were especially vulnerable to disturbance. He assigns medics and botanists an operative role as trouble-spotters, consciousness-raisers and instigators of remedial action.

Whereas Brockway stressed the botanical garden's commercial roots, Grove emphasizes the 'edenic discourse' of recreating paradise. The colonial scientist emerges as a far less obsequious figure who, far from prostituting himself to capital and colonial state, formulated a vigorous critique, and even got the 'upper hand' in policy formation. Yet not all naturalists and colonial officials were alarmed over environmental degradation in the tropics. David Arnold cites surgeons and other doctors from India's Bengali plains who, 'far from being the advocates of conservation that Grove describes, often favoured the wholesale destruction of scrub and jungle in order to improve ventilation and dispel harmful miasmas'. Even Grove acknowledges that the motives of the regimes that adopted conservationist recommendations were geared to long-term security considerations.[72]

In addition to challenging the orthodox view of the colonial scientist, Grove locates the antecedents of a late twentieth-century international environmentalism preoccupied with deforestation, species extinction and climate change in the views of these eighteenth-century scientists and the policies they shaped, arguing for their 'disproportionate' influence on the subsequent history of environmentalism. Reacting against a perceived US hegemony over environmentalism's origins, which gives Americans most of the credit as founding fathers, Grove is keen to establish its non-American parentage.[73]

But a handful of British, Dutch and French scientists is a slender basis for such a massive claim, especially since 'environmentalism' and 'environmentalist' did not assume their current meanings until the 1960s. Despite the concern with climate change and wildlife depletion that eighteenth-century colonial scientists share with late twentieth-century scientists and environmentalists, environmentalism as we know it is the product of ecological threats largely peculiar to the period since 1945 (see chapter 7). Grove's search for 'relevance' transmutes every past action that is vaguely conservationist into fully-fledged environmentalism and suggests direct influence. Yet Western environmentalism has more immediate and obvious roots and ancestors.

Nature and nationalism

With reference to the 'invention' of tropicality, Arnold shows how European ideas of the 'otherness' of non-Europeans were informed by experience of unfamiliar physical environments and debilitating diseases and climes. He argues that negative (pestilential) images of tropicality were more pervasive among colonial officials than is appreciated by scholars who purvey predominantly positive (paradisiacal) images of tropicality. Negative conceptions of the 'alien' based on nature also emerged from white settler colonies in North America. Wilderness was reviled as the diabolical abode of the savage Indian and enemy of every painstaking gain of European civilization. In due course, however, naturalists and literary figures reappraised the disadvantages of otherness – and more decisively so than in the tropics. This enlargement of conceptions of nature was predicated on the subjugation of large tracts of land and a growing sense of independence from the colonial centre. As the new American nation matured politically and economically in the early nineteenth century, cultural nationalists reappraised the once reviled wilderness as a precious and shrinking cultural asset. White Americans seized on nature as a source of national identity and self-esteem as well as material gain.

The notion of the United States as 'God's country' and of Americans as his chosen people was one of the most powerful legacies of seventeenth-century Puritan colonization. But Americans also came to think of their home as 'nature's nation'.[74] The youthful nation had severed political ties with Britain and was loosening its economic reliance, but it remained servile in the literary and artistic realms. In his 'American Scholar' address at Harvard in 1837, Ralph Waldo Emerson challenged Americans to terminate their 'long apprenticeship to the learning of other lands'. Nature was a key ingredient in his remedy for the intellectual starvation likely to result from continued feeding on 'the sere remains of foreign harvests'.[75]

Pride in American nature stirred in the debate between Old and New World naturalists over the quality of American nature. The American contribution often took the form of puerile claims that US phenomena simply eclipsed their European counterparts, as in Philip Freneau's denigration in the 1780s of the Nile as a 'small rivulet' and the Danube as a 'ditch' in comparison with the mighty Mississippi.[76] The most erudite contribution was Thomas Jefferson's retort, bristling with statistics, to the eminent French naturalist Count Georges Buffon, in *Notes on Virginia* (1784). Buffon contended that America's plants and animals (and native peoples) were degenerate and inferior to their European equivalents (in so far as they existed). But Jefferson, on a visit to Buffon, dismissed European ungulates such as reindeer as puny alongside the New World's moose, pointing out that the former could easily pass under the latter's belly. (So much for his claim that nature has no favourites.)[77]

None the less, it was wondrous places rather than magnificent beasts on which Americans staked their claims to greatness. But a wealth of monumental scenery *per se* was not a ready-made solution to American cultural inferiority complexes. Cultural nationalists had to rebut the charge that America's natural scenes were culturally bankrupt, hardly meriting description as landscapes since too much nature was involved. In the account of her American sojourn in the late 1820s, British novelist Frances Trollope declared that the Ohio River between its confluence with the Mississippi and Louisville, Kentucky would have been 'perfect', 'were there occasionally a ruined abbey, or feudal castle, to mix the romance of real life with that of nature'.[78] Never mind the absence of castles, cathedrals and other ennobling adornments, cultural nationalists gained confidence by focusing on what the scientist and explorer of the trans-Mississippi west, Clarence King, dubbed America's 'green old age' (1872). Not only were California's giant sequoias and redwoods the biggest faunal representatives on earth (and an American world exclusive), but, as the journalist Horace Greeley had boasted in 1859, sequoias had been 'of very substantial size when David danced before the ark, when Solomon laid the foundations of the temple, when Theseus ruled in Athens'.[79]

Venerability had been added to the advantages of size and beauty, but this was not the ultimate compensation. The very quality of rawness constituted the trump card. This is evident in Henry Wadsworth Longfellow's semi-autobiographical novel *Kavanagh* (1849), which con-

tains a blistering critique of literary nativism. One of the book's characters, Hathaway Passing, an arch-nationalistic editor who wants to set
up a mass-circulation magazine dedicated to the cause (*The Niagara*),
anticipates 'a national literature altogether shaggy and unshorn, that
shall shake the earth, like a herd of buffaloes thundering over the
prairies'.[80] Nationalists puffed that the wild majesty of American nature, unencumbered by the impress of the past, was bound to uplift the
life of the mind. Thoreau was convinced that America was designed for
a far nobler purpose than the making of a fast buck. Echoing British
poet William Blake's conviction that 'great things are done when men
and mountains meet', he argued, in 1862:

> If the heavens of America appear infinitely higher, and the stars brighter,
> I trust these facts are symbolic of the height to which the philosophy and
> poetry and religion of her inhabitants may one day soar . . . For I believe
> that climate does thus react on man – as there is something in the
> mountain air that feeds the spirit and inspires. Will not man grow to
> greater perfection intellectually as well as physically under these influ-
> ences? I trust that we will be more imaginative . . . our intellect generally
> on a grander scale . . . Else to what end does the world go on, and why
> was America discovered?[81]

Though even the most ardent cultural nationalists favoured a cultivated rural scene or gracious town as their everyday outdoor environment, wild nature supplied a better national symbol. James Fenimore
Cooper had risen to the challenge more than a decade before Emerson's
admonition of 1837, becoming the first American novelist to pledge
allegiance to the nation's untilled soil. In *The Pioneers* (1823), the first
home-grown American bestseller, Cooper found his winning formula
in the elemental clash on the frontier between 'savagery' and 'civilization'. Sticking to the literary trail he had blazed, Cooper generated
another four, equally popular, tales in this 'Leatherstocking' series,
whose hallmark was the awesome sublimity of America's wilderness
and the nobility of its human occupants, Indian and pioneer.

Cooper had counterparts in the artistic community. Prior to the
1830s, American artists essentially emulated European styles and subjects. The Hudson River School broke out of this straitjacket and located
beauty and value in the Hudson River valley and Catskill mountains of
upstate New York. Human figures were largely absent from the landscapes of Thomas Cole, the school's founder, an English immigrant
who grew up on the upper Ohio that left Frances Trollope nonplussed.
Even when included, people were invariably dwarfed and humbled by
their natural environs.[82] The canvases of his colleague Asher Durand

celebrated scenes that had escaped what he called 'the pollutions of civilization'.[83]

Neil Evernden claims that, whereas nature is culturally constructed (and by definition, therefore, a domesticated thing), wilderness is an objective, primordial condition: '*Wildness* is the quality of this divine other. Wildness is not "ours" – indeed, it is the one thing that can *never* be ours. An entity with the quality of wildness is its own, and no other's.' But the wildness of upstate New York was often just as contrived as the informality of Capability Brown's gardens (see chapter 6). By the 1830s, civilization's pollutants had already infiltrated the Hudson valley and artists sometimes deleted elements which spoiled the impression of uncontaminated wildness; their canvases betray no sign of wharf, mill, cottage or quarry.[84]

We should resist the urge to identify incipient conservationism in Cole's paintings and Cooper's novels. Through the mouthpiece of Leatherstocking (aka Natty Bumppo), Cooper reflected on the ecological consequences of frontier conquest, notably deforestation and wildlife depletion. With reference to a massacre of passenger pigeons, Leatherstocking criticizes the pioneer's 'wasty ways', bemoaning on another occasion how they 'scourge the very 'arth with their axes'.[85] Yet there is no doubt in Cooper's mind that the price is worth paying for the blessings of civilization. We should also be careful in our interpretation of the work of photographers. Their photographs may have galvanized public support for nature protection in the formative years of the mid- to late nineteenth century, but the desire to obtain perfect views led some Americans (and Australians) to chop down interfering trees. And sometimes cut trees were introduced to embroider the foreground of views considered otherwise too bare.[86]

The United States also developed a moralistic, republican version of nature that went far beyond the aesthetics of scenery. Enlightenment thinkers perceived nature as the supreme authority. Nature in this guise justified resentment against Britain. In 1774 Richard Henry Lee of Virginia told delegates to the Continental Congress, who were accustomed to grounding their protestations against colonial misrule in the rights of Englishmen, that we 'lay our rights upon the broadest bottom, the ground of nature'.[87] The prominent reference in the Declaration of Independence (1776) to 'the Laws of Nature and of Nature's God' dictating America's right to nationhood was a powerful statement of nature as the unimpeachable source of unambiguous truth, a legitimating principle overriding the claims of tradition and history.

The distinctiveness of American attitudes to nature can be highlighted with reference to Canadian experience. Upper Canada, home to the majority of English-speaking settlers, was well endowed with natural resources and scenic spectacles. Nevertheless, nature lacks comparable moral integrity in Canadian novels written at the same time as Cooper's. Nor is wild nature so hallowed. In John Richardson's *Wacousta* (1833), wild nature jeopardizes the human civilization to which it is vastly inferior. Richardson's ideal of nature is the subdued nature of Europe. While Cooper is refining the theme of a benign nature's moral strength, nature is indifferent and silent in Canadian literature. Marcia Kline compares the writings of three women who migrated westward – two Canadian sisters and an American. In the Canadian recollections of Susanna Moodie and Catharine Parr Traill, she detects a yearning for the more picturesque and humanized landscapes of the old country. The American writer, Caroline Kirkland, is more positive towards raw nature.[88] Unwilling to repudiate political ties with Britain, Canadians were content to maintain cultural bonds, which included keeping faith with British notions of nature. Feelings of 'Canadianness', as the literary critic Northrop Frye suggests, did not emerge until the 1860s, when Darwinian attitudes were more powerful than the Romantic impulses prevailing when Americans were busy forging their national identity.[89]

Nature was a vital cohesive force in a country that lacked the glue of ethnic, religious and racial homogeneity. Reinforcing the shared commitment to republicanism, democracy and free enterprise, a literal sense of common ground could mitigate the centrifugal tendencies of heterogeneity. The fabled frontier thesis of Frederick Jackson Turner (1893), which rooted American culture, character and intellect firmly in the unmodified nature that colonists encountered on the frontier, represented the culmination of a way of thinking about nature as a moral quality imbued with a redemptive virtue that rubbed off almost magically on those who came into contact with it, metamorphosing Europeans into Americans.

In settler nations whose white citizens are increasingly cut off from their pioneer pasts in suburban environments, the national park enshrines nature's recruitment for patriotic purposes. The appropriation of nature as heritage elevates a particular version of the past – in this instance, the culture, history and environmental settings of the nation's largely WASP (White Anglo-Saxon Protestant) founders. What resonance or relevance can a nature whose cultural value resides in its ability to conjure up the New World as it was when the first European pioneer clapped eyes on it have for today's Laotian immigrant, or for an Afro-American or a Native American?

The cultural argument for nature preservation in Old and New Worlds alike is often conservative, myopic from an ecological standpoint and prone to alliance with nativism. The American identification of freedom and independence with wild nature produces the fear that the values of nationalism itself will be damaged if you destroy the symbols of nationalism because they depend on embodiment in tangible objects. Killing a bald eagle becomes as heinous a crime as burning the Stars and Stripes. This objectification of cultural beliefs through attachment to certain landscapes or animals results in an odd sort of conservation: the bald eagle's value derives not from any ecological role but from its status as national emblem. Nature as national heritage offers no reason for an American to be worried about the fate of Canadian or Mexican eagles.

Visions of an authentic nature propel arguments for the preservation and rehabilitation of national heritage, just as the growing practice of ecological restoration increasingly distinguishes between correct and incorrect versions of nature. In the late nineteenth and early twentieth centuries, pride in native American nature fuelled campaigns to curb the influx of non-native plant species, finding a symbolic focus in 1909 in opposition to a Japanese gift of 2,000 ornamental cherry trees to the city of Washington, DC. This was part of a wider confrontation between advocates of 'ecological independence' and proponents of 'ecological cosmopolitanism' that complemented and overlapped with debates over immigration restriction.[90]

Today, anti-restorationist groups and journalists sympathetic to their cause are increasingly vociferous in their criticism of the champions of native nature and historic landscapes, accusing them of intolerance towards nature's 'aliens'. English Heritage and English Nature have formulated long-term plans to gradually reinvest the gardens of Kenwood House on London's Hampstead Heath with some of their original eighteenth-century glory by checking the growth of non-native species such as turkey oak, sycamore, chestnut, laurel and rhododendron. What official management terminology refers to as 'control' has been presented as sinister botanical 'cleansing' by the advocates of wild, multicultural disorder. But where the latter perceive a reactionary, xenophobic campaign fed by resentment against the successful immigrant and an unhealthy obsession with order, the restorationists see a crusade to reclaim the rights of those members of 'first nature' suffocated by aggressive invaders, an anti-Darwinian intervention necessary to even the odds in the struggle for existence.

6

Nature as Landscape

Ronald Hepburn, a specialist in the philosophy of aesthetics, believes we perceive and evaluate natural objects and objects of art differently. Aesthetic experience of nature, he argues, involves immersion rather than detachment. Whereas a piece of art is framed, nature is frameless and offers more scope for the individual imagination because it has not been deliberately created. The question of seeing what the artist intended us to see does not arise; the perceiver provides the frame.[1] In practice, the distinction between objects of art and nature is not quite so clear. The very language we use to conceptualize various aspects of nature derives from the realm of cultural forms. 'Scenery', for instance, is a theatrical term, and some natural scenes have been deliberately 'staged' (to use Kenneth Olwig's term), inviting detachment and providing interpretative frames.[2] Focusing on enclosure and landscape gardens in eighteenth- and early nineteenth-century England, but with some reference to the United States for comparative purposes, this chapter surveys the new landscape and looks at how it displayed the distribution of power within society. It also explores the intersections between ideas of nature and conceptions of landscape and countryside.

The word 'landscape' denotes places that are the combined product of human and bio-geological forces, as suggested by its frequent, rather indiscriminate, use as a synonym for nature, land, scenery, the physical environment and even ecosystems. Some historical ecologists still cling to a distinction between 'natural' and 'cultural' landscapes. But approaches to landscape as perceptual terrain and what W. J. T. Mitchell calls a 'medium of cultural expression' are firmly in the ascendant, often to the neglect of physical aspects. Landscape, argues Donald Meinig, is *'comprehensive and cultural* . . . it encompasses everything to be seen in our ordinary surroundings . . . virtually all that can be seen has been created or altered by human intervention'. This perspective, pioneered in the 1950s by perceptual geographers concerned with 'the country of the mind' (James Wreford Watson), has been rediscovered and popularized of late by Simon Schama in *Landscape and Memory*.[3]

'Landscape' was once a far more precise term. For the medieval peasant, it meant a system of cultivated plots. In its original medieval sense, the related expression, 'countryside', was also primarily associated with the peasantry. Deriving from the French *contra*, meaning 'opposite' or 'against', it was attached to a tract of land stretching before the observer.[4] These largely vernacular ideas were eventually redefined by social elites, who transformed them into aesthetic and recreational concepts. English landscape preferences were acquired from sixteenth- and seventeenth-century Dutch and Flemish painters such as Pieter Brueghel and Peter Paul Rubens, who applied the term *landskip* to rural scenes. 'Landscape' was also applied to the painting itself – a sense retained in references to 'a landscape' by John Constable – a process Olwig refers to as 'the colonisation of nature by landscape scenery'.[5]

Nature enclosed

The latest generation of human geographers and the 'new' garden historians seek to reveal the victors and victims in the competition for control over the definition and use of nature. They remind us that the 'timeless' landscape of the English countryside – the 'real' England cherished by foreign tourists and makers of period films, such as Merchant Ivory – is the outcome of specific historical circumstances, notably the commercial revolution as expressed through the acceleration of the rate of enclosure and imparkation. They call this historicized countryside a 'landscape of exclusion'.[6]

We are also gradually recognizing that the landscapes of the American west, which nineteenth-century white adventurers, nature writers and national park promoters hailed as exemplars of pristine and unadorned nature, were actually created by Euro-American incursion and reconceptualization. When US cavalry first entered Yosemite Valley, California in the 1850s, it was a place of work and people. The meadows and open woodland struck white visitors who came in the soldiers' wake as park-like because Indians had intensively managed the valley to maximize the number of game animals and acorns (as well as to create recreational opportunities). But the recent eviction of Indians had disguised this long aboriginal occupation. A Yosemite Indian revisiting Yosemite Valley in 1929 (the sole survivor of the tribe expelled in the 1850s) was unimpressed by subsequent changes in the land. Management (or lack of it) for the sake of wilderness values had fostered a landscape she thought untidy and overgrown.[7]

The English iconographic counterpart to American wilderness is the countryside. We rarely conceptualize British environmental history in these terms but it also helps to approach rural Britain as a landscape of dispossession. The brushing aside of the Native American created a blank canvas onto which Euro-Americans projected their ideas of wildness (initially negative but increasingly holy by the time whites penetrated Yosemite Valley). In a similar fashion, according to John Rennie Short, Britain's eighteenth- and early nineteenth-century enclosure, urbanization and industrialization 'decanted the rural population, leaving a vacuum to be filled by imaginative reconstructions of rurality'.[8] George Ensor, an authority cited by Karl Marx, had explained in 1818 how, to make room for sheep and deer during the Highland Clearances (1780s–1850s), 'the Scottish grandees dispossessed families as they would grub up coppice-wood'.[9]

Emphasis on the brutality of enclosure and clearance can easily conjure up a mythical past. Short excoriates the post-1750 enclosure movement as 'a profit-based exercise which destroyed the English peasantry and replaced a moral economy of traditional rights and obligations with the cash nexus of commercial capitalism'.[10] For maudlin sentiment, however, it is hard to beat the edenic vision crafted by W. G. Hoskins in the 1950s. Though he demonstrates a keener awareness of socio-economic realities elsewhere in his work, he has also given us an image of a 'Merrie England' *c*.1690 that was free of stress and distress, with universal access to nature's fruits and delights:

> Few boys lived beyond easy walking distance of thick woodland, or of wild and spacious heaths, where they could work off freely the animal energies that in the twentieth century lead too many of them in the foul and joyless towns into the juvenile courts. There was plenty of scope for poachers of fish and game, and plenty of fresh air and space for everybody, and silence if they wanted it. No industrial smoke, nothing faster on the roads than a horse, no incessant noises from the sky . . . how infinitely more pleasant a place England then was for the majority of her people![11]

England before commercial and industrial upheaval was no haven of tranquillity (though early modern game laws lacked the teeth of their eighteenth-century replacements, and enforcement was lax). Moreover, enclosure's role in shaping the essential features of the English country-side after 1700 may have been overstated (some hedges are the ghosts of former wildwood rather than eighteenth-century plantings).[12] Much of England had already been enclosed in piecemeal and often non-traumatic fashion by 1450. This process slowed down considerably over the next century and a half, before picking up again in a more or less gradual and frequently non-disruptive manner around 1600.

None the less, we should not underestimate the scale of convulsions during the eighteenth and early nineteenth centuries in human or natural terms. In the century following the first Enclosure Act of 1701, 3.5 million acres of open commons, fields and woodland were dis-sected into private parcels, redistributed and ploughed up. Between the first parliamentary Enclosure Act of 1761 and 1844, some 2,500 Acts subdivided over 4 million acres. Some 20 per cent of England's total land surface was enclosed between 1760 and 1820.

Food prices, which had been climbing steadily since the 1760s, rose even higher during the Napoleonic Wars, peaking around 1813. The most striking feature of English enclosure during the 1800–13 wartime period, as pressure on marginal land intensified, was the consumption of open moorland. In *A Tour through the Whole Island of Great Britain* (1742–6), Daniel Defoe had dismissed Bagshot Heath, Surrey, just under 20 miles from London, as 'given up to barrenness, horrid and frightful to look on, not only good for little, but good for nothing . . . a foil to the beauty of the rest of England'.[13] The 'improvers' regarded them as an affront to efficient agriculture rather than unsightly. Still, most heaths, moors and fens were highly productive, integral to the rural economy.

Many people resisted the passing of the old social and natural order. Between 1631 and 1653, the earl of Bedford and various other so-called 'Adventurers' (those who put up the capital for drainage projects) enclosed and reclaimed 100,000 acres of Cambridgeshire fenland. Dis-placed fenfolk sabotaged the new drainage installations. Repeatedly in the 1630s, protesters demolished dikes, filled in ditches, broke down fences and destroyed grain.[14] Prominent among those who mourned a vanishing world was John Clare (1793–1864), the 'peasant poet' who grew up on the edge of the heath country of northern Northampton-shire and the fens of Lincolnshire. Clare was the son of barely literate peasants and grabbed what schooling he could between demanding farm chores. In the early 1800s, he spent much of his time wandering Helpston Heath, tending stock and scribbling verse on any available scrap of paper. His prodigious literary output (though it never earned him enough to free him from farm labour) displays a gift for keen observation and representation of the natural world in what he called 'a language that is ever green'. The abrupt, homogenizing changes underway as enclosure ripped his home ground apart after 1809 lent poignancy to Clare's celebration of his natural habitat in 'The Village Minstrel' (1821):

> *desolation struck her deadly blows,*
> *As curst improvement 'gan his fields inclose:*
> *O greens, and fields, and trees, farewell, farewell!*[15]

There is no evidence that he took direct action but his poetry trembles with indignation (such was his anguish, he wound up in a lunatic asylum). In 'The Lamentations of Round Oak Waters' (1820), a poem considered too radical for publication in his first collection, Clare directly empathized with the 'genius' of the brook, which, stripped of its shade through the ploughing of its banks, has dried up:

> *Dire nakedness o'er all prevails*
> *Yon fallows bare and brown*
> *Are all beset with posts and rails*
> *And turned upside down.*

Clare's sensitivity to man's savagery to man and other creatures was so sharp that he is now embraced as a spiritual forefather of today's radical environmentalism. Anne Barton is confident that he would back the activists (such as those at Newbury, Berkshire, in 1996) who chain themselves to trees and perch in their crowns to prevent ancient woodland from being bulldozed to make way for bypasses.[16]

Nature as landscape of leisure: eighteenth-century parks and gardens

'Amenity' is a term that derives from the Latin *amoenitas*, meaning the aesthetic and sensory pleasures of country living. The role of the countryside as an amenity for wealthy urbanites, originally enshrined in the the Roman *villa rustica*, had been in retreat during the later Middle Ages, when Norman hunting reserves were eroded by economic pressures. But the return of prosperity towards the end of the fifteenth century was accompanied by a new wave of parkland creation. Hunting remained immensely popular, and the parks of wealthy Tudors were often located on the sites of Norman deer parks (explaining why many trees in eighteenth-century park illustrations look so big and old).[17] But the new parks, besides being larger than their predecessors, were more than just hunting grounds. Grazing, hay-making and timber harvesting were increasingly prominent functions by the seventeenth century, and deer were often killed for food rather than sport. This changing character was reflected in the Elizabethan tendency to erect houses rather than hunting lodges in their parks; these were also innovative in becoming the proprietor's main place of residence instead of just a retreat. And given that it was often hard by 1700 to draw a clear divide between an estate's recreational and its productive functions (the home farm overlapped with the park), we should be aware of the drawbacks of the convenient dichotomy between landscape of leisure and landscape of work.

The new rash of parks indicates that it would be paranoid to assume that the wealthy regarded every bit of the natural world as potential fodder for the monstrous maw of an insatiable capitalism. Nevertheless, as the eighteenth century advanced, the generous acreages allocated to gardens and parks, and thus spared conversion into extractable wares, were just as infused with the ethos of control over and consumption of nature as the landscapes of work and production that looked so different. A 'place' was not found, but made. As the arch-improver Henry Crawford commented of the Thornton Lacey estate in Jane Austen's *Mansfield Park* (1814): 'By some such improvements as I have suggested . . . you may give it a higher character. You may raise it into a *place*.'[18]

Landscapes of leisure were no more innocent and no less enclosed than the landscapes of agricultural progress. The privatization of nature was particularly evident in the conversion (or reconversion) of woodland into hunting estates and the controversy over game laws. The most savage piece of legislation was the Black Act of 1723, which created fifty new capital offences. According to one of its provisions, mere presence in the vicinity of game in possession of a weapon and with a blackened face was a hanging offence (as was harbouring someone charged with this crime).[19]

Whereas the designation of a Royal Forest in the Middle Ages grafted deer and deer hunting onto existing land uses such as grazing and tree-cutting, park creation – ever since the establishment of the first Norman hunting preserves – involved a mixture of physical displacement and annulment of users' rights based on common law. Following their eviction to make way for a Tudor park, the villagers of Wilstrop, Yorkshire, in alliance with various discontented elements among the local gentry, attacked the local estate on various occasions in 1498.

During one raid, they uprooted the boundary fence (pale) and recently planted walnut and apple trees.[20] Not only villages but also productive farmland, roads and other public rights of way were obliterated.

In many instances, the sole crime that villagers had committed was to spoil the estate-owner's view. At Normanton, Rutland, park creation entailed demolition of church and village (1764); the village was rebuilt outside the estate, the church within it. Oliver Goldsmith's poem, *The Deserted Village* (1770), was reputedly based on the removal of the villagers of Newham to Nuneham Courtenay (one-and-a-half miles away) to make way for the construction of Lord Harcourt's Nuneham Park (1760–1) on a hill overlooking the Thames.[21] Yet perhaps the most astonishing story – due to the sheer temerity of the landlord – is that of Middleton, near Blandford, Dorset. Two cottages, one of them fifteenth-century, comprise the sole reminder of the original village of Middleton, which had consisted of over a hundred dwellings. This village, one of the oldest in Dorset, was slowly demolished by Joseph Damer (Viscount Milton) between 1771 and 1790, as sitting tenants gradually died off. Lancelot 'Capability' Brown (1715–83) laid out the park around his new house.[22] Living up to his name, Damer dammed the valley on his estate to create a fishpond. According to local folklore, when some villagers refused to give up their leases and move half a mile to the new village of Milton Abbas, he breached the dam and flooded them out. Before we leap to condemn such men unreservedly, we might pause to consider whether at least some 'displaced' tenants found their rebuilt 'model' villages an improvement on their former living conditions and were grateful rather than resentful.

Francis Bacon's essay on gardens (1625) is never mentioned by his hostile green critics. Yet he considered them 'the greatest refreshment to the spirits of man'. Some garden historians have even traced the English fondness for the 'wild garden' (an oxymoron to some, never-theless) back to Bacon's prescriptive essay. His ideal garden of circa 30 acres included a 6-acre 'heath or desert' awash with wildflowers, an area that he wanted to see 'framed, as much as may be, to a natural wildness'. Nevertheless, he retained a particularly strong affection for a closely cropped 'green': 'nothing is more pleasant to the eye than green grass kept finely shorn'.[23] Isaac Newton was equally fond of gardens, one of his biographers assuring us that his own garden was 'never out of order'. The sight of a weed apparently greatly bothered him.[24]

The manicured aesthetic of nature represented by Bacon and Newton, born of a wider belief in the perfectibility of nature, flourished in the eighteenth century. Refined taste in landscape, as in architecture, was informed by a mechanistic conception of nature as a well-regulated and predictable system that functioned in accordance with laws stemming from a supreme intelligence. The idea of proportionality and symmetry was embodied in the Palladian style and exemplified by the palace and grounds of Versailles. The formal gardens of eighteenth-century continental Europe signified the triumph of culture over a self-willed natural world as emphatically as the sprouting factories and urban tenements. Straight avenues radiated from a central axis formed by the house itself. Pumps forced water uphill and into fountains. The outdoor art of topiary distorted trees and bushes into every conceivable shape. Geometrically shaped garden terraces and parterres (level parts consisting of flower beds) were embroidered with statues, urns, terraces and mounds.

British aestheticians were in the vanguard of the reaction. They invariably couched their reform proposals in terms of a rigid dichotomy between Nature and Art. Joseph Addison in 1712 entered a plea for the 'beautiful Wildness of Nature' over 'the nicer Elegancies of Art', frowning that on most estates 'we see the Marks of the Scissors upon every Plant and Bush'. The assault on stern form gathered momentum with Alexander Pope, who, in 1719, dismissed as 'green walls' the towering and immaculately clipped evergreen hedges that hemmed in paths, and ridiculed 'modern' gardeners as 'ever-green tailors'. In 1722 Pope extended his attack to the entire notion of artificiality, wanting to know who would 'prefer a painted face to the natural colour of a beautiful countenance'. Conventional taste was also confronted in the call for walls to come tumbling down. The wall was thought to lend dignity to an estate by uniting garden with house. In 1715, however, the gardening author Stephen Switzer wanted to 'throw the Garden open to all View, to . . . the expansive Volumes of Nature herself'. These radical views were collected in Batty Langley's *New Principles of Gardening* (1728) which condemned 'abominable Mathematical Regularity and Stiffness'. Langley pronounced the felling of ancient oaks for the sake of regularity (only trees in rows were acceptable) 'a Crime of so high a Nature, as not to be pardon'ed'.[25] Banish Art and follow Nature's dictates was Langley's battle-cry.

The landed gentry eventually began to adopt these less formal preferences. Though some clung to traditional designs, many were finding, by the 1760s, that the new aesthetic meshed happily with other, more material, considerations, namely, shooting, riding, forestry and stock grazing. (Grazing animals 'mowed' the growing expanses of turf.)[26] In the meantime, English estate-owners developed a fashionable regard for classical antiquity. Gardens studded with grottoes, bridges, temples and obelisks were fashioned at this time. These features were often scattered at random – as at Castle Howard, Yorkshire – but they sometimes marked deliberate stages in a circular walk. The aim was to render the landscape more interesting by summoning up the classical past, a tradition whose British origins might be traced to the publication of the first English translation in 1726 of *Ten Books of Architecture* by the fifteenth-century Italian humanist Leone Battista Alberti. To be reminded of 'great men' and the depth and glory of the human past through imitations of the 'remains of Antiquity' was thought highly desirable.[27] The impulse to wrap yourself in the trappings of antiquity can be explained by the rise of an urban-based commercial class conscious of its perceived vulgarity and anxious to acquire social respectability and cultural status by purchasing rural estates. Accordingly, the 'New Romans' of a rising British mercantile empire hungrily embraced what Schama calls a 'British Virgilian' style.[28]

The reforms associated with Addison, Pope and Switzer, as implemented by the English gentry, are usually characterized as a revolt against continental formalism. Jean-Jacques Rousseau, the continent's leading champion of the informal *jardin anglais*, took it as his model for the garden of 'Elysée' in *Julie; ou La Nouvelle Héloïse* (1761). In the terrestrial Eden that the noblewoman, Julie, has crafted for her young tutor and lover, St Preux, 'the gardener's hand is nowhere to be discerned, nothing contradicts the idea of a desert island, and I cannot perceive any footsteps of men . . . you see nothing here in an exact row, nothing level, Nature plants nothing by the ruler'.[29] But Rousseau had been duped, for the new convention was hardly more natural. The English garden-park may have looked less kempt and orderly, but was thoroughly contrived.

The garden-park at Stourhead, though hardly typical, is one of the most exquisitely engineered. This garden-park in the south-western corner of Wiltshire was the creation of Henry Hoare I (1677–1725), a London banker who financed the landscaping ventures of many fellow landowners, and his eldest son and heir, Henry Hoare II (1705–85). In a real estate deal that symbolized the shifting balance of power between 'new' and 'old' money, Henry Hoare I bought the estate of the Stourtons, bankrupt aristocrats; he razed the ancestral seat and started to erect a house exuding Palladian uniformity, which was completed in the 1740s. In a drastic departure from both the Versailles model and the future style of Capability Brown, in both of which the landscape served as backdrop for the central architectural jewel, the Hoares displaced the house to a peripheral position in the overall design, entirely incidental to the grounds.[30] The house and garden are separated from the park by a transitional zone of trees, bushes and grass which, reflecting refined notions of order, was dubbed a 'wilderness'. The central feature of the confection, begun in 1743, was an artificial lake, which assumed its present shape in the 1750s when a river was dammed to join and enlarge two existing bodies of water. Today's parkscape is more or less as it was when Henry Hoare II died in 1785 (with the exception of various plantings, notably evergreens).

The visitor is drawn around the lake by a string of classical inducements representing a complicated series of allusions to Virgil's Aeneas and his journeys.[31] The voyage through Elysium climaxes with a full view of the lake from Apollo's temple. The Pantheon, sited to serve as the focal point of the entire experience, houses a statue of Hercules (a figure associated with gardens since the Renaissance). Pagan water deities are Stourhead's speciality, however, and items such as the nymphs' grotto also furnish places of rest and shelter. In the Mediterranean, these structures were no doubt intended to supply shade. In England, they provide welcome protection from rain, as I appreciated when visiting Stourhead on a very showery summer day.

Stourhead, like many other English parkscapes, has since been deprivatized through the agency of the National Trust, which took charge shortly before the Second World War. Most visitors today will be largely unaware of the classical associations with which Henry Hoare II heightened the landscape. He intended them to be a permanent feature of both the physical and the mental landscape but, as our knowledge of the classics fades, Stourhead is perceived differently. Hoare conceived it as a work of art, with the natural elements firmly subordinate. (Nature, in the shape of a spring, determined the location of the grotto – but that is all.) He might be shocked to find that (with the exception of classical scholars) the majority of us are most impressed by the lake and the trees, seeing the monuments as little more than curious ornaments, even intrusions. Even so, the veneer of artifice is inescapable. Views are literally framed, sometimes by overarching vegetation. We move around the park from view to view like visitors in an art gallery. But since the frame is a living entity it threatens to impinge on the scene, and boughs must be cut back periodically.

In one corner of the park is the village of Stourton with its church. Though the Hoares significantly reduced its size it has not been moved. And unlike many of his peers, who blithely fashioned sanitized landscapes of prestige, gentle recreation and repose, Henry Hoare II wished to impart the aura of a less exclusive, living and working, landscape. Though no river exited the lake at this point, he erected a five-arched bridge across the corner nearest the village, modelled on Palladio's bridge at Vicenza. As he wrote to a daughter in 1762: 'When you stand at the Pantheon the water will be seen thro the arches and it will look as if the river came down through the village and that this was the village bridge for publick use.' His grandson, Richard Colt Hoare (1758–1838), who inherited the property in the early nineteenth century, did demolish cottages that marred the view of the church and gardens from the lakeside walk. Yet work and workers were largely exorcized from the Stourhead scene. One early nineteenth-century picture shows rustics fishing, but most ordinary folk depicted in various paintings in the house itself cater to the leisured – the permissible forms of work engaged in by gardeners, boatmen and those sweeping the gravel-topped circular path.[32]

The pastoral illusion

Eighteenth-century English landowners did more to recreate the ambience of Virgilian pastoralism than erect temples of flora. In his *Georgics*, Virgil celebrated an inclusive pastoral landscape which, unlike a cultivated one, bore 'no fence or boundary-stone'.[33] Belts of trees that screened off the surrounding agrarian landscape of crops enhanced the appearance of informal pastoralism. But the key device was the sunken fence. Such a fence (or wall) hidden in a ditch was popularly known as a ha-ha; the name derives from the exclamation of surprise that was typically the reaction of strollers who found their saunterings beyond a house suddenly interrupted, realizing they had been taken in by what Schama calls a 'poetic lie'. The ha-ha lent the impression of an unbroken landscape and 'very polite kind of rudeness' to someone gazing out from the windows of the mansion while keeping grazing animals off the lawns.[34] The ha-ha's effect is entirely lost, however, if it is approached from the other side. A 'visible stamping of power', in Raymond Williams's phrase, it was not intended to give the cowherd the sense that the estate was part of a shared landscape.[35] Williams has reflected on the cruel sham involved in the construction of an idealized communal landscape that paralleled the disintegration of the authentic English commons. As the gentry were pretending to take down their fences in conformity with the last word in landscape aesthetics, the real things were going up beyond parkland boundaries. As the countryside came to look more like a formal garden, gardens themselves were looking more like the old rural landscape.[36]

As capitalism besieged the natural world, nature was increasingly defined as those places 'where industry was not'. Williams also pon-

ders the 'very bitter irony' that some people managed to 'both live on
the process and escape its products'.[37] The price of a comparatively
small patch of landscape beauty and composure might include more
extensive ugliness and environmental dislocation elsewhere. A particularly good American example of Williams's point is the former Barron
Garden at Menlo Park, California. Carved out of oak savannah, the 380-
acre Barron Garden consciously aped the aristocratic parks of Europe,
and English visitors were astonished and delighted to find a place of
such old-world refinement in barbaric, rugged nineteenth-century
California. (To maintain the lawns at their optimal English green, the
grounds were routinely swamped in water outside the winter rainy
season.) Barron Garden was funded from the profits of William
Barron's mercury mines twenty miles away at New Almaden.[38]

Ralph Allen's 28-acre Prior Park overlooking Bath in England casts
further light on the symbiosis between landscapes of leisure and landscapes of work. Allen made most of his money quarrying the stone that
built the fashionable Palladian spa town of Bath. He constructed a
tramway (1731) to carry the enormous blocks of Bath stone (oolite)
down from his Combe Down quarry (located almost immediately
above Prior Park) to the River Avon. (Unlike Combe Down, which
mostly preserved the pasture above the workings, his Hampton Down
quarry was open-cast.)

Opened to the public in 1996 following acquisition by the National
Trust, which is restoring the garden and buildings, Prior Park was
created by Allen between 1734 and 1764 in conjunction with Pope and
Brown. The formality and clean lines of the initial layout, in which
lawns predominated, were relieved by Pope's 'wilderness area'. That it
did not take much informality to make a wilderness from a genteel
eighteenth-century perspective is indicated by an engraving of 1752,
which depicts this area as a few well-spaced clumps and lines of trees
and gently winding paths.[39] The severe fringes of the woodland were
eventually softened, and in the 1760s Brown removed a cascade that
broke up the gardens at midpoint, creating the current effect of an
uninterrupted sweep of unadorned parkland between the house and
the Palladian bridge over the lakes at the lower end of the estate. The
tracks of his tramway ran parallel to one side of his estate, shielded by
a wall.

Prior Park illustrates how Brown advanced the 'freer' style of English landscaping. Brown (whose nickname derived from his apparent
obsession with the 'capabilities' of a place) dotted the landscape with
loosely arranged clumps of oak and meandering paths, but the overall
thrust was clearance. He not only eliminated sentimental classical

buildings and statues and erased the garden that served as intermediary terrain between house and park; he also uprooted avenues of trees. His stark minimalism drew fire from both traditional formalists and, increasingly as the century drew to a close, the advocates of the emerging aesthetic of the picturesque. The latter, typified by designer Humphry Repton, favoured a busier, more intimate and varied, landscape composed of streams with uneven banks, mossed stones, hollows, mounds covered in tangles of ferns and vines, thickets, fallen trees and exposed roots (and from which the garden near the house had not been banished). Richard Payne Knight, a Hereford landowner and early disciple of William Gilpin's notion of the picturesque (see chapter 7), focused his hatred of Brown's totalitarian new order on its central feature, the oceanic and featureless lawn, that 'flat, insipid, waving plain' (1794).[40]

Not all stately homes became marooned in a vast prairie of turf (and in many that had, the garden was staging a comeback by 1800). But in many of the 'crown jewel' sites on which garden history has traditionally focused, the effect of Brown's reorganizations was to run the park right up to the front steps of the house, a style exemplified at Wimpole Hall, south Cambridgeshire. (This change in landscape aesthetics was happily reinforced by considerations of financial economy; the cost of buildings and the upkeep of stone terraces, fountains and parterres was becoming prohibitive.)[41] Brown's distinctive contribution to landscape is usually considered to be the introduction of a style faithful to William Shenstone's belief (1764) that 'whatever thwarts nature is treason'.[42] Yet Brown's remodelling of the landscape (what he called 'place-making') was no less interventionist than the style he literally overwrote.[43] We have been misled because he covered his traces so deftly. Of his work at Burghley House, where he obliterated the formal gardens and created a lake, a guide of 1797 declared:

> It was the genius of [Brown], which, brooding over the shapeless mass, educed out of a seeming wilderness, all the order and delicious harmony which now prevail. Though the beauties, with which we are here struck, are more peculiarly the rural beauties of Mr Brown, than those of Dame Nature, she seems to wear them with so simple and unaffected a grace, that it is not even the man of taste who can, at a superficial glance, discover the difference.[44]

The English vision of nature as 'natural' garden was so powerful that it seduced potentially hostile Americans. Even that arch-cultural nationalist Thomas Jefferson was impressed, despite his Anglophobia, his republican contempt for the dissolute and parasitic aristocracy of

Europe, and, not least, his trumpeting of the superiority of American nature and scenery. Jefferson, a landed gentleman himself, toured some of England's best-known landscape gardens in 1786 with John Adams (then serving as American envoy to Britain). Adams's responses are riddled with Yankee disapproval for opulence. 'It will be long', he hoped, 'before Ridings, Parks, Pleasure Grounds, Gardens . . . grow so much in fashion in America', where Nature had 'done greater Things'. But Jefferson was struck by the 'natural style' at places like Stowe in Buckinghamshire, incorporating many features of informal English design into his own estate in Virginia's Blue Ridge Mountains. At Monticello, the Englishness of winding walks, sloping lawns and the Palladian house is enhanced by the thick surrounding hillside forests out of which the estate was carved.[45] Even the Californian Sierra Nevada was described by that most enthusiastic American celebrator of ungilded wildness, John Muir, in terms of the aesthetic conventions rooted in eighteenth-century English parkscapes. In 1894 Muir compared its canyon bottom 'parks' to 'artificial landscape-gardens, with charming groves and meadows, and thickets of blooming bushes'.[46]

Despite the genteel Englishness of Jefferson's taste in estate aesthetics, other aspects of his pastoral vision were more egalitarian. In his physiocratic view of nature, agriculture was revered for its proximity to nature, and he hailed America's (white) yeoman farmers as God's chosen people. For Jefferson, American virtue and vigour stemmed directly from redemptive contact with the soil. His democratic view of nature as pastoral paradise was most clearly expressed in a letter to fellow Virginian planter, James Madison in 1785: 'Whenever there is in any country, uncultivated lands and unemployed poor, it is clear that the laws of property have been so far extended as to violate natural right. The earth is given as a common stock for man to labour and live on.'[47] Eugene Hargrove praises Jefferson's purchase of Virginia's Natural Bridge as 'perhaps the first major act of nature preservation in North America'.[48] But for Jefferson (like the medieval Benedictine farmer-monks), wild and unmodified environments did not constitute nature. Wilderness was the raw material out of which nature was fashioned – nature being the improved, privately owned landscape of farms, gardens and rural estates that occupied the middle ground between industrial urban society and untamed savagery. Jefferson was immensely influenced by John Locke's theory of property ownership articulated in *Two Treatises of Government* (1690), in which Locke argues that inalienable property rights derive not from government or monarch but from the labour an individual invests in the land: 'Whatsoever then he removes out of the State that Nature hath provided, and left it in, he hath mixed his *Labour* with, and joyned to it something that is his own, and thereby makes it his *Property*.'[49]

Many early nineteenth-century English immigrants to America were fleeing the dislocations of enclosure, urbanization and industrialization, anxious to revive a dissolving agrarian way of life. Clare declared in his poem 'Enclosure' that the 'only bondage' known by English moorland that had 'never felt the rage of blundering plough' was 'the encircling sky'.[50] To the homesteader staking a claim to a patch of American earth and converting it from nature to property through labour, the impoundment of public space meant freedom and autonomy. By contrast, the displaced American Indian who saw the prairie sod being busted by blundering plough by these refugees from the old country's blundering plough might easily have thought that Clare's poem was written as an elegy for them and for American nature newly placed in bondage.

7

Reassessments of Nature: Romantic and Ecological

Modern environmentalism has been conditioned by a range of dangers to land, air, seas and inland waters that are largely unique to the period since the Second World War. Hydrogen chloride, a by-product of glass, soap and textile production, and better known as 'acid rain', was identified in the 1850s in the rainwater of Manchester, England. Ecological awareness in its present form, however, was shaped by a new order of pollutants, notably nuclear fall-out, insecticides, inorganic fertilizers, plastics and chemical detergents. Whether in the form of radioactive contamination, DDT residues or crude oil spilled along coasts, pollution has moulded a consciousness quite distinct from the conservationism that arose from perceptions of dwindling natural resources and the desire to preserve nature prompted by challenges to the integrity of wild lands and wildlife from farming, logging, mining and hunting.

Nevertheless, late twentieth-century attitudes to nature, particularly the valorization of its wilder aspects and conceptions of hallowed natural systems under threat, remain essentially shaped by two intellectual developments from the eighteenth and nineteenth centuries respectively that questioned the ideology of industrial capitalism and sometimes modernity itself: Romanticism and the emergence of ecological science via evolutionary theory.

The Romantic ideal of resuming contact with a re-enchanted nature was central to the counter-cultural impulse of the 1960s. As Charles Reich explained in his cult bestseller, *The Greening of America*, the new youth movement sought out nature not 'as a holiday from what is real. They go to nature as a source. The salt water of the sea is the salt in their blood. The forest is where they came from, it is the place where they feel closest to themselves, it is renewal.'[1] In 'The Moralists: A Philosophical Rhapsody' (1709), an under-appreciated forerunner of the Romantic credo by Lord Shaftesbury (Anthony Ashley Cooper, 1671–1713), the leading moral philosopher of the English Enlightenment, the character Philocles enquires of the nature-worshipping Theocles: 'how comes it that, excepting a few philosophers of your sort, the only people who are enamoured in this way, and seek the woods, the rivers, or seashores, are your poor vulgar lovers?' Yet ever-increasing numbers of Westerners are what Theocles called 'deep in this romantic way'.[2]

Some insist on ideological discontinuity between Romanticism and current environmentalism (not least because of Romanticism's elitist connotations), stressing in particular the novelty of biocentric thinking.[3] Yet for counter-cultural critics of the 1960s such as Theodore Roszak, the quest for the original ecological consciousness led straight to Romanticism (the 'great lost cause' with which he closely identified). Deep ecologists will thrill to the feeling of oneness with a vital nature expressed by William Wordsworth in *The Prelude* (1805), from which Roszak quotes at length.

> *I held unconscious intercourse with beauty*
> *Old as creation, drinking in a pure*
> *Organic pleasure from the silver wreaths*
> *Of curling mist, or from the level plain*
> *Of waters coloured by impending clouds*
>
> .   .   .   .
>
> *To every natural form, rock, fruit, or flower,*
> *Even the loose stones that cover the highway,*
> *I gave a moral life: I saw them feel,*
> *Or linked them to some feeling; the great mass*
> *Lay bedded in a quickening soul, and all*
> *That I beheld respired with inward meaning.*[4]

Meanwhile the search for the origins of ecological understanding has led others directly to Charles Darwin.

The solid ground of nature

Nature, nonetheless, has meant far more over the last two-and-a-half centuries than daffodils, waterfalls, food chains and energy flows. Romantic poets themselves tried to connect the aesthetic and sensual enjoyment derived from the contemplation and experience of the natural world with notions of order and goodness. Shelley wrote poems about west winds, clouds and skylarks but was more interested in nature's laws. Truth, liberty and love, he instructed in his lyrical drama, *Prometheus Unbound* (1818–20), are 'Nature's sacred watchwords'.[5] In Byron's poem *Childe Harold's Pilgrimage* 'the book of nature' speaks with greater meaning to the hero than books by men. The Romantic desire for communion with nature was based on an arresting distinction between nature and culture. Distaste for city life had long been a pastoral convention, yet the Romantics chose *wild* nature not only over its tamer aspects but also above the finest charms and accomplishments of the human mind. The sound of the wind in the trees was sweeter to them than any symphony.

Theologians, jurists, economists and politicians have also appealed to nature as an antidote to the flux and imperfections of past and present. Between the Renaissance and 1800, according to Basil Willey, Nature was 'the grand alternative to all that man had made of man; upon her solid ground therefore – upon the tabula rasa prepared by the true philosophy – must all the religion, the ethics, the politics, the law, and the art of the future be constructed.'[6] The idea of natural law predating man-made law stems from the classical (Stoic) idea of nature as universal moral arbiter. The belief that people are free by nature but enslaved by man inspired a range of causes from medieval peasant revolts to the eighteenth-century anti-slavery movement. The idea of nature as a liberating principle and the association of the right, the good and the immutable with the natural peaked during the eighteenth century, especially in the minds of political philosophers looking for the origins of civil society.[7] *Philosophes* and Romantics invoked nature as a force subversive to the power wielded by state, monarch, Church and God. Nature is often regarded as a problematic term due to its multiple meanings. In the eighteenth century, however, argues Willey,

> it was not the ambiguity of 'Nature' which people felt most strongly; it was rather the clarity, the authority, and the universal acceptability of Nature and Nature's laws. The historical role of 'Nature' at this time was to introduce, not further confusion, but its precise opposites, – peace, concord, toleration and progress in the affairs of men, and, in poetry and art, perspicuity, order, unity, and proportion.[8]

The reasoning that, if nature is good, then human nature must also be good was hotly debated by eighteenth-century ethicists. The argument as to whether human nature was essentially selfish or social had been provoked in the previous century by Thomas Hobbes (1588–1679), an English Royalist *émigré* in France who wrote in an era racked by reli-

Reassessments of Nature

gious strife and civil war. In *Leviathan* (1651), he characterized the state of nature in pejorative terms:

> In such condition, there is no place for Industry; because the fruit thereof is uncertain: and consequently no Culture of the Earth; no Navigation, nor use of the commodities that may be imported by sea . . . no Knowledge of the Face of the Earth; no account of Time; no Arts, no Letters; no Society; and which is worst of all, continuall feare, and danger of violent death; And the life of man, solitary, poore, nasty, brutish, and short.[9]

For Hobbes, nature was a predicament to be redeemed through culture in the form of government. The anti-Hobbesian view emanated most powerfully from the French encyclopedists, who, distinguishing sharply between a corrupt culture and innocent nature, approached history as a foul deviation from nature's original plan for liberty, equality and fraternity. The gist of Baron Holbach's thinking is that history's vices and crimes transgress nature, indeed are 'forbidden by nature, which wants him [i.e. man] to work for his lasting happiness'. 'Nature', he wrote in *Système de la Nature* (1780), 'bids man to be sociable, to love his fellows, to be just, peaceful, indulgent, beneficent, to make or leave his associates happy.'[10]

Cultural primitivism, the conviction that happiness is greatest nearest to nature, has been characterized by Arthur Lovejoy and George Boas as 'the discontent of the civilized with civilization'.[11] It is closely related to the classical idea of decline from a golden age of undefiled and spontaneously bountiful nature. These sentiments had been most famously expressed in the seventh century BC by the Roman poet, Publius Ovid, in his *Metamorphoses*:

> The first age was golden . . . Earth herself, unburdened and untouched by the hoe and unwounded by the ploughshare, gave all things freely. Spring was eternal, and the placid Zephyrs with warm breezes lightly touched the flowers, born without seeds; untilled the earth bore its fruits and the unploughed field grew hoary with heavy ears of wheat. Rivers of milk and rivers of nectar flowed, and yellow honey dripped from the green oaks.[12]

Primitivism waned in the early Christian period, re-emerging in the sixteenth century when European expansion provided indigenous peoples as role models. The writings of Michel de Montaigne, Peter Martyr and Antonio Pigafetta (the latter accompanied Ferdinand Magellan on his round-the-world voyage in 1519–22 and raved about happy and free Brazilians), introduced Europe's intelligentsia to what

eventually became known as the 'noble savage'.[13] In the seventeenth
century, a spate of utopian tales located prelapsarian paradise in an
extra-European world where people devoid of sin and clothing lived in
a state of nature without the debilitating institutions of Church, government, law and private property. The eighteenth-century search for a
better civilization often led to tropical islands. The jettisoning of
Hobbes's nightmarish vision of human life when left to nature reached
its zenith with Rousseau's popularization of the state of nature and the
concept of the noble savage in *A Discourse on the Origin of Inequality*
(1755).[14] Rousseau's *Julie* (1761) was strongly influenced by George
Anson's account (1748) of his transglobal voyage of 1740–4 – especially
visits to the islands of Juan Fernandez off Chile and Tinian, east of the
Philippines. By contrast, the idyllic account of native life on Tahiti
(1772) by the French explorer Louis-Antoine de Bougainville was itself
coloured by Rousseau's primitivism.[15]

Mountain glory

Belief in nature as a blueprint for social rejuvenation reached its zenith
in the French and American physiocratic ideology of agrarian virtue
(something never mentioned by environmentalist critics of the Enlightenment). Rousseau (1712–78) shared their notion of nature as norm. But
in the mid-eighteenth century, he railed against prevailing conceptions
of progress, specifically the conviction that science and technology
would inexorably advance the cause of humanity. Favouring agrarianism and decentralized authority, he inveighed against the corrosive
influence of commerce and industry. (Voltaire accused him of wanting
to return to cave dwelling and walking on all fours.)[16] These views have
led some to embrace him as the key figure in the formulation of a proto-
green critique prior to this century's environmental movement.[17]

Though much of Rousseau's primitivism was fustian and warmed-
over classical pastoralism, when allied to political radicalism it identified an exhilarating category of democratic landscapes that went far
beyond the more natural *jardin anglais* that he championed. Literary
juxtapositions of the ideals of frugality and equality against ostenta-
tious wealth and aristocratic injustice were often set in Rousseau's
home region, the Swiss Alps. *St Leon* (1799), a novel by the English
libertarian William Godwin, was inspired by Rousseau's Alpine
works, *Julie* and *Émile* (1762). Godwin's protagonist, the French aristo-
crat Reginald de St Leon, repents a life of 'riotous living' in Paris,
during which he has squandered his inheritance, by withdrawing into

the Swiss Alps to subsist on beans among upright and free-living pastoralists devoid of artifice.

In a European variation on the Yankee theme of republican virtue, the humble cottage and unadorned mountainside are elevated above the decadent palace and formal garden. The primitivist juxtaposition of nature and culture is encapsulated in the heroine Marguerite's lecture to Reginald: 'How idle it would be, to wish to change our arbours, our verdant lanes and thickets, for vaulted roofs, and gloomy halls.'[18] In the poetic account of his summer tour of continental Europe in 1790, when he was 20, Wordsworth celebrated the Swiss Alps as a surviving fragment of the original Eden, harbouring vestiges of Man 'entirely free, alone and wild ... Nature's child'.[19] The Swiss mountaineer and English Lakeland shepherd were the closest European approximations to the noble savage of North America.

Marjorie Hope Nicolson has commented as follows on the famous declaration by Byron's Childe Harold, 'To me, high mountains are a feeling, but the hum of human cities torture':

> We comfortably agree, believing that the emotions we feel – or are supposed to feel – in the presence of grand Nature are universal and have been shared by men at all times. But high mountains were not 'a feeling' to Virgil or Horace, to Dante, to Shakespeare or Milton ... We assume that our feelings are the perennial ones of human beings.[20]

The Romantic re-evaluation of nature can be most strikingly documented by examining this shift in literary and popular attitudes to mountains. Today's glass-domed observation cars provide maximum exposure to mountain glory for the nature pilgrim as trains cross the North American Rockies. But in pre-Romantic times, gentlefolk traversing the Pennines or the Alps drew the curtains across their carriage windows to protect themselves from offensive sights. For when they did not ignore mountains, poets and travellers disparaged them as boils, warts and blisters that disfigured the fair face of Nature, expressing mighty relief upon descending into friendly lowlands. In 1681 Charles Cotton, the Derbyshire poet, reviled his native hills as 'Nature's Pudends', and quite a few English peaks were dignified with the name 'Devils-arse' at this time.[21]

It was not simply bad roads that generated such negative views (though easier access to regions such as the Alps thanks to steamers and railways and more secure and comfortable means of local travel certainly facilitated more appreciative attitudes). Prevailing aesthetic canons elevated level and ordered landscapes. In *Modern Painters*

(1856) – from which the terms 'mountain gloom' and 'mountain glory' used by Nicolson derive – John Ruskin deplored the classical and medieval treatments of mountains that held sway until the later seventeenth century. Ruskin complained that in the classical tradition with its fondness for gentle, pastoral landscapes, mountains rarely featured except as a backdrop or as symbols for human moods.[22]

Feelings for nature reflect deeper convictions about the earth. The Byronian outlook marked the culmination of intellectual reappraisals involving theology, philosophy, geology and astronomy. Aesthetic concepts of nature, focusing on the external beauty of natural forms, cannot be divorced from metaphysical concepts of nature – the universe known to philosophy and science.[23] Thomas Burnet's *The Sacred Theory of the Earth* (1684) encapsulated the orthodox Christian view that the Flood destroyed earth's original perfection. Once smooth and regular as an egg, it became ugly and disorderly. Burnet's assumption that mountains were just a pile of post-diluvian junk, the product of human sin, was refuted by George Hakewill's physico-theology. In his *Apologie of the Power and Providence of God* (1627), Hakewill argued for mountains as an integral part of the original paradise. Further inverting theological conventions, John Wilkins (bishop of Chester) in *Of the Principles and Duties of Natural Religion* (1675) preached the belief (deism) that not only adequate but ultimate proof of God's existence could be found in nature's revealed glory, which rendered revelation superfluous:

> Whatever is Natural, doth by that appear adorned with all imaginable Elegance and Beauty . . . whereas the most curious Works of Art, the sharpest, finest Needle, doth appear as a blunt rough Bar of Iron, coming from the Furnace or the Forge . . . So vast a Difference is there betwixt the Skill of Nature, and the Rudeness and Imperfection of Art.[24]

Though it is currently fashionable to criticize the Enlightenment for promoting a demystifying rationality that debased nature, the findings of its physicists and astronomers further undermined the belief that art perfects imperfect nature. Theological and scientific innovations promoted feelings of awe for physical creation as an ordered system whose perfection mirrored that of its creator and overshadowed man's works, enabling Romantics to transfer human allegiance from art to nature.

Other new sensibilities were evident in a reaction against animal suffering as the British in particular started to become a humane and pet-loving people. The likes of Voltaire, Tom Paine, Jeremy Bentham and John Stuart Mill changed the question from the one asked by Descartes – Can they reason? – to Can they suffer?[25] Stressing the overriding importance of sentience as a common denominator between man and beast, reformers protested against man's inhumanity to various animals as well as to other people. The founding members of Britain's Royal Society for the Prevention of Cruelty to Animals (RSPCA, 1836) were also prominent in campaigns against the slave trade, child labour and excessive working hours.

The ground for Romanticism was also prepared by the aesthetic of the picturesque. Its chief theoretician, William Gilpin (1724–1804), set himself the task of 'not barely examining the face of a country; but of examining by the rules of picturesque beauty; that of not merely describing; but of adapting the description of natural beauty to the principles of artificial landscape.'[26] In the late eighteenth century, Gilpin roamed Britain judging its landscape merits. Through his guides to the Lake District, the Scottish Highlands, North Wales, Dovedale and the Wye Valley, he created and publicized the 'beauty spot'. The term picturesque is taken from landscape art and referred to a scene's potential for framing. Gilpin approached landscapes with a particularly rigorous yardstick: how well would this prospect look mounted on a wall? The landscapes Gilpin measured often fell short, since Nature is 'seldom so correct in composition as to produce a harmonious whole. Either the foreground or the background is disproportioned, or some awkward line runs through the piece; or a tree is ill placed . . . or something or other is not as it should be.'[27]

The aesthetic mood that rebelled against the picturesque was that of the sublime. The search for the picturesque excluded many landscapes and many of nature's features and moods. But Romantics followed Immanuel Kant's distinction (1764) between the merely beautiful and the sublime in nature.

> The stirring of each is pleasant, but in different ways. The sight of a mountain whose snow-covered peak rises above the clouds, the description of a raging storm . . . arouse enjoyment but with horror; on the other hand, the sight of flower-strewn meadows, valleys with winding brooks and covered with grazing flocks, the description of Elysium . . . also occasion a pleasant sensation but one that is joyous and smiling. In order that the former impression could occur to us in due strength, we must have a *feeling of the sublime*, and, in order to enjoy the latter well, *a feeling of the beautiful*. Tall oaks and lonely shadows in a sacred grove are sublime; flower beds, low hedges and trees trimmed in figures are beautiful.[28]

Edmund Burke (1729–97), whom we more readily think of as the arch-conservative he became in his later years, was a leading and influential exponent of the sublime in his more radical youth.

In a treatise published in 1757 (but probably written when he was 19), Burke noted how 'the passion caused by the great and sublime in *nature*, when those causes operate most powerfully, is Astonishment . . . the inferior effects are admiration, reverence and respect'. Instead of concentrating on landscapes primarily pleasing to the eye and on nature's benign guises, the Romantics wanted their entire beings to be thrilled with a delicious terror. In a letter to Richard Shackleton (1746), Burke remarked on how Ireland's River Liffey in spate 'gives me pleasure to see nature in those great but terrible scenes. It fills the mind with grand ideas, and turns the soul in upon herself.'[29] This desire stemmed from the belief that man's essential nature resided in his emotions ('I feel therefore I am') rather than his reason ('I think therefore I am'), a conviction that invested Shaftesbury's 'The Moralists'. Persuaded of the wisdom of Theocles's nature philosophy, Philocles declares:

> I shall no longer resist the passion growing in me for things of a natural kind; where neither art nor the conceit or caprice of man has spoiled their genuine order, by breaking in upon that primitive state. Even the rude rocks, the mossy caverns, the irregular unwrought grottos, and broken falls of waters, with all the horrid graces of the wilderness itself, as representing Nature more, will be the more engaging, and appear with a magnificence beyond the formal mockery of princely gardens.[30]

The Romantic soul felt empowered by those qualities of mountain scenery that had so appalled and disoriented their predecessors. For Byron's character Manfred, in the dramatic poem of that name, who lives in a castle in the Alps, a turn-off had become a turn-on:

> *From my youth upwards*
> *My spirit walk'd not with the souls of men;*
> *My joy was in the Wilderness, – to breathe*
> *The difficult air of the iced mountain's top,*
> *Where the birds dare not build,*
> *nor insect's wing*
> *Flit o'er the herbless granite . . .*[31]

Not that the Romantic explorer deliberately sought out truly dangerous situations. 'I must have torrents, fir trees, black woods, mountains to climb or descend, and rugged roads with precipices on either side to alarm me', Rousseau declared in his account of a trip into the French Alps near Chambéry, but proceeded immediately to indicate the degree to which Romantic sensibilities were nurtured and protected by improvements to the infrastructure: 'The road has been hedged by a parapet to prevent accidents, and I was thus enabled to contemplate the whole descent, and gain vertigoes at pleasure; for a great part of my amusement in these steep rocks is they cause a giddiness and swimming in my head which I am particularly fond of, provided I am in safety.'[32]

The limits of Romanticism

The Romantic generation, a transnational fraternity moulded by the shared experience of industrialization and urbanization, has been hailed as 'the first great subversives of modern times' (Donald Worster). Like many of today's environmentalists, they questioned dominant religious and scientific values and offered an alternative, holistic philosophy. The notion of a 'Romantic ecology' that informed Worster's discussion of Henry David Thoreau has since been attached to William Wordsworth in Jonathan Bate's 'literary ecocriticism' of his life and writings.[33] Bate politicizes and historicizes Wordsworth by locating him within the British green tradition, a process which upgrades him from nature poet to proto-ecologist. Like Thoreau, Wordsworth rejected Cartesian dualism and mechanism in favour of a living and breathing nature, especially in *The Excursion* (1814). A reviewer of *The Excursion*, Charles Lamb, typified those who suspected the poem of pantheism: 'In his poetry nothing in Nature is dead.'[34] The casual observer may well wonder why it is necessary to restate what was so obvious to Wordsworth's contemporaries and still is to the layperson – his deep communion with nature. But, as Bate explains, perverse scholarly tendencies over recent decades have tried to dissociate the essence of Romanticism from powerful feelings for nature.

Thoreau's ideas captivated John Muir, the Scottish-born crusader for wilderness preservation and national parks in the United States. Muir founded the Sierra Club in 1892 to combat threats to his most sacred space, the Sierra Nevada mountains of California. In similar fashion, Wordsworth's poetry and example, in tandem with immediate challenges to Lakeland places eulogized by the Romantics, moved Canon Hardwicke Rawnsley of nearby Carlisle and others to set up the National Trust in 1895. Given that one of the first spots the Trust acquired was Gowbarrow Park on Ullswater, the site of the daffodils that inspired that still beloved poem, Bate perceives a direct connection between Wordsworth, the ideology and activities of the National Trust and the subsequent national park campaign.[35]

It is tempting to claim that everyone who goes hiking in the Lake District or the Sierra Nevada nowadays is in some intangible but nonetheless meaningful sense an heir to the Romantic tradition whether or not they have ever read or heard of Wordsworth, Byron, Thoreau or Muir. Romanticism's nature-based religion, encapsulated in Samuel Taylor Coleridge's reference to torrents and cataracts in the Savoy Alps as 'glorious as the Gates of Heaven' in his poem 'Hymn before Sunrise, in the Vale of Chamouni' (1802), and Wordsworth's allusion to mountains as 'temples of Nature', struck many Christians as idolatrous. On the other hand, they appealed strongly to nineteenth-century critics of modernity who concurred with Wordsworth that the world was too much with them, as well as to those discontented with conventional religious creeds and forms.[36] Yet do the hordes of contemporary visitors who come close to overwhelming many national parks on summer weekends experience a spiritual euphoria comparable to that of the nineteenth-century nature poets? Willey is sceptical, arguing that what we moderns are getting from nature is 'for the most part . . . physical and nervous regeneration rather than . . . spiritual assurance'.[37] Moreover, the 'back to nature' enthusiasm of even its original Romantic proponents was confined. None wanted to trade permanently the benefits of modern life for the charms of existence in rude nature. Most sought only a temporary antidote. 'Cataracts and mountains are good occasional society', Wordsworth conceded, 'but they will not do for constant companions.'[38]

Furthermore, the Romantic ideology of nature (specifically its value as a precursor of ideas of nature's intrinsic value) is more ambiguous than is usually appreciated by today's environmentalists. The equivocal nature of the Romantic legacy is suggested by a close reading of Ralph Waldo Emerson's first book, *Nature* (1836). *Nature* was the first detailed exposition of that distinctive US variation on Romanticism known as transcendentalism. In the 1830s, it attracted little attention beyond Concord, Massachusetts, but has since acquired considerable kudos among nature preservationists and ecocentric thinkers.

Evidently influenced by his readings in Orientalism, Emerson perceived a primal unity between man and nature: 'The greatest delight which the fields and woods minister, is the suggestion of an occult relation between man and vegetable . . . They nod to me and I to them.' Despite these allusions to pagan kinship, Emerson makes no real effort to collapse the distinction between people and nature. On the contrary, through solitude in nature we recognize our apartness and our essence: 'I am not solitary whilst I read and write, though nobody is with me. But if a man would be alone, let him look at the stars.' Emerson's stress is constantly on how nature can serve humanity: 'To the mind and body which have been cramped by noxious work or company' nature is a soothing balm. Nature facilitates access to the godhead: 'Standing on the bare ground . . . all mean egotism vanishes. I become a transparent eye-ball. I am nothing. I see all. The currents of the Universal Being circulate through me; I am part or particle of God.' Nature really has no worth independent of human judgement: 'All the facts in natural history taken by themselves have no value.'

Nature indicates that for transcendentalists human spirituality was the element of highest value in the universe, leaving nature as a conduit, a raw material to assist the human spirit in its quest for perfection: 'beauty in nature is not ultimate. It is the herald of inward and eternal beauty, and is not alone a solid and satisfactory good.'[39] According to Peter Kaufman, Emerson consistently believed that human dominion over nature 'did not rest upon columns of steel and shafts of timber but rather upon the soul's aptitude to use nature in exploits of self-discovery and to contemplate the essential, spiritual harmony exhibited by the created universe'.[40] It is often assumed that the transcendentalists, in defiance of theological warnings about confusing the creator with his works, took the plunge and saw nature itself as touched with the divine spark. It was more a case of seeing nature as proof of human divinity.

Nature also suggests that American Romantics, despite stock antimodern noises, were less disenchanted with modernity than their counterparts in Britain and Germany. In common with many other nineteenth-century white Americans, Emerson believed in the providential discovery of America and the desirability, indeed inevitability, of human evolution beyond primitive conditions. A great admirer of Bacon in his youth, Emerson never wavered (at least prior to his harrowing visit to England's industrial centres in 1847), in his faith in progress through scientific and mechanical power over nature, speaking euphorically of entering 'the kingdom of man over nature'. Though its highest use for him was spiritual, he recognized that one of nature's most important uses was as a set of material commodities. Michael Pollan attacks Emerson for making a fetish of wildness, failing to appreciate that he, too, cherished a vision of America as a pastoral paradise, a destiny Emerson believed the railroad would help fulfil.[41]

Emerson's admonition 'Know then, that the world exists for you. For you is the phenomenon perfect', was loaded with Renaissance and Enlightenment humanism. It was unthinkable that such an exuberant believer in the potential and divinity of every human being should wish to impose restrictions on dealings with nature; 'Build, therefore, your own world' ran another famous injunction in *Nature*. But what if that world was constructed by eradicating trees and wildlife? This was not a question Emerson cared to pose, but it is clear that the end of nature for Emerson, as Gertrude Hughes has explained, was 'its own destruction, destruction in the service of liberation. The more we make nature disappear the more we use nature for the designated end.'[42] Emerson's belief that nature is found in essences rather than objects and that human impact cannot alter that essence promoted a naïve faith in its immortality: 'The charming landscape which I saw this morning, is indubitably made up of some twenty or thirty farms. Miller owns this field, Locke that, and Manning the woodland beyond. But none of them owns the landscape. There is a property in the horizon which no man has but he whose eye can integrate all the parts, that is, the poet.'[43]

Optimistic Whiggish accounts exaggerate the extent to which the dominant tendency to measure the natural world's value according to exclusively commercial criteria was challenged before Darwinism and the advent of scientific ecology. For instance, assertions that English (or Western) society's sensibilities towards animals became more sentimental and tender between 1500 and the Romantic era require sociological refinement. Blood sports loved by the masses, such as cock-fighting and bear-baiting, might have been increasingly frowned on and quashed by polite society, but fox-hunting remained largely unscathed. The ameliorative tendencies that Keith Thomas (in his *Man and the Natural World*) detects in early modern England, which bore fruit through organized humanitarian campaigns in the nineteenth century, mostly affected domestic creatures, principally horses, donkeys and mules, for which Anna Sewell's novel *Black Beauty* (1877) precipitated the passage of protective legislation.[44] Besides, these middle-class initiatives often displayed more concern with the detrimental effects that the enjoyment of cruelty would have on the moral status of the lower orders and their behaviour towards other humans than sincere interest in the well-being of the animal victims. Whereas the ancient Roman elite trusted that gory spectacles would exhaust plebeian emotional urges, rendering the populace more tractable, the British Victorian establishment believed that sadistic amusements exacerbated people's natural bestiality.

The observation in George Orwell's satirical novel *Animal Farm* (1945) that some creatures are more equal than others, is borne out by historical experience. Animal rights philosopher Mary Midgeley introduces the notions of 'relative dismissal' and 'absolute dismissal', explaining that the much-vaunted species barrier has never quite lived up to the wholesale impenetrability the image suggests.[45] It has been more like a fence with gaps, so that the family dog could merit more consideration and affection than the servants (and certainly better treatment than non-whites).

Birds and animals of prey certainly enjoyed no reprieve from deep-seated hostility during the Victorian era. The humane movement on both sides of the Atlantic found the character and eating habits of these 'bad' animals morally repugnant. Meanwhile, members of the upper classes who defined nature as a sporting arena had no more tolerance for predators than the farmer who regarded nature as provender. To protect pheasant, grouse and partridge for shooters, British game-keepers had pushed the osprey, red kite, buzzard, golden eagle, wild cat, pine marten and polecat to the edge of extinction by the end of the nineteenth century.[46] Nor did animals abroad benefit from the new sensibilities as British big-game hunters (who would never tolerate cruelty to their horses or dogs) blasted away merrily at the charismatic megafauna of Africa, Asia and North America. A fully fledged theory of 'speciesism' (deemed an evil on a par with racism and sexism) did not emerge until the mid-1970s, when Peter Singer published *Animal Liberation*. Using Benthamite utilitarian logic (a creature's desire to avoid pain), Singer extended the ethical circle to embrace grizzly bear and laboratory rat alike – though he drew the line 'somewhere between a shrimp and an oyster' (the capacity of a mollusc to feel pain being even more questionable than that of a crustacean).[47]

My priority in this section has been to delineate the broad differences between Romantic and traditional approaches to nature, while recognizing that existing attitudes and tastes were not entirely superseded. Despite its potency, the Romantic creed never gained unquestioned ascendancy. The eighteenth-century British man of letters Samuel Johnson, an incorrigible urbanite, was no fan of mountain scenery. His notoriously bigoted account of his Scottish tour of 1773 abounds with references to the 'dreariness of solitude' and he pines for the soft landscapes of southern England:

> The imaginations excited by the view of an unknown and untravelled wilderness are not such as arise in the artificial solitude of parks and gardens, a flattering notion of self-sufficiency, a placid indulgence of voluntary delusions, a secure expansion of the fancy, or a cool concentration of the mental powers. The phantoms which haunt a desert are want, and misery, and danger. The evils of dereliction rush upon the thoughts; man is made unwillingly acquainted with his weaknesses, and meditation shows him only how little he can sustain, and how little he can perform.

After all their rough riding around the highlands and islands, Johnson and his companion James Boswell were delighted to step into a carriage again when they reached Loch Lomond: 'We had a pleasing conviction of the commodiousness of civilization, and heartily laughed at the ravings of those absurd visionaries who have attempted to persuade us of the superior advantages of a *state of nature*.'[48] Plenty of rationalists with milder expectations of scenery survived into the nineteenth century.

Darwinism, ecology and nature

Charles Darwin (1809–82) joined the RSPCA and, in a letter to a fellow scientist in 1871, lambasted vivisection for 'mere' curiosity as 'damnable and detestable'. He had also enjoyed rambling and geological study in Snowdonia during his earlier years. However, unlike his younger contemporary, Henry Salt (see chapter 8), Darwin never adopted vegetarianism or opposed vivisection on principle. Nor did he graduate to the cause of animal rights or become involved in campaigns to protect Snowdonia from mining for the sake of public recreation and nature conservation.[49] And though evolutionary theory came to affect most areas of intellectual endeavour, from literature (naturalism) and philosophy (existentialism) to sociology (social Darwinism), Darwinism is not readily associated with the ideas about nature that flowed into ecological science – the study of the relations between organisms and their physical surroundings – and invested the ideology of popular ecology.

Darwin's agreement with Thomas Malthus, the eighteenth-century population theorist, that life involved a 'struggle for existence' (a phrase he adopted from Malthus), seems a far cry from the Romantic view of nature as a harmonious community of life. The doctrine of the 'survival of the fittest' (one of the key phrases in *The Origin of Species* (1859), but which Darwin borrowed from the British social and political thinker Herbert Spencer) could be construed as the supreme justification of man's dominion: humankind sat at the apex of life forms by virtue of its evolutionary superiority.

Other aspects of Darwinian thought, however, anticipated ecological science and more recent environmental ethics. The most striking passage in *Origin of Species* for today's environmentalist has nothing to do with the principle of natural selection or the struggle for existence. It deals with the ecological community of clover, bees, mice and cats, foreshadowing the concept of the food chain. To illustrate what he called the 'web of life' – 'how plants and animals remote in the scale of nature, are bound together by a web of complex relations' – Darwin related a homely story. The most direct influence on the red clover was a certain bee (the humble) indispensable for fertilization. The number of bees was regulated by the size of the field mouse population, for mice destroy bee nests and combs. Whether or not mice are abundant is in turn determined by the quantity of cats in the locality, which tended to be greater in the vicinity of towns and villages. In short, the more cats, the more clover.[50] (Thomas H. Huxley, the leading proponent of Darwin's ideas in Britain, thought that old maids, the sector of the population fondest of cats, should be added to this ecological chain!)[51]

This is not to say that *Origin of Species* precipitated a debate over the ecological consequences of human intervention in the natural world. Open a British book written after 1859 containing 'Man' and 'Nature' in its title – of which there were many – and you will find no discussion of human impact on the environment. Huxley's *Man's Place in Nature* (1863), for instance, is about man's position relative to other creatures in the chain of life. These discussions might have profound implications for religion (stimulating many efforts to harmonize Genesis and geology, evolution and Revelation) but they did not generate conservation measures.[52]

Evolutionary theory reinforced the ancient notion of the 'tree of life', and Darwin was convinced of the similarities between humans and the higher primates. In the late 1830s he spent many hours at Regents Park Zoo in London observing its first orang utan, Jenny. Aspects of Jenny's behaviour reminded him exactly of his own children's. When denied an apple, Jenny threw a fit 'precisely like a naughty child'.[53] But this does not support the popular view that Darwin collapsed the sacred divide between mankind and animals. His evolutionary model did not insist that humans were directly descended from the apes. Instead, it stressed divergence from a common progenitor, a relationship conveyed by the idea of parallel but separate limbs of a tree, united by trunk and roots. It is often forgotten that Darwin did not actually discuss the connections between men and animals in *Origin of Species*, which restricted itself to the suggestion, on the penultimate page, that as a result of evolutionary theory, 'much light will be thrown on the origin of man and his history'. (A direct discussion of human evolution followed in *Descent of Man* (1871), in which Darwin compared man's mental faculties and emotions with those of the 'lower' animals though, as Singer complains, this did not convert him to vegetarianism.)[54]

Nevertheless, the implications of this single bland sentence were sensational enough to shock many Victorians, for whom the ascent of man amounted to what Donald Worster calls a series of declarations of independence from the natural world.[55] To suggest that man was related to the apes, no matter how indirectly, was considered degrading and insulting to man. The belief that humans were tied up with nature was also thought dangerous: conceding this point could provoke human descent into the animalism of unrestrained sexual activity and violence.

Evolutionary theory's most obvious consequences, however, were for orthodox Christianity. Evolution taught that the giant tortoises and iguanas of the Galapagos Islands off the coast of Ecuador had migrated there instead of being installed by a divine creator: the idea of nature as the outcome of historical forces replaced that of the one-off creation. Now, in revealing the 'brute' origins of mankind, Darwin was hardly spoiling for a fight with Christianity. He procrastinated for twenty years before publicizing his findings, having compared the discovery of life's mutability, in a letter to the botanist Joseph Hooker, to 'confessing a murder' (1843).[56] Natural law and natural selection in fact left God's role in the origins of life open. Could he not have set the whole process in motion? Many accounts stress confrontation, yet many Victorian Christians found themselves able to reach an accommodation.[57]

Others have approached Darwin and Darwinism within the context of emerging ecological and animal rights viewpoints. On returning from his seminal trip to the Galapagos in the late 1830s (shortly after the first parliamentary legislation against animal cruelty, notes Singer) Darwin confided in his diary that 'Man in his arrogance thinks himself a great work, worthy of the interposition of a deity. More humble and, I believe, true, to consider him created from animals.'[58] The English novelist Thomas Hardy, who hailed Darwin as the greatest single influence on his outlook, hammered out the long-term ethical implications of his reading of Darwinism's emphasis on kinship between species. In a letter to Salt's Humanitarian League on the occasion of its twentieth anniversary (1910), Hardy opined that Darwinism 'logically involved a readjustment of altruistic morals by enlarging as a necessity of rightness . . . the application of what has been called "The Golden Rule" beyond the area of mere mankind to that of the whole animal kingdom'.[59] In 1923 Hardy was invited to assume the vice-presidency of the Animal Defence and Anti-Vivisection League.

The pioneering US environmentalist Aldo Leopold shared Hardy's view that the recognition of inter-species kinship was Darwin's major intellectual bequest. For Leopold, writing in the 1940s, Darwin's

striking denial of mankind's splendid isolation encouraged a less con-
ceited human role: 'men are only fellow-voyagers with other creatures
in the odyssey of evolution'.[60] In his exposé of 'the machine civilization', *The Pentagon of Power*, which isolates the world-views of Kepler
and Galileo as the sources of the modern nightmare inflicted by
bureaucratized technology, Lewis Mumford hails Darwin as the 'first
and perhaps the greatest of ecologists'.[61] Loren Eiseley, an American
anthropologist and leading Darwin scholar, connected his own feeling
of an egalitarian unity with nature with an awareness of evolution.
He reflected on his habit of taking seeds with him when climbing
(to scatter around): 'I have carried such seeds up the sheer walls of
mesas and I have never had illusions that I was any different to them
than a grizzly's back or a puma's paw.'[62]

Darwin never used the term 'ecology', and most Americans and
western Europeans had probably not encountered it before Earth Day
in April 1970. Still, proto-ecological ideas attached to evolutionary
theory were in the mid-nineteenth-century air, and the coining of 'ecology' is usually attributed to Darwin's contemporary and major champion in Germany, the zoologist Ernst Haeckel (1834–1919). In *Generelle
Morphologie* (1866), Haeckel used *oekologie* to characterize 'the science of
relations between organisms and their environment'. Though he did
little in a practical sense to advance the cause of ecology, let alone that
of conservation, Haeckel spearheaded the intellectual forces that disputed the belief that the universe consists of two different substances,
mind and matter ('supernature' and 'nature').[63]

Unlike Darwin, Haeckel was an aggressive atheist who decried
Christianity for generating contempt for other creatures. In *The Riddle
of the Universe* (1901), he mocked the so-called 'mystery' or 'riddle
of human consciousness' and rejected the conviction that it was
unknowable and therefore inexplicable in the context of material life
forms, as well as discontinuous with the rest of nature.[64] Haeckel's anti-
dualistic ecology, influenced by Goethe's Romantic holism and an interest in Buddhism, was expressed in monism – a belief that all matter
is invested with spirit and that matter and spirit are part of a common
substance within a unified cosmos. He firmly believed, in the words of
a mentor, that man is 'not some stranger in the universe, a supernatural
vagabond, but an integral part of nature'.[65]

Haeckel, who insisted that animals enjoyed status, consciousness
and reason and who located morality among other primates, expressed
vividly his low rating of humanity: 'Our own "human nature", which
exalted itself into an image of God in its anthropistic illusion, sinks to
the level of a placental mammal, which has no more value for the

universe at large than an ant, the fly of a summer's day, the microscopic infusorium, or the smallest bacillus.' Small wonder that a critic argued in the late 1920s that Haeckel's thesis 'robs man of his good name and tells him that he is of no more value to the universe than bugs which live in a puddle of mud and die in a day.'[66]

Each interest group takes from evolutionary theory and ecological study what best serves its needs. Many late nineteenth-century male Darwinians insisted that females of the species were passive, an approach embodied in Patrick Geddes's and J. Arthur Thomson's influential book, *The Evolution of Sex* (1889). Nowadays, ecofeminists have one of the highest profiles in the business of extracting lessons from nature. Bettyann Kevles has challenged male-constructed orthodoxy by stressing how females play decisive roles in courting, mating and parenting. She cites studies since the early 1970s indicating that the female members of many species, from English moorhens to Californian elephant seals, exercise considerable control over who fathers their offspring. She also finds evidence of precisely those features, such as homosexuality (in gulls), whose alleged absence among animals earlier authorities (not least Thomas Aquinas) had cited as clinching evidence of the distinction between culture and nature.[67]

Scientific endeavour is no less subjective and historically contingent than work in the humanities and social sciences.[68] Ecologists themselves have been active in modelling nature's identity. Early twentieth-century US ecologists such as Frederick Clements firmly believed in nature's original and intrinsic identity. In his view, which dominated professional ecology until the late 1940s, all processes in nature conspired towards this climax stage, an ultimate end he called a 'superorganism'. The ideas that dominate popular perceptions of ecology today, however, were developed in the 1950s by the likes of Eugene P. Odum, who replaced the idea of a climax stage with the notion of the ecosystem, defined as a 'community' of organisms interacting both with one another and with inanimate elements of the physical environment through an elaborate system of energy flows.[69] The key concepts characterizing this ecological community were balance, diversity and co-operation, with the human role very much that of George Perkins Marsh's 'disturbing agent'.

How biological research stressing nature's co-operative and altruistic features could become intertwined with social values is suggested by the 'biological humanism' of Warder Clyde Allee and his colleagues in the zoology department at the University of Chicago between the 1920s and 1950s. Allee's work on interactions between organisms, pointing to the beneficial effects of aggregation and collaboration among insects, was stamped by the horrors of the First World War, and by his Quaker beliefs. Allee believed his research on animals challenged the misunderstanding and misuse of Darwinism as a justification for war and authoritarianism, and sought to exploit his findings in the interests of pacifist internationalism. But these scientists were no environmentalists. For them, the ecologist was a 'social healer' and Gregg Mitman explains that they 'did not want to heal nature as much as be healed by it'.[70]

Then, in the 1970s, a postmodern version of ecology emerged that reduced the characteristics of stability, balance, order, collectivity and direction in nature to the level of mere cultural constructs. Chapter 9 will consider the implications for popular environmentalism of the fashionable accent on plural identities, competition and unpredictability, and its relevance to the debate over 'the end of nature'. For in the absence of an overarching, timeless identity for nature, can we speak of threats and damage? How can we invoke the higher reality of 'Nature' if nature is just another of those suspect universal signifiers and ultimate truths?

8

The Disunited Colours of Nature

A historical perspective that recovers anticipations of current thinking 'implicitly validates and strengthens the Green position', argues Malcolm Chase, 'reinforcing through the addition of historical pedigree ideas which "mainstream" thinking was (and is perhaps still) inclined to dismiss as fads'.[1] But there is no single 'green position'. Conservation, environmentalism and ecology come in many, often competing, shades of green. Accordingly, a dip into the past does more than just raise the green profile. A historical exercise can also serve to clarify a particular ideological position, distance it from its rivals and produce findings designed to discredit those rivals. Some eco-socialists, for example, try to establish parallels between the views of contemporary deep ecologists and the Nazi ideology of nature. Rather than implicitly validating and strengthening a common green position, the variety of green searches for a usable past expose deep disagreement over the nature of environmentalism and green ideas.

For those on the left who identify a natural convergence between red and green, the search for latent environmentalists, the first ecologists and incipient greens has led to Karl Marx rather than to American Indians, the Romantics or Darwin. Other scholars have found progenitors in Nazi Germany. Not all who draw attention to the Nazis are engaged in a critique of deep ecology, however. Neither are they celebrating the connection between brown and green in an attempt to rehabilitate the far right. The Nazi experience is important to them because it highlights the difficulties of trying to situate green thought and practice neatly within an ideological spectrum running from bright red to vivid blue (and brown). Looking at selected episodes in the emergence of conservation, environmentalism and green thinking highlights the complexity of their relationship with social class, political positions and economic values. We must also be aware of how ideas of nature in the broadest sense have been a central feature of various ideologies.

Nature, capitalism and socialism

Every culture projects its values onto nature and then holds them up as nature's own authority, deploying this apparently unimpeachable and independent source of authority to justify its vision of society and the world. The idea of nature as immutable template can serve to support the status quo. Though most recently invoked by sociobiologists, 'nature' has a record of service as a justification for social hierarchy, inequality of wealth and the pursuit of private property that extends at least as far back as Aristotle, who instructed that slaves were slaves 'by nature'. In his *Reflections on the Revolution in France* (1790), Edmund Burke, the philosopher and politician, compared society to an ancient tree of complex growth, the repository of wisdom with which people should not tamper. 'Because half a dozen grasshoppers under a fern make a field ring with their importunate chink, whilst thousands of great cattle, reposed beneath the shadow of the British oak, chew the cud and are silent', he importuned, 'pray do not imagine that those who make the noise are the only inhabitants of the field.' Conflating history and nature, Burke recruited the latter to his defence of tradition. 'The levellers', he argued, 'only change and pervert the natural order of things.'[2]

The liberal position was most famously articulated at that time by the Scottish arch-theorist of capitalism Adam Smith. In the Middle Ages, nature had been summoned as a curb on acquisitive instincts. But for Smith the laws of nature sanctioned the accumulation of wealth and he thought they should function unfettered. Reasoning of this kind reached its nineteenth-century climax in Social Darwinian theory, where Victorian society and the natural world mirrored each other: competition drove the evolution of higher life forms, ensuring biological and social progress. The emergence of powerful individuals (variously referred to as robber barons and captains of industry), corporate entities (industrial monopolies) and the imperialistic ventures of Anglo-Saxon nations testified to the survival of the fittest and served the interests of the race as a whole.[3] During the 1980s, sociobiology revitalized Social Darwinism. According to one eco-socialist, its thrust was epitomized by British Prime Minister Margaret Thatcher's 'cunning' invocation of the 'laws of economic gravity'.[4] Thatcherite (and Reaganite) celebration of the free market as the invisible hand of evolution equated the laws of classical economics with physical laws. Through this process of naturalization, cut-throat capitalism, a human creation (like all economic systems), is deified as an ineluctable force that must be obeyed. Nevertheless, the most ruthless followers of nature in this respect, as we shall see, were the Nazis.

Many eco-socialists are wary of appeals to nature because they feel that nature has most frequently been marshalled in defence of conservative causes.[5] Their objections also arise from a conviction that nature and human nature are both malleable entities, historically and socially constructed. In their objection to paying homage to nature's norms, they follow John Stuart Mill, who complained in 'Nature' (1874), that 'if it can be said with any plausibility that "nature enjoins" anything, the propriety of obeying the injunction is by most people considered to be made out'. The natural world was so flawed, in his view, that no just and benevolent creature could have made it with the intention that humankind should follow it blindly.[6]

Yet socialists and anarchists have also liberally summoned nature's hallowed laws, if usually to counter the conservatives' claims. Friedrich Engels, for example, imagined a society 'of real human freedom and of an existence in harmony with the established laws of Nature' (1878).[7] The idea that the fittest specimens in both human society and the natural world are the most co-operative – and that sociability boosts intelligence – was formalized in Peter Kropotkin's theory of mutual aid (1902). A naturalist and geographer as well as prominent anarchist, Kropotkin (1842–1921) formulated his ideas as a refutation of biological and sociological Darwinism. He based his thesis on observation of nature (he had led a number of expeditions to Siberia in the 1860s) as well as the study of history. He saw the forms of organization among animals such as the herd and pack paralleled in tribalism among primitive peoples and medieval communalism. Animals, Kropotkin contended, avoided rather than courted conflict and, in this context, he interpreted migration as a safety-valve.[8]

From the invocation of an abstract nature we turn to the role of nature and the natural world within socialist thinking. Eco-socialists believe that elements of Marxist thought lend themselves to a vigorous green critique of capitalism. The case for Marx (1818–83) as proto-environmentalist is based partly on various statements that echo current 'eco-speak' but relies most heavily on his criticisms of capitalist mishandling of natural resources.[9] According to Marx (1857/8), a quiet feudal relationship with an unmolested nature, characterized by 'nature-idolatry', preceded capitalism. Then, 'for the first time, nature becomes purely an object for humankind, purely a matter of utility; ceases to be recognized as a power for itself; and the theoretical discovery of its autonomous laws appears merely as a ruse so as to subjugate it under human needs'. He also apparently demonstrated, within the framework of anti-Semitic comments, a non-instrumental appreciation of nature's autonomy (1844):

> The idea of nature to which one comes under the domination of private property and of money is the actual contempt, the practical degradation, of nature... In this sense, Thomas Münzer [a sixteenth-century Anabaptist dissident and leader of peasant revolt] declares it intolerable 'that all creatures have been made into property, the fish in the water, *the birds in the air*, the plants on the earth – the creatures, too, must be free'.

In *Capital* (1867), Marx lambasted capitalism for its profligate use of raw materials and failure to recycle waste products, but focused on loss of soil fertility: 'All progress in capitalistic agriculture is a progress in the art, not only of robbing the labourer, but of robbing the soil.'[10] Identifying US agriculture as a particularly severe example of despoliation since it adopted industrial processes early on, Marx explained how capitalism was prepared to entertain fundamental damage to the sources of wealth for short-term gain. Instead, he advocated the 'conscious rational cultivation of the soil as eternal communal property'.[11]

It was Engels (1820–95) rather than Marx, however, who provided most of the ammunition for East German eco-communists in the 1970s.[12] The 'green red' consciousness of Engels's early writings, notably *The Condition of the Working Class in England* (1845), which he published in his mid-twenties, has been recovered of late through the medium of social justice environmentalism. One of the most striking passages in his account of the English proletariat is a lurid description of the foul River Irk (a tributary of the Irwell) as it flowed ('or rather stagnates') through Manchester.[13]

Written during the two decades following George Perkins Marsh's *Man and Nature* (1864), Engels's *Dialectics of Nature* (not published until 1925) was also a proto-environmental history. While stressing capitalism's sale of the earth, he notes the ill effects of most modes of production. Many of his examples of overgrazing and deforestation, like Marsh's, are drawn from the former empires of the ancient world. Sounding like a modern ecological Cassandra, Engels warns against forgetting our ties with nature and urges us to remember that our actions may rebound on us: 'Thus at every step we are reminded that we by no means rule over nature like a conqueror over a foreign people, like someone standing outside nature – but that we, with flesh, blood, and brain, belong to nature, and exist in its midst.' He proceeded to attack the traditional dualisms of mind/matter, soul/body, man/ nature that have dogged Western thought, blaming them, perceptively, on a combination of ancient Greek thought, Christianity and the scientific revolution.[14]

Anna Bramwell's case against Marx as underappreciated ecologist turns on accusations of anthropocentrism. Ecology, she declares, cannot put man first, as Marx clearly did.[15] His conviction that natural resources should be managed on a sustainable yield basis for the good of the greatest number certainly anticipated the utilitarian resource conservation invariably associated with the ideology and programme of the chief of the US Forest Service, Gifford Pinchot, during the turn-of-the-century Progressive reform era. Whether we can align this stance with environmentalist ideas and practices that have emerged since 1945 is more questionable.

Whether an 'earth first' orientation is essential to a sound ecological/environmentalist position can be disputed. But there are other respects in which Marx's green credentials are more obviously dubious. Some commentators, pointing to anti-mechanistic images in his writings, emphasize that (like Haeckel) he advocated the unity of man and nature through materialism (monism). Nature, Marx remarked in 1844, is man's 'inorganic body', 'with which he must constantly remain in step if he is not to die . . . for man is a part of nature'. More characteristic of his thinking, however, is a reference in *Capital* to how the labourer 'annexes' nature 'to his own bodily organs'. Marx always displays a keen awareness of and enormous pride in man's transformative capacity.[16] At the core of Marx's historical schema is the human advance beyond animalism through a series of liberations from nature's shackles, starting with the discovery of fire (which Engels accorded a more momentous role than the invention of the steam engine). Both Marx and Engels defined freedom largely in terms of emancipation from the problems of securing food, shelter and fuel. So completely had historical forces shaped nature's identity that, according to Engels, 'there is devilishly little left of "nature" as it was in Germany at the time when the Germanic peoples immigrated into it. The earth's surface, climate, vegetation, fauna, and the human beings themselves have infinitely changed, and all this owing to human activity.'[17]

Mankind was embedded in nature but the latter remained firmly subordinate. Drawing on Georg Hegel, Marx and Engels employed the

terminology of 'first' and 'second' nature to denote respectively original nature (raw materials, ecological systems) and the layer superimposed by human culture and economic systems.[18] Whatever else it
rejected in capitalism, socialism shared its essential orientation towards
nature. Marx's labour theory of value (first propounded in *Grundrisse*,
1857/8) – that matter has no value aside from that imparted by
the human labour needed for purposes of extraction and processing
– denied nature any intrinsic worth as surely as did capitalist
commodification. Despite allusions to nature as mankind's 'original'
larder and tool store, Marxism rejected the prior and independent
existence of something called nature; the history of nature was effectively the history of man. From an environmentalist's standpoint,
this exposes Marxism, paradoxically, as insufficiently materialistic.
For Marxism fails to recognize the labour that plants and animals
themselves undertake and the capital constituted by nature itself (the
'wealth of nature' as Donald Worster calls it), the fruits of which
are appropriated by humans. By grounding its analysis in economic
modes of production, Marxism ignores their indispensable ecological
foundation.[19] Marx complained of capitalism's objectification of labour
– in which workers are reduced to the status of things for sale in the
marketplace. He did not wring his hands over the objectification of
nature.

How green you consider Marx and Engels to be also depends on
what you mean by environmentalism. An environmentalism consisting
primarily of an awareness of the debilitating impact of overcrowding
and pollution on human health will not greatly impress those for
whom the following concerns are uppermost in their priorities: the
preservation of majestic landscapes, the protection of increasingly rare
flora and fauna, and the recognition that non-humans have interests (if
not rights) worthy of our respect. Marx undeniably relished his walks
on London's Hampstead Heath while writing *Capital*, but this was
strictly exercise. He deplored mysticism and sentimentality of any kind
and evinced no aesthetic appreciation of nature.[20] He hated the countryside and ridiculed what he called the 'idiocy of rural life', which
he consigned to history's dustbin. Engels's tour of English industrial
centres left him with a visceral mistrust of cities, but the rurophobic
Marx had enormous faith in industrialization and technological
advance, locating the future hopes and happiness of humanity squarely
in cities.

Given that the most pressing environmental problems that Marx and
Engels witnessed were associated with urban poverty and industrial
pollution, we cannot excoriate them for insensitivity to the destruction

of wildlife habitats. Nevertheless, it requires a great leap of faith to argue, with Howard Parsons, a Marxist philosopher, that the pair would have been even more ecologically attuned had they lived to see the environmental crisis of the late twentieth century.[21] It would be just as preposterous to hold them responsible for incidents such as the Chernobyl nuclear disaster in 1986 as it would be to blame the explosion at Three Mile Island in 1979 on Columbus. But to insist that Marxism is clean despite the dirty records of various socialist and communist regimes does not wash. Environmental historians serving up a 'metanarrative' of capitalist destruction often deal ineffectively with the palpable enthusiasm of socialist regimes for the same ethic of economic growth and consumption and their conspicuous legacies of environmental damage. Bar the profit motive, every feature of capitalist agriculture, from loss of ecological diversity through monoculture to technophilia and chemical dependency, has characterized agriculture in the former Soviet Union and eastern European bloc. The diversion of waters flowing into the Aral Sea to irrigate land to grow rice and cotton in southern Kazakhstan, a project begun in the early 1970s, involved a restructuring of the natural world to match anything undertaken in the West.

Like those who blame Asian lapses from ecological virtue and good practice on Western colonialism, we can of course absolve Marx's followers by blaming the aggressive capitalist West whose ethos has 'become sovereign almost everywhere'.[22] Or we can protest that this century's socialist and communist regimes, while professing Marxism, have really been Leninist–Stalinist. Hence, all that their abuses of nature (and violations of human rights) reveal is the distance between what has passed for communism/socialism and the genuine article. Parsons mounts a spirited defence of the Soviet Union's crimes against nature as aberrant: accusations fail to take into account the extraordinary circumstances and external pressures faced by the fledgling and beleaguered communist regime.[23] Yet Marxist theory and socialist/communist practice have generally meshed over nature. In the proletariat's struggle to catch up with the bourgeoisie's living standards, the desirability of increased production and consumption is largely unquestioned. Marx and his disciples did not worry about natural resource depletion and were mostly compulsive technocrats, sharing with their capitalist opponents a conception of nature as a bottomless storehouse.

Marxism was heir to a proud tradition of belief in progress. Towards the end of the eighteenth century, inspired by the belief in human perfectibility and encouraged by the notion that through technology the pool of material abundance could be increased, the conviction grew that the human condition was amenable to improvement. Marxism inherited the Enlightenment's growing optimism and gave it its highest expression. In so far as those on the left have favoured a plastic notion of nature and society, rejecting the image of nature as niggardly and denying the role of restrictions (associated with Malthusian pessimism), they have rejected the notion of environmental limits to economic growth and believe in the unlimited power of culture to mould nature in the interests of all people. (The contemporary social ecologist and green anarchist Murray Bookchin dismisses the 'lifeboat ethic' – that the world harbours insufficient resources to support all its inhabitants – as neo-Malthusian 'eco-fascism'.)[24]

Leon Trotsky elevated to new heights the Promethean belief in the superman who, like a geological force, would rearrange nature through technology when liberated from capitalism. A Soviet school text for 12- to 14-year-olds published in 1929, *The Great Plan*, contained nature-busting sentiments that rival any triumphalist account of national mission and manifest destiny arising from the subjugation of the American frontier:

> We must discover and conquer the country in which we live. It is a tremendous country, but not yet entirely ours. Our steppe will truly become ours only when we come with columns of tractors and plows to break the thousand-year-old virgin soil. On a far-flung front we must wage war. We must burrow into the earth, break rocks, dig mines, construct houses. We must take from the earth.[25]

At the twenty-fifth Party Congress of the CPSU in 1977, Leonid Brezhnev echoed Francis Bacon in declaring that 'it is possible and necessary, comrades, to improve nature, to help nature reveal her living forces completely'. To concede natural limits was defeatist, counter-revolutionary bourgeois revisionism.[26]

The greening of socialism

Just as progressive Christians try to fashion a green theology through creative reinterpretation and the promotion of minority traditions, 'red greens' (social ecologists) strive to do the same for socialism. This task combines the resurrection of neglected virtues in socialist theory with efforts to overcome what some theorists concede to be Marxism's manipulative, imperious approach to the natural world. The pioneers were the cluster of German critical theorists in exile from Hitler in the

United States in the 1930s. 'Frankfurt School' thinkers, notably Theodor Adorno and Max Horkheimer, saw the modern ecological dilemma as something bigger and more complicated than capitalism and class conflict. They and the likes of Martin Heidegger were convinced that the roots of disharmony resided more insidiously in science and technology and the 'modernist' values informing them (Heidegger sometimes imbued technology with an intrinsic essence and malevolence).[27] *Dialectic of Enlightenment*, by Adorno and Horkheimer (1944), and *The Eclipse of Reason*, by Horkheimer (1947), anticipated the postmodern denial of the authority of the 'metanarrative' of progress and foreshadowed many concerns and contentions of the environmental historian. Their authors discussed (if with no actual reference to *philosophe* writings) how the 'Age of Reason' had generated a scientific, technological and economic system that benefited only a few and desacralized nature. The disturbing degree to which the relations of man and nature had been corrupted by Western civilization was suggested to Horkheimer by 'the story of the boy who looked up at the sky and asked, "Daddy, what is the moon supposed to advertise?"'[28]

Intellectuals, such as the French existential Marxist André Gorz and the British New Left literary critic Raymond Williams, were strongly influenced by the Frankfurt School. They sought to upgrade Marxism by blending it with ecological insights. A socialism that sought only the social redistribution of natural resources was for them inadequate because it removed none of man's impositions on the natural world. Gorz and Williams accepted that indefinitely spiralling levels of production were ecologically unsustainable and therefore unattainable. Genuine human freedom and wealth, they contended, involved more than economic emancipation.

The Frankfurt School also spawned an American tendency that has questioned the assumptions of social ecologists. Counter-cultural critics of the 1960s and 1970s such as Herbert Marcuse and Theodore Roszak regarded the emphasis on the struggle between capitalism and socialism as a distraction for this deflected attention from the fundamental problem – the industrial ethos and mode of production they shared. Jonathon Porritt, prominent in the British environmental movement during the 1980s, has restated this critique. In view of a wholesale commitment to the overarching 'super-ideology' of industrialism and infinitely expanding production ('growthism'), he argues that the question of who controls the means of production and industrial process is a subsidiary issue: 'a filthy smokestack is still a filthy smokestack whether it is owned by the state or by a private corporation'.[29]

The green critique typified by Marcuse and Porritt usually attributes this crippling 'super-ideology' to cultural factors such as Judaeo-Christianity, patriarchy, the scientific revolution and Enlightenment rationality. Preferring the juxtaposition of 'people versus nature' to the conventional notion of intra-human class struggle, deep ecologists in particular tend to revile a collective and undifferentiated 'humanity' and its anthropocentric values. Deep ecology, a term coined in 1972 by the Norwegian philosopher and environmental activist Arne Naess, tends to be apolitical, and critical of the 'reformist' environmentalist mainstream for the shallowness of its ecological underpinnings, its entry into the existing political arena and its willingness to compromise. Attacking the stewardship position, deep ecologists deny humans any rights over nature, regardless of how they exercise authority.[30]

According to the deep ecological world-view, 'we the people', who drive too many cars, use too many disposable nappies and eat too many hamburgers, must shoulder direct responsibility for our ecological predicament, instead of palming it off onto some wicked military–industrial complex, fat-cat elite, or exploitative economic order. 'Real' solutions are sought at the individual level.

David Pepper dismisses the radical green ('New Age') diagnosis of the environmental crisis as 'a powerful cocktail of false consciousness': make no mistake about it, capitalism is the problem, for it is *'inherently* "environmentally unfriendly"'. In common with Andrew Dobson, he advocates an unashamedly homocentric yet stewardly 'new green socialism' as a more viable and socially equitable alternative to what they dismiss as the elitist, ineffectual, anti-humanistic creed of deep ecology.[31]

Eco-socialists and green anarchists contend that it is sociologically and historically facile to present vast and vague impersonal forces like industrialization, technology, population growth and 'human greed' as the source of the problem without distinguishing between privileged and underprivileged people, or the West and the rest. Historical context must be examined, specifically the integral connection between environmental losses and the rise of capitalism. Technology and environmentally damaging values, they protest, do not simply develop according to some inner logic; their evolution reflects the preferences of those in power. In short, who owns the means of production is not such a trivial issue. Believing that subjugation of groups of humans by other humans antedated the domination of nature rather than that they arose in tandem, it is their view that the natural world will benefit only when elites are deprived of their control over natural resources.[32]

The British 'green' tradition and nature as outdoor amenity

Since so much attention has been lavished on the pioneers of American conservation and environmentalism by US historians, who have often presented them as the inventors of conservation and environmentalism, it is worth devoting some space to the forerunners of British green thinking. Though British scholars have been far less active than their US counterparts in assembling a genealogy, they have begun to press a range of individuals and ideas into service. Derek Wall has exhumed a green history for the unvarnished purpose of arming the green activist on the left: 'Read, enjoy . . . and act!'[33] His catholic approach claims as a proto-green almost anyone who expresses reservations at the prospect of every inch of land and every animal becoming domesticated. Peter Marshall also vigorously unearths green exceptions to the dominant thinking of every era, though, as you might expect from a historian of anarchism, the accent is libertarian. William Godwin, Percy Bysshe Shelley and William Morris feature as his leading British lights.[34]

Green socialists aim to steal deep ecology's thunder by showing how much current green thinking is prefigured in the history of socialism. True greens, in their view, are also red. In British radical circles an alternative to the mainstream of scientific socialism emerged during the last two decades of the nineteenth century, which Peter Gould has hailed as the most important era in the history of environmental thinking and activism in Britain prior to the 1980s. He has identified a strand of radical 'back to nature' thinking loosely housed within early socialism that was characterized by pacifism, vegetarianism, rural communitarianism, decentralism, nature worship and animal rights. The contemporary bias of Gould's approach is suggested by his observation that this coterie of avant-garde thinkers 'shared all but two of the twenty-nine features that Porritt identifies as distinguishing the politics of ecology and those two are the outcomes of technological development'. (The absent features appear to be anti-nuclearism and a commitment to renewable energy.)[35]

The linchpin of the 'back to nature' movement is William Morris (1834–96). His futuristic eco-utopian novel, *News from Nowhere; or, an Epoch of Rest* (1891), was written as a rejoinder to *Looking Backward, 2000–1887* (1888), a utopian novel by the US social reformer, Edward Bellamy, which celebrated a thoroughly industrialized and technocratic state capitalism. Morris offered an updated pastoral vision of a green and pleasant land that would have evinced nothing but scorn from Marx. Morris's hero falls asleep in his house on the banks of the Thames at Chiswick in the nineteenth century. On awakening in the twenty-first century, he is astounded to find that the vile, stinking soapworks have disappeared, delighted that all industrial sights and sounds have been banished. The industrial state has been superseded by an economy combining small-scale, 'low-tech.' industrial pursuits with agricultural work. London, which Morris once described as a 'sordid loathsome place',[36] has been greened. Trafalgar Square doubles as an orchard – and salmon frolic again in the Thames. His description of a boat trip on the upper Thames is a bucolic vision in the Virgilian mode. Village life has been revitalized and the countryside throbs with happy activity.[37]

Edward Carpenter (1844–1929) was another prominent maverick, who not only founded the Sheffield Socialist Society but attacked mechanistic science and big technology. Greatly enamoured of Henry David Thoreau's *Walden*, he practised self-sufficiency on a smallholding at Millthorpe, near Chesterfield. In his best-known work, 'Civilisation: Its Cause and Cure' (initially delivered as a Fabian Society lecture in 1889), Carpenter celebrated the savage as a fitter being. Without advocating a literal return to a state of nature, he attacked civilization as a 'disease' and his proposed cure was 'movement toward Communism with Society [and] Nature Movement – Savagery Within'.[38] In the 1920s this ideology lived on in the alternative scouting group, the Kibbo Kift Kin, and its offshoot, the Woodcraft Folk. These outfits were pervaded by hostility to machinery, industry and cities and a sympathy for paganism, the renewal of folk life, the revival of craft industries and nature preservation in national parks. Heavily influenced by Rousseau's *Émile*, they insisted on the benefits to mental and physical health of camping out amidst wild nature.

Of more specific interest to the animal rights lobby is Henry Salt (1851–1939), one of Victorian and Edwardian Britain's leading humanitarian reformers and most famous nonconformists. Educated at Eton and Trinity College, Cambridge, Salt was a pacifist, socialist and vegetarian (he became vice-president of the Vegetarian Society and directed the Humanitarian League). He was also an ardent opponent of zoos, vivisection, hunting and fishing. (He entitled his autobiography *Seventy Years among Savages* (1921), by which he meant the British upper classes.) A great admirer of Thoreau, whose reputation as a powerful critic of capitalism and excessive materialism prompted the Fabian Society to popularize *Walden*, in 1890 Salt wrote the first biography of Thoreau by a non-American. He even emulated his mentor's experiment at Walden Pond: relinquishing a comfortable and respectable career as a master at Eton in 1884, he retreated to a cottage in the hinterlands of Surrey near Tilford, where he pursued a frugal and semi-reclusive existence with his wife for a few years. Salt's top hat provided shade for a marrow plant and he recycled his academic gown by cutting it into strips to bind his vines to a wall.[39]

Swayed by social justice environmentalism, some US scholars (including various environmental historians) have begun to attack the American environmentalist community's 'hegemonic' Romantic interpretation of environmentalism as the protection of wild places and things, fretting over the white middle class's 'elitist' quest for a 'wilderness experience'. They deplore what they see as the denigration of all non-'pristine' environments as (in Michael Pollan's phrase) 'fallen, lost to nature, irredeemable'. They regard the desire for a wild tonic as a dangerous bourgeois (often 'macho') fetish, and dismiss wilderness preservation as a false priority that offers nothing to the blue-collar population and 'people of colour'.[40] Many social justice environmentalists see wilderness as no more than a construct – and a violent and imperialistic one at that, a conceit of an empty, unsullied place born of the dispossession of the American Indian – and therefore no more intrinsically worthy of our concern than any other environment.[41] These preoccupations, they argue, deflect attention from more pressing environmental problems from which non-whites suffer disproportionately. For social justice environmentalists the source of these problems is 'environmental racism' – the deliberate location of environmentally hazardous facilities in disempowered, low-income and ethnic/racial minority communities.

Their goal is to redeem the city by reconceptualizing 'nature' and 'the environment' as people's ordinary daily living, working and playing spaces. The desired outcome is an idea of nature that includes people and their activities and redefines environmental problems so that they become inseparable from issues of socio-economic deprivation and racial discrimination.[42] It also expands our investigations of relations between humans and nature to include issues such as how Dominicans and Puerto Ricans experience nature through everyday communal activities, such as gardening and fishing in the New York City area.[43] In the meantime, many social justice environmentalists decry the term environmentalist in favour of 'post-environmentalist', aligning themselves with the civil rights movement and even avoiding the term 'nature'. As slums, community health and hazardous working conditions are transformed into environmental issues, underprivileged people, rather than the natural world itself, are being designated the primary victims of environmental abuse.

Similar views have been brought to bear on the assessment of some of Britain's best-known Romantic poets. For Basil Willey, writing long before the current wave of political correctness, Wordsworth's and Coleridge's daily devotion to the discovery and celebration of the sacred bond between nature and the human soul during their sojourn at Nether Stowey and Alfoxton in Somerset's Quantock hills in 1797 and 1798 exemplifies nature's metamorphosis from a revolutionary principle into a conservative force in the wake of the French Revolution.[44] Commentators who regard nature-loving as degenerate and diversionary accuse the Romantics of seeking to retreat into an idealized, timeless world of nature that ignores the oppression of the peasantry and other harsh socio-economic realities. The construction of a reactionary Wordsworth has been advanced by those who accuse the elderly poet (he was 80 when he died in 1850) of a desire to exclude working-class visitors from his beloved Lake District. So great was his indignation over the proposed extension of the railway from Manchester beyond Kendal to Windermere that he wrote two long letters to the editor of the London *Morning Post* in December 1844, this paper having already published his 'protest' sonnet (also 1844) enquiring

> *Is then no nook of English ground secure*
> *From rash assault?*
>   .   .   .   .
> *Plead for thy peace, thou beautiful romance*
> *Of nature; and, if human hearts be dead,*
> *Speak, passing winds; ye torrents, with your strong*
> *And constant voice, protest against the wrong.*[45]

Wordsworth feared that Lakeland would be inundated with 'the whole of Lancashire, and no small part of Yorkshire'. The masses brought by train would crave distractions (readily provided by eager entrepreneurs) in the form of 'wrestling matches, horse and boat races without number', while 'pot-houses and beer-shops would keep pace with these excitements and recreations, most of which might too easily be had elsewhere'.[46]

It is valuable to be reminded of the racial, social and cultural specificity of our conceptions of nature and place. For Afro-American slaves and peons incarcerated in rural plantations in the American South, it was the northern city that symbolized escape and revitalization.[47] Ingrid Pollard's photographs of British Blacks in the Lake District ('Pastoral Interludes', 1984) promote a sense of incongruity. 'It's as if the Black experience is only lived within an urban environment', she remarks. Pollard expresses her feelings of disorientation, alienation and exclusion when she tried to follow in Wordsworth's footsteps in a parody of one of the best-known lines from 'Daffodils': 'I thought I liked the LAKE DISTRICT, where I wandered lonely as a BLACK face in a sea of white.'[48]

Notwithstanding this awareness of the social and racial exclusivity of 'heritage' landscapes, we should note that Wordsworth enthusiastically agreed with essayist William Hazlitt's characterization of nature in 'On the Love of the Country' (1817) as 'a kind of universal home' in which everyone felt they had a stake: nature always spoke the same language and wore the same face for Hazlitt, whether in England or France. Jonathan Bate, in the vanguard of scholarly efforts to secure Wordsworth's reputation from rash assault, stresses the warmth of his welcome to all who wished to partake of nature's blessings. He insists that Wordsworth's love of nature stimulated a love of mankind, while an awareness of the rights of nature alerted him to the rights of man.[49]

Moreover, charges of snobbery fail to appreciate that there ought to be a few special places from which certain things can quite reasonably be excluded. After all, as Wordsworth pointed out, such things are easily pursued much closer to home. That more people attend bingo halls and cinemas than concert halls and theatres is no argument for converting concert halls and theatres into bingo halls and cinemas. What Wordsworth wanted to keep at bay was not the working class as such but forms of mass tourism that disregarded the Lake District's existing values and charms.

At the same time, Wordsworth maintained that a taste for wild nature could be acquired only by a gradual process of cultural education. As such, he probably underestimated the English working class's capacity for an outdoor experience unembellished with wrestling matches and grog shops. That the desire for contact with wild nature cannot be shrugged off as a bourgeois foible is suggested by a letter from a factory worker (1900) accompanying his contribution to the National Trust's appeal for the purchase of 108 acres of land at Brandlehow on Derwentwater: 'I am a working man and cannot afford more than 2s., but I once saw Derwentwater and can never forget it. I will do what I can to get my mates to help.'[50]

Elements of the industrial working class were strongly attracted to unspoiled nature. Genteel sensibilities hardly came into it. Victorian Britain's 'two nations' truly inhabited different worlds. According to Robert Blatchford, the populist lecturer, it was indisputably more pleasant to bathe in the Avon than the Irwell and to see a squirrel instead of a sewer rat, for 'the value of beauty is not a matter of sentiment; it is a fact'.[51] In his bestselling *Merrie England* (1894), Blatchford explained to the denizens of Wigan and Widnes how capitalists manufactured the twin landscapes of privilege and deprivation:

You will find these people living as far from the factories as they can get . . . The pleasures they enjoy are denied to you. To make wealth for themselves, they destroy the beauty and the health of your dwelling-places; and then they sit in their suburban villas, or on the hills and terraces of the lovely southern counties, and sneer at the 'sentimentality' of the men who ask you to cherish beauty and to prize health.[52]

Blatchford's magazine, the *Clarion*, which enjoyed a wider circulation than any other turn-of-the-century socialist periodical, disseminated the ideas of Carpenter and Morris. His critique in the *Clarion* and *Merrie England* of the 'Manchester school' of thought, and the cities and factories it had spawned, was distinctive among socialist tracts for its focus on how capitalism alienated people from nature and despoiled natural beauty.[53] In *Merrie England*, whose cover contrasted images of belching chimneys with birds and trees set against pure skies, Blatchford compared the benign rurality of Suffolk and Hampshire to the blighted scenes of industrial Lancashire and Staffordshire. Like Salt and Carpenter, Blatchford paid homage to Thoreau, advising his readers that if they read *Walden* (which he apparently kept under his pillow) they would be better able to appreciate *Merrie England*.[54]

City parks offered some outlet for suffocated energies and suppressed aesthetic desires. London's first non-royal parks (royal parks having been opened to the public in the eighteenth century) were private, urban versions of landscaped country estates. Marylebone Park (1811, now Regent's Park) aped a 'rural paradise', providing, in the words of its designer John Nash, 'open Space, free air and the scenery of Nature'.[55] In 1838, however, it was opened to the public. Some canny members of the Victorian establishment welcomed public parks as safety-valves for socio-economic discontent, minor concessions that might reconcile the working class to the existing distribution of property by providing them with the illusion of land ownership. The likes of Octavia Hill, a founder of the Commons Preservation Society (1865) and the National Trust (1895), regarded the opportunity for workers and their families to walk in pleasant surroundings on their day off not simply as a harmless and perhaps ennobling alternative to the grog shop and wrestling match but as vital security for the future of private landownership.[56]

Victoria Park, laid out in London's East End in the early 1840s, was designed expressly for the public, but the best-known British example opened on Merseyside in 1847. Birkenhead Park was designed by Joseph Paxton in pastoral/Romantic style to mimick 'natural' scenery, with lakes, undulating meadows, groves, rockeries and meandering paths. Frederick Law Olmsted, the creator of New York City's Central

Park in the 1850s, who was inspired by Paxton's creation, praised the democratic spirit of this 'People's Garden': 'The poorest British peasant is as free to enjoy it in all its parts as the British Queen.' Though Birkenhead Park covered 125 acres, far more urban terrain was consumed by housing and industry than was allocated to open space. City parks were insufficient to satisfy working-class recreational urges. Victoria Park, Salt noted sardonically in his first essay on Thoreau (1885), 'does not offer the advantages of Walden'.[57]

Rambling, launched in the mid-nineteenth century as a middle-class pursuit inspired by the Lake poets, was transformed by the urban working class into a mass recreation beyond paternalistic control. On Sundays, large numbers of factory operatives, many of them recent migrants from farms, joined mass exoduses from northern industrial cities. However ugly and depressing their immediate living environs might be, cities like Sheffield and Leeds had moorland on their doorsteps. Less advantageously situated workers were willing to march for a few hours to reach open countryside. The spreading railway network catered to this expanding clientele. The railway, which many saw as the vanguard of pernicious, debilitating progress, also functioned as a temporary escape route from modern conditions, rendering accessible a nature becoming invested with pre-modern virtue. Already by the 1860s, Sunday excursion trains were ferrying workers from Lancashire to the Lake District and operatives in Sheffield to the Derbyshire Peak District.[58]

The needs of working-class people for relief from the pressures of modern urban–industrial life were arguably even greater than those of the literati with their delicate sensibilities. Their motives in seeking out wild nature may have been more prosaic but they were no less urgent. The craving for camaraderie, clean air and exercise as an antidote to cramped and grimy existences and demeaning jobs is enshrined in songs like 'The Manchester Rambler': a mill worker cooped up and ordered about for six days of the week is transformed into a 'freeman on Sunday'. Moreover, many wanted more than to simply stretch their legs. Natural history societies with an interest in conservation, typified by the Clarion Field Clubs (1895), flourished in most industrial cities by 1900.[59]

Far from diverting attention from the class struggle and dissipating potential radical impulses, rambling assumed a prominent role not only in cementing class consciousness but also in undermining the status quo by agitating for access to sporting estates. Working-class ramblers secured some allies in the ruling class. In 1865, radical Liberals such as John Stuart Mill formed the Commons Preservation Society, which won public access to open spaces around London such as Epping Forest and Wimbledon Common. From the 1880s onwards, the Liberal peer James Bryce, a keen mountaineer, endeavoured to gain access to Scottish mountains and moorland.[60] By the 1920s, however, much of the movement's drive came from the veterans of cycling clubs inspired by Blatchford's *Clarion*, and from grassroots organizations such as the Liverpool Hobnailers. Their campaigns for entry culminated in 1932 in the mass trespass on Kinder Scout, the highest summit in the Peak District (the Ramblers' Association was founded in 1935).

Nor was rambling's appeal restricted to the British working class. In Austria and Germany, Friends of Nature (1895) had attracted 30,000 members by 1914, the vast majority of them working-class. Marching under the slogan 'Free Mountains, Free World, Free Peoples', Friends of Nature also committed mass trespass. Shortly before the First World War, a socialist deputy in the German national legislature inveighed against 'the fat cats who sported through the countryside in their luxury automobiles, spraying dust and stench at the poor, pedestrian, working-class friends of Nature'.[61]

Nature beyond the left

Despite this evidence of working-class engagement with nature, and notwithstanding the antecedents of today's green ideas and agenda that can be detected in the lives and thought of Carpenter, Blatchford, Morris and Salt, eco-socialists can overstate their case. True, disagreement with the 'utopians' was so bitter that the Social Democratic Federation split in 1884 (Morris founding the breakaway Socialist League). But Henry M. Hyndman, spokesman for the centrist, statist tendency represented by 'scientific socialism', exaggerated when he accused an assortment of 'old cranks' of scheming to take over the socialist movement.[62] The extent to which socialist thinking remained wedded to machine civilization and material progress is suggested in *The Road to Wigan Pier* (1937), in which George Orwell (who accepted machines as a fact of life, however unpleasant) caricatured the 'nexus of thought, "Socialism-progress-machinery-Russia-tractors-hygiene-machinery-progress"'. Socialists, Orwell claimed, 'will usually assume' that critics of machine civilization 'want to revert to a "state of nature" – meaning some stinking palaeolithic cave'.[63]

Indeed, some of those most at variance with the dominant ethos of industrial capitalism might be decried by those on the left as nostalgia-ridden reactionaries. In his essay 'Signs of the Times' (1829), Thomas Carlyle addressed the alienating impact of machinery and the industrial process as passionately as Marx and Engels ever did. He lamented the demise of the artisan and ridiculed the mania for machines ('for the simplest operation . . . some cunning abbreviating process is in readiness') that had even produced a cabbage-mincer: 'We remove mountains . . . nothing can resist us. We war with rude Nature . . . and come off always victorious.' Intriguingly, the images Carlyle employed (in a letter to his brother Alexander in 1824) to convey the profoundly unnatural scenes of industrial horror he witnessed in the coal mines and iron foundries of the Birmingham area were naturalistic ones, specifically those of troubling and destructive forces such as volcanos, earthquakes and tornados.[64]

Bate, another scholar engaged in locating the 'fathers and mothers of our environmental tradition', views the British left in its formative stages as more green than red, more Romantic than socialist. John Ruskin (1819–1900), who also took up residence in the Lake District, was certainly a more potent influence on Morris than Marx.[65] Ruskin's hankerings after a mythological, pre-industrial, pre-capitalist past saturated his most influential piece of social criticism, 'Unto this Last' (1862). In this critique of classical economics, which thrilled Gandhi and the young William Morris, Ruskin invented a moral landscape perfectly balanced between wild and tame: peasants nestle happily in the bosom of wildflowers and orchards, forests and fields, cows and wildlife ('the world cannot become a factory nor a mine').[66] In terms of their environmental vision, the anti-capitalist, anti-bourgeois right (conservative in the broadest sense) and the green left share more than they realize or may care to admit.

Derek Wall's recent collection of source materials defines green beliefs so as to exclude most elements with right-wing associations. Environmentalists on the right cannot be 'green', he asserts, because green politics and parties today are mostly left-leaning. He dislikes the association of conservationists with conservatives 'keen to keep grouse moors and salmon streams safe from the working class and secure for the exclusive use of an elite' because this perpetuates the traditional leftist view of conservationists as 'apolitical or reactionary'.[67] He acknowledges that Octavia Hill was possibly the most prominent British conservationist of the late nineteenth/early twentieth centuries, but has no room for her views in his compendium. For many eco-socialists, the British National Trust is tarnished by its close ties with the aristocracy and its preoccupation with preserving and restoring the elite landscape of the country estate.

Though the emergence of Britain's environmental movement was less intimately tied to the idolization of wild nature than its US cousin, a long-standing British tradition of conserving flora, fauna, mountain and moorland deserves attention. Today's agitators on behalf of endangered wildlife may dismiss the efforts of late Victorian and Edwardian sports hunters to preserve what remained of the empire's big-game animals as naked self-interest (the members of the Society for the Preservation of the Wild Fauna of the Empire were afraid there would be nothing left to shoot) or unconvincing penance ('Sorry we've killed nearly all of them, we'll make amends by saving the last handful'). But nobody else was doing much at that time.

Nor should we denigrate initiatives in nature protection (more or less simultaneous in Britain and the United States) because they were pursued by upper- and middle-class women who were less engrossed by urban problems and, in the United States, were just as concerned with conserving the supremacy of white Anglo-Saxon Protestant America as they were worried about the future health of American soil, flora and fauna. Powerful organizations such as the General Federation of Women's Clubs and the arch-conservative Daughters of the American Revolution maintained bustling conservation committees, and women spearheaded many local campaigns. Birds, above all, attracted female attention. By 1915, women accounted for slightly over half the members of the leading US bird protection organization, the Audubon Society (founded in 1885). The profile of its British sister organization was even more female. The Society for the Protection of Birds (SPB, founded in 1891, the forerunner of today's Royal Society for the Protection of Birds) had its roots in the Fur and Feather Group set up a few years earlier by a Manchester solicitor's wife, Emily Williamson, and run by the duchess of Portland from 1889 to 1954.[68]

Women were the main consumers of bird products. The millinery trade's suppliers plucked feathers from nesting mother-birds abroad and at home ('white gulls' such as kittiwakes, for instance, at sites like Flamborough Head, Yorkshire). These plunderings left fledglings to starve or be preyed on. Conceptualizing the family home as a microcosm of humanity's planetary abode, some ecofeminists have recently explained women's role as carers within the domestic sphere as the springboard for their activism in conservation and environmentalism. They argue that women's biological functions and nurturing responsibilities heighten their sensitivity to suffering and give them a natural role as planetary protectors and housekeepers. Given that 'eco' means house, argues Andrée Collard, 'ecology is woman-based almost by definition'.[69] While their motivations can hardly be described as ecological, late nineteenth- and early twentieth-century female lobbyists against the plumage trade on both sides of the Atlantic worked to arouse a sense of shame among their fellow women by playing on their maternal instincts.

Following the introduction of protection for British birds, foreign species were even more heavily targeted. Thanks to organized women's pressure, importation of the feathers of birds such as egrets, herons and birds of paradise was outlawed in the United States and Britain in 1913 and 1921 respectively (though the British ban exempted ostrich and eider duck). The fate of the plumage trade was finally sealed by the whims of fashion. Just as the shift to silk hats among the fashionable had granted the North American beaver a last-minute reprieve in the 1840s, so the survival of egrets and various songbirds was assured in the 1920s when large, ungainly hats – often festooned with entire birds – became extinct; the modish bob provided no anchorage for a hatpin. Non-plumage birds, however, remained beyond the emotional pale. By the turn of the century, many men had joined the SPB and its women had no desire to ruffle their feathers by threatening male recreational pursuits. The SPB's royal charter of 1904 disavowed any intention of interfering with the 'legitimate sport' of shooting game birds.[70]

The counterpoint to the construction of a leftist heritage for today's environmentalism is the right-wing parentage that Anna Bramwell, who regrets the left's appropriation of ecological ideas over recent decades, has unearthed for 'ecologism'. Wall dismisses the British fascist and arch-conservative involvement with ecology during the inter-war period as an interlude out of step with the nation's emerging green tradition. Yet Bramwell pays serious attention to fascist and High Tory concern with ecological matters and identifies a vivid green strand within an anti-capitalist, right-wing tradition.[71] By far the most heavily contested issue, however, is the intimacy of the historical relationship between nature and the right in Germany, with controversy focusing on nature's status within Nazi ideology and the pursuit of conservation under the Third Reich.

Studies of the German green phenomenon of the 1980s rarely explore its origins further back than the counter-cultural impulses of the 1960s. The shallow memory of many of Die Grünen can be attributed at least in part to an understandable sensitivity regarding forebears. Exceptions focus on the influence of Romanticism and the anti-modernism of Friedrich Nietzsche. Romantic intellectuals felt that Germanic qualities had been progressively debased and denatured by a series of foreign influences ever since the Roman imperium – most recently by the rationalism of the French Enlightenment. In their view, authentic

Germanism predated Christianity, capitalism and the bourgeoisie. This *völkisch* search for cultural purity and attempt to recover a sense of original, organic *Gemeinschaft* (community) became entangled with reverence for an undefiled Germanic world of nature located in the *Urwald* (primeval forest). Burke thought the oak a particularly British tree, but *Sturm und Drang* (Storm and Stress) writers such as Johann Gottfried Herder adopted it as the arch-symbol of Germania. Love of native nature was the crux of cultural nationalism in Wilhelm Heinrich Riehl's *The Natural History of the German People* (*Die Naturgeschichte des Deutschen Volkes*, 1851–5). Riehl, an ethnographer who hated cities, industry, capitalism and liberalism in equal measure, insisted that 'The German people need the forest like man needs wine . . . to warm the inner man.'[72] *Völkisch* ideology was saturated with Social Darwinism and offered a foretaste of sociobiology in its conviction that human culture and national character are fashioned by nature, which made some people better than others. *Völkisch* theorists urged Germans to treasure and defend the source of their superiority.

In the late nineteenth century, *Kulturpessimismus* (cultural pessimism) boosted the manufacture of a mythological past rooted in nature. A response of certain educated, middle-class Germans to industrialism and urbanization, *Kulturpessimismus* expressed a sense of loss of status, individuality and community.[73] The revulsion against soulless modernity was furthered by the Wandervögel, a nature-embracing, middle-class student organization. Founded in 1901, it flourished within the wider German youth movement after the First World War, when world-weary and embittered young Germans sought out the countryside. Partly a reassertion of the values of the strenuous life, originally articulated by and associated with US president, conservationist and outdoor enthusiast Theodore Roosevelt, the Wandervögel also anticipated 1960s counter-culturalism in its anti-modern thrust and anti-bourgeois bohemianism. Such impulses overlapped with a health reform and 'nature cure' fraternity preaching the virtues of naturism, fresh air and *Vollkornbrot* (wholemeal bread), and also converged with nature protectionism (*Naturschutz*).[74] In some instances, they also intersected with occult Nordicism.

Whereas Lewis Mumford identified the Third Reich as a 'megamachine' of peerless ruthlessness (whose roots he found in Bacon's *New Atlantis*), Bramwell has highlighted Nazi leadership in applied ecology. She focuses on Richard Walther Darré, Minister of Agriculture and Peasant Leader between 1933 and 1942, asking 'Was this Man Father of the Greens?'[75] Though he did not coin the phrase 'Blood and Soil' (*Blut und Erde* had been in vogue among pro-peasant nationalists in the 1920s), Darré made it his own and popularized it among early Nazis. He was contemptuous of urban Romanticism and no nature-lover in the mould of the SS chief Heinrich Himmler, but the two books he wrote before joining the Nazi Party in 1930 are larded with Jeffersonian and Rousseauian sentiments regarding the superiority of those nearest nature. Darré also believed that the first Germans were Nordics, that Nordicism was the lifeblood of an unexcelled, pre-industrial Germanic culture, and that Christianity should be overthrown and old Norse gods such as Thor reinstated. A naturist like a number of other Nazi ideologues, Darré maintained that pagan German Nordics blissfully pranced around in a state of nature until Christianity brought shame to nakedness and Jews perverted innocent nudity by imposing sexual overtones and exploiting female sexuality.[76]

Darré envisaged a stable, peasant-based society arising from the ashes of a rootless and predatory but doomed industrial capitalism (from which Jews were inseparable). Imbued with the anthroposophic ideas of Rudolf Steiner, he treated the soil as a living entity. He crusaded unflaggingly for organic farming – whose merits became a vital issue in the campaign to raise agricultural production for the war effort – until his death in 1953.[77] Hitler gave Darré political authority so he could win rural and small-town constituencies over to Nazism. (German industrialization was more widely diffused than in Britain, much of it lodging in small towns where workers retained their ties with ruralism.) From his power-base at Goslar, a medieval town in the foothills of the Harz, Darré duly delivered their votes.

Darré was not alone in his views within higher Nazi officialdom. Himmler, his closest associate, laid out an experimental organic farm within the Dachau concentration camps where he raised herbs for medicines to treat SS members. Moreover, nature-based nationalism flourished in 1930s Germany. A flurry of books bearing titles such as *Der Wald in der Deutschen Kultur* and *Deutscher Wald, Deutsches Volk* married German culture with a woodland heritage. (Willy Lange, the landscape architect who created the Heldenhain – a grove to commemorate a soldier who died in the First World War – advocated the planting of an oak for every fallen soldier.)[78]

The SS adopted the oak leaf as its emblem, and Nazi Germany led Europe in the creation of nature reserves and the implementation of progressive forestry sensitive to what we would now call biodiversity; for the sake of wildlife habitat, deciduous trees were included in plantations, and hedgerows and copses were protected. Himmler's plans for the Germanization of German-occupied western Poland (1939–40) extended to the reconstruction of the landscape, complementing a general emphasis within German landscape design on cleansing the environment of 'unharmonious foreign substance'. The creation of a 'German face' involved the incorporation of far larger numbers of trees, hedges, shrubs and copses into the countryside. This was not only an expression of what Himmler called 'our love, inherited from the German tribes, for trees, shrubs, and flowers (village oak or village linden)', but was also designed to furnish habitats for weasels, hedgehogs, buzzards and falcons, which, not least, would help control the vermin that preyed on crops.[79]

Yet even if we accept such actions as anticipations of modern green policies and recognize Darré as a green forefather, this does not mean they were particularly close or influential antecedents and ancestors. It is not as if post-war German Greens suddenly discovered Darré's ideas and made them their own, but more a case of their running parallel. (Bramwell has been misconstrued in this regard; she does not argue for direct continuity or inspiration.) Nor does it mean that environmental protection was prominent in Nazi propaganda or central to the Nazi domestic programme. Darré remained a fringe figure. At variance with key Nazi policies of imperial expansion and autobahn construction, and also at odds with the leadership principle, he was increasingly sidelined after 1939. Darré's position reflects the uneasy coexistence between ecology and mainstream Nazism.

Raymond Dominick shares Bramwell's view that many German conservationists were linked to the right in the interwar era, and we ought to take seriously her belief that 'the existence of the uniforms and the swastikas' should not preclude an attempt to understand a German ecological viewpoint that existed prior to the 1930s and has survived Nazism.[80] Martin Heidegger was the most prominent German intellectual attracted to Nazism because of its orientation towards nature. Steeped in Buddhism and Taoism, he objected to anthropocentrism, which he felt had dominated Western philosophy and life since Plato. Though critical of Nazi racial theories, he believed the Nazis could engineer a massive shift in human consciousness that would obliterate the entire withering package of capitalism, communism, democracy, liberalism, rationalism, commercialism and cosmopolitanism, as well as the totalitarianism of technocracy.[81] Dominick is right, however, to warn against confusing 'ideological overlap on a few points with fundamental congruence'.[82] Most Nazis were not conservationists and most German conservationists did not subscribe to Nazi militarism or racial ideology.

Nazism (as distinct from a generic European 'fascism') was a peculiar mixture of modernity and anti-modernity. The Third Reich's guardians of culture seized on the German landscape as a weapon to bludgeon modern art, for instance. For the Reichskulturkammer, abstract and non-representational styles such as Cubism and Dadaism were cynical and bloodless filth. From 1936, a torrent of wholesome Aryan art (*Volkskunst*) spewed forth, the accent on landscape and scenes of contented peasants harvesting wheat. At the same time, the works of Romantic artist Caspar David Friedrich, whose paintings had nurtured a nascent German nationalism during the Napoleonic era, enjoyed a revival in popularity.[83]

Yet German fascism also worshipped the rational and the technological sublime. Huge road construction projects and land reclamation programmes ruptured the landscape. Cities swelled and industrial output soared in the 1930s, though Hitler saw this as an expression of the immense spiritual capacities of the new German man rather than capitulation to bourgeois materialism. That the German version was the only brand of fascism allied to ecological concerns in any significant way suggests (as Bramwell does) that we should focus on the German intellectual tradition rather than fascist ideology *per se*. With the notable exception of the pro-Germanist philosopher Julius Evola (who was eventually banned by Mussolini), the ideology (and practice) of Italian fascism was unflinchingly modern.[84]

Shifting the focus of debate from applied ecology to green spirituality, certain commentators believe that Nazism intersects with various tenets of deep ecology. Employing 'religion' in a loose sociological sense that renders its meaning largely synonymous with ideology, Robert Pois has identified a Nazi 'religion of nature', which rejected organized religion and Judaeo-Christian dualism in favour of a pagan submergence of humanity within a divine nature.[85] Himmler epitomized what Pois labels Nazi 'mystical, nature-worshipping *Schwärmerei*'.[86] Buddhism fascinated Himmler and he celebrated the occult, the intuitive and the irrational, dabbled in Oriental mysticism and erected forest shrines.

The case for a Nazi religion of nature is reinforced by the conviction of Nazi intellectuals that mankind as part of nature must obey its iron will. Nazism perceived culture and society as organisms, natural entities in which forces operate to maintain the overall structure. 'Society', 'nature' and 'system' are not merely abstractions; they have their own interests and imperatives. On the basis of conformity to nature's eternal laws, for example, Hitler condemned pacifism as 'contrary to Nature'. His reverence for nature as a Darwinian lesson – a far cry from environmental protection – is encapsulated in *Mein Kampf* (1925/6):

> This planet once moved through the ether for millions of years without human beings and it can do so again some day if men forget they owe their higher existence, not to the ideas of a few crazy ideologists, but to the knowledge and ruthless application of Nature's stern and rigid laws.[87]

Nature also justified Nazi views on sexual orientation, racial purity and women's status. Homosexuality violated natural law; their Nordic ancestors who drowned homosexuals in bogs had had the right idea. 'Nature', according to Hitler, had 'little love for bastards'. And in 1934 he told an assembly of the NS Frauenschaft, a Nazi women's organization of distinctively rural character, that nature had decreed a natural equality between the sexes by setting up separate spheres: 'she, in those areas of life determined for her by nature, [should] receive every deep respect due to her'. For Nazi ideologues, the new German woman was a renatured creature who willingly relinquished cigarettes and cosmetics for the javelin and a tanned face.[88]

Those few Nazis who accepted that Jews had a place within the natural order put them at a very low level. Leading Nazis denied that Jews had greater rights than fleas or mosquitoes and rarely set them above parasites and weeds. Weeds flourished, unfortunately, even on the healthiest soil, explained Darré in 1940; the job of the good land steward was to uproot them. Other favourite representations of the alien Jew were as virus, fungus and vermin.[89] Propaganda films compared the elimination of Jews to a delousing operation, while a production about the Warsaw ghetto was interleaved with footage of swarming rats.

Nazi propaganda rendered the 'Jew' synonymous with the 'city', an association that the strategy of ghettoization rendered a physical reality by transplanting rural Jews into the cities. For many Nazis, the very existence of Jews, huddled in 'lifeless' cities apart from nature, was an affront to the natural order. And nature decreed that the weak, the degenerate and the unnatural be extinguished. This helps explain how Himmler, who sent millions of Jews to their deaths, could denounce hunting to Felix Kersten (a renowned hunter and Himmler's masseur and close confidant) as 'pure murder' (proclaiming every animal's 'right to live') and instigate anti-vivisection laws.[90] Propaganda played on the methods of Jewish ritual slaughter: the laws of Kashrut, it pointed out, refused to allow animals to be stunned before they had their throats slit.[91] The Nazi stance on cruelty to animals betrayed more hatred of Jews than love of animals, and propagandists exploited conservation and animal rights 'to whip up enthusiasm for causes it thought more important'.[92]

The commandant of Auschwitz, Rudolf Höss, was apparently shocked at the indifference to the suffering of their compatriots displayed by the largely Jewish Sonderkommando. In his memoirs (1959), Höss charges that this elite group, responsible for removing bodies from the gas chambers, extracting gold teeth, and then dispatching corpses to crematoria, carried on eating and smoking as if they were gardening or reading the newspaper. For Höss, this callous behaviour confirmed the unnaturalness of the Jew. He sought solace from these traumas through contact with the wholesome world of nature: 'I would mount my horse and ride, until I had chased the terrible picture away. Often, at night, I would walk through the stables and seek relief among my beloved animals.'[93]

Shoving humanity off its pedestal may sound exhilarating to those who believe that a fundamental philosophical shift is necessary to save the planet. But defining humans as animals no more worthy of consideration than other creatures potentially strips certain people of the rights and immunities to which they might otherwise lay claim. You do not need to be a social ecologist to appreciate the dangers of Hitler defining Jews as pests or of a radical environmentalist of the 1980s comparing humanity to a cancerous growth. Deep greens sometimes give the impression that it really does not matter if we wipe ourselves out, since humanity is entirely expendable from nature's standpoint. In James Lovelock's words, we are nothing more than parasitic, 'intelligent fleas' to Gaia, whose 'unconscious goal is a planet fit for life. If humans stand in the way of this, we shall be eliminated with as little pity as would be shown by the micro-brain of an intercontinental ballistic nuclear missile in full flight to its target.' In fact, if humanity itself is the ultimate form of pollution, our extinction may be something for the rest of nature to celebrate. 'The possibility that life on the earth may be preserved only by the expedient of catastrophe for the human species, like the possibility that the Western tradition cannot be renewed', concludes John Gray in his vilification of modernism, humanism and Westernization, 'is one to which any mode of thinking that is authentically free from humanism must open itself'.[94]

For the eco-socialist, such sentiments constitute 'eco-fascism', an allegation sharpened through direct allusions to the 'green' ideology, policies and personnel of the Third Reich.[95] At a glance, certain pronouncements of Nazi ideologues like Ernst Kriek resemble the biocentric outpourings of today's deep ecologists. For these Nazis believed, according to Richard L. Rubenstein, that 'in nature men have the same rights as flies, mosquitoes or beasts of prey'.[96]

Bookchin, who wonders whether Earth First! translates into 'People Second', rates the biocentricism of deep ecology on a par with the anti-humanism of Himmler, who told his SS leaders in 1942, when the elimination of the Jews was at its peak, that 'man is nothing special'.[97] Condemned as eco-fascist are a range of authoritarian policies and their advocates: wildlife preservationists who value the life of an endangered animal so highly that they would forcibly relocate an African or Asian village impinging on its habitat, or who advocate a 'shoot to kill' policy for poachers of the white rhinoceros; Western proponents of zero or negative population growth in the developing world through compulsory sterilization; those Americans who support draconian action against Mexicans breaching the 'tortilla curtain'; and, above all, the mavericks within Earth First! who (in 1987) regarded famine and AIDS as Mother Nature's tough love for the planet and Gaia's immune system fighting back ('If radical environmentalists were to invent a disease to bring human populations back to ecological sanity, it would probably be something like AIDS').[98]

The eco-socialist dystopia is a police state run by a green Hitler that mobilizes a vast network of informers to stamp out ecological incorrectness, where picking a rare wildflower is a hanging offence and those failing to recycle their yoghurt containers are banished.

Catchy and off-handed (if rather dated) polemics by fringe elements within Earth First! – not to mention equally notorious (and even older) aphorisms such as Edward Abbey's 'I'd rather kill a *man* than a snake' (1968)[99] – definitely make for tempting and shocking copy. And the more unscrupulous members of the 'green left' certainly seek to discredit those passionately concerned about the future of wild creatures and wild places by tarring them with the brush of misanthropic right-wing extremism. Nevertheless, the majority of Western nature preservationists retain their faith in humanity and the democratic process. Despite the colourful efflorescence of radical groups over the past twenty years, the bulk of those in the United States and Britain who call themselves 'green' still belong to organizations such as the Sierra Club and the National Trust.

9

The Future of Nature

In 1989 Francis Fukuyama, a US State Department official, published a provocative article entitled 'The End of History?'[1] Defining history as the struggle between competing systems and ideologies, most recently that between capitalism/liberal democracy and communism, he argued that the definitive triumph of capitalism and liberal democracy signalled 'the end point of mankind's ideological evolution'. History defined less grandly as a series of events would of course go on, but 'all of the really big questions had been settled'.

Those unconvinced by Fukuyama's dramatic pronouncement wondered whether communism was really dead and buried, and drew attention to issues such as the rise of Islamic fundamentalism and ethnic strife in places such as the former Yugoslavia. Sceptics also queried whether liberal democracy and capitalism were truly in such healthy shape, citing the depradations not only of drugs, poverty and crime in the Western world but also of environmental degradation.

Fukuyama acknowledged that the twentieth century 'has made all of us into deep historical pessimists':

> Our own experience has taught us, seemingly, that the future is more likely than not to contain new and unimagined evils, from fanatical dictatorships and bloody genocides to the banalization of life through modern consumerism, and that unprecedented disasters await us from nuclear winter to global warming.

Yet despite his sombre announcement of history's demise, Fukuyama was eager to demonstrate that there was still plenty of life left in the idea of history as progress. The collapse of communism aside, another prime reason to think that history was still moving forward was the 'progressive conquest of nature' that promised material abundance for all people. Rejecting the need to control human capacity for destruction, Fukuyama singled out environmentalists as the greatest threat to history, defined not as ideological struggle but as the extension of human control over nature. He presented environmentalists (whose intellectual roots he traced back to Rousseau) as such dangerous enemies because they question the notion of an ever-upward historical trajectory thanks to science, technology and capitalism, and because they (allegedly) brim with nostalgia for an earlier stage of historical evolution when nature was far more in control. Placing his faith in scientific ingenuity and technological fixes, Fukuyama blithely dismissed eschatological fears of the earth's collapse.[2]

The 'end of nature' debate is more readily associated, however, with Bill McKibben's *The End of Nature* (1990), a book about the dire implications of climate change induced by global warming for traditional ideas of nature and culture. A range of other factors germane to apocalyptical notions of nature's 'end' and 'death' will also be discussed below in the context of speculation over nature's future: the reconfiguration of nature through genetic engineering; the postmodernist critique of nature's autonomy; recent developments in animal biology and behaviourism that further blur the distinction between nature and culture; and revisionist ecological science that undermines the idea – so dear to many Western environmentalists and environmental historians – of a nature that embodies truth, beauty, permanence and reality. 'Historians thought ecology was the rock upon which they could build environmental history', remarks Richard White; 'it turned out to be a swamp.'[3] We conclude with an appraisal of sanguine views that dispute the likelihood of nature's death or imminent demise, whether as physical entity or symbol.

The mortality of the earth and the end of nature

The grave announcement of Lake Erie's 'death' through eutrophication (oxygen starvation) catalysed American public awareness of an ecological crisis in the 1960s. In the 1980s, Germans coined a term for pine trees dying of acid rain – *Waldsterben* – and the idea of death is now ubiquitous in public discussion about the condition of the planet. Post-war generations living under the shadow of the mushroom cloud are not the first, however, to engage in anguished debate over the planet's future (or lack of one). Approaching the earth as a single organism, intellectuals at various times have viewed it as a mortal being well advanced in age and suffering from virtual exhaustion. Lucretius, in *De Rerum Natura*, contended that the earth was 'gradually decaying, nearing the end, worn out by the long span of years'.[4] The early Church Fathers during the era of transition from the ancient period (third, fourth and fifth centuries) were preoccupied with the problems of a postlapsarian world of curses, disease, famine, thistles and dwindling natural resources. Sounding remarkably like the 'limits to growth' school of environmental economists in the early 1970s, they feared for the future and issued jeremiads such as this: 'Everything has been visited, everything known, everything exploited. Beaches are plowed, mountains smoothed and swamps cleaned . . . Everywhere there are buildings, everywhere people, everywhere communities, everywhere life' (Tertullian, *c*.200).[5]

These ideas of mortality and terminal decay resurfaced with a vengeance in the late sixteenth century. The world in its 'crooked old age', lamented Lambert Daneau in *Physica Christiana* (1570s), is 'weake, sicke, and wounded'.[6] Yet works such as Bishop Godfrey Goodman's *The Fall of Man, or the Corruption of Nature* (1616) invariably focused on the moral decline of man (internal nature), which they believed had generated the physical decay of the world (external nature), rather than on the condition of the earth itself. Nevertheless, the pessimists enumerated the earth's inadequacies and obstacles – among them thorns, weeds, disease, predatory animals, poor soil, inclement weather and uninhabitable mountains and deserts (not to mention lacklustre rainbows) – as prime evidence of the Fall.[7] Despite the fresh lands and abundant natural resources supplied by European expansion, even Walter Ralegh conformed to the notion of planetary senescence in his *History of the World* (1614), where he compared the world to a clock that cannot be rewound.

George Hakewell's counter-argument in *An Apologie of the Power and Providence of God* (1627) attributed earthly imperfections to human sloth. Dismissing the idea of a golden age as a 'pretty invention', he warned against confusing change and mutability with decay. Nature was inviolable, governed by the laws of compensation, not deterioration. Had there been any progressive decay, '*Cedars* would have beene no taller than *shrubs*, *Horses* no bigger than *Dogges*' and 'nothing else could now be lefte to use but the very *refuse* and *bran*, the *drosse* and *dregges* of nature.'[8] Francis Bacon hated the hopelessness and restrictions on human potential implicit in the idea of the earth's mortality. Decoupling the earth from the idea of human corruption (a radical intellectual departure), Bacon insisted on a world external to man that offered unlimited scope for human achievement.

Bacon thought he was revitalizing the idea of nature but, as we have seen, environmentalists have argued that the rationalism, mechanism and patriarchalism he symbolized were instrumental in killing it off. Though Nicolson and Merchant had already discussed the 'death of the world' (1950, 1963) and 'the death of nature' (1980), most readers will associate the idea with Bill McKibben, a writer who retreated from the city to live in a log cabin on the fringes of second-growth woodland in the Adirondack mountains of upstate New York.[9] His thesis in *The End of Nature* is that we have so thoroughly domesticated the earth and modified natural processes that it is no longer possible to speak of nature as something with a separate existence. Given the ubiquity of transnational pollutants such as acid rain, the world is now entirely of our own making.

McKibben's book belongs to a distinct genre of post-1945 'disaster scenario' literature raising the spectres of population explosion, resource exhaustion, desertification, nuclear winter and species extinction. His specific subject is global warming from the greenhouse effect, and he conjures up the nightmarish vision not only of rising sea-levels (drowning low-lying tropical islands) but of his local creek drying up and the trees he loves being replaced by others migrating northward as things hot up.

McKibben denies that nature has been slowly dying for centuries by drawing a qualitative distinction between the kind of damage inflicted through abusive logging, farming and hunting and a new order of assault constituted by various pollutants since 1945. He argues that much of the former's damage was localized and reparable provided the destructive activity stopped. By contrast, the changes brought by the expanding hole in the ozone layer are global and irrevocable: 'by changing the weather, we make every spot on earth man-made and artificial. We have deprived nature of its independence, and that is fatal to its meaning. Nature's independence *is* its meaning; without it there is nothing but us.' The death of nature is not to be confused with the end of life on earth or the disappearance of phenomena such as rain, wind and sun. Plants, animals and beautiful places will still exist (though he insists they have all been hopelessly devalued): 'When I say "nature", I mean a certain set of human ideas about the world and our place in it.'[10] So what he really means by the end of nature is the destruction of the idea of nature as an untrammelled entity. In short, the demise of the idea of wilderness.

But if, by nature (and wilderness), we mean something unaffected by humans and their history, then not only the idea but also the very substance of nature (and wilderness) have been emphatically dead for a long time. Fukuyama insists that McKibben's timing is about 400 years out, but that is conservative.[11] (We can probably go back as far as the evolution of humans. McKibben overlooks the extent to which deforestation, farming and hunting have brought permanent change. Recovery is not as easy as he implies. Assuming, for instance, that the nucleus of a wildlife population exists to serve as the basis for a reintroduction, extensive habitat restoration will be a precondition.) The confusion arises because, for McKibben, like many other Americans, nature is synonymous with wilderness, and human intervention, whether in the shape of a drystone wall or a nuclear power plant, can only be conceived of in terms of loss and intrusion, a mentality that relegates a garden to the same category as a car park.

Whereas McKibben craves the illusion of being in 'another, separate, timeless, wild sphere', his fellow refugee from the city, the gardening enthusiast and *Harper's* editor Michael Pollan, would argue that the death of the idea of nature as 'the other' is something to celebrate. From his perspective, we must leave the wilderness and return to the garden in order to improve our relations with nature.[12] An assault on the Romantic fetish for the wild is central to Pollan's argument, which is fashioned around his efforts to grow flowers and vegetables on an old Connecticut dairy farm, a hilly area with rocky, unyielding soil. Through selective quotation, overlooking the evidence that they too extolled the virtues of the pastoral and the joys of civilization, this reformed 'child of Thoreau' sets up Thoreau and Emerson as misanthropic wilderness obsessives who harboured a deep contempt for the cultivated. Yet he usefully reminds us that there is more history in nature than we think: witness the weeds that invaded Thoreau's beanfield at Walden Pond, which he assumed were more natural than his beans but which were in fact mostly European imports.[13]

Most Europeans, however, will not need reminding that the 'wilderness ethic' is of limited value, if not entirely redundant, as a guide for appropriate environmental behaviour, since the overwhelming preponderance of nature in the western world has been substantially modified by human activity.[14] Pollan's belief that there are choices beyond the stark alternatives of deflowering nature or setting her on a pedestal beyond human reach may have upset many wilderness preservationists in the United States but is essentially a restatement of the Christian ideal of stewardship.

Tampering with the essence: biotechnology

Climate change as the alleged cause of nature's death has been rivalled (if not eclipsed) in the popular mind over recent years by advances in genetic engineering. In 1996 the product of twenty-one years of research became available on British supermarket shelves: cans of purée made from genetically altered Californian tomatoes. By isolating the enzyme that governs the rotting process, this research has enabled the growth of a longer-lasting, firmer tomato that is easier to pick and transport. But the taste of the future that really made the headlines in 1997 was the birth of Dolly, the cloned sheep, an event prompting public debate over the propriety of scientists 'playing god'.[15]

The argument that the idea of nature as something autonomous 'died' long ago, or that this dying process has been slow if not imperceptible, affects assessments of the long-term importance of recent innovations in biotechnology. Some believe that the industrial genetics, represented not only by drought- and frost-resistant plant strains but also by 'test-tube babies' and surrogate motherhood, represents the logical culmination of the arrogant Baconian view of nature as infinitely malleable matter. Walter Truett Anderson, while referring to a 'biological revolution' and seeing these developments as a 'colossal step forward', denies that they constitute an unprecedented departure from the previous course of evolution.[16] Another viewpoint holds that genetic engineering is best discussed as an extension of well-established methods of selective breeding of pigs for leaner meat, cows for higher milk yield and sheep for more wool, while successful artificial insemination of animals dates back two centuries.

Others approach these innovations as changes of kind entailing breathtaking disrespect for existing life forms. McKibben, dubbing them the 'second end of nature', fears that scientists fooling around with recombinant DNA ('gene-splicing') will cook up all sorts of 'designer' animals – not only leaner chickens but a chicken that is nothing but lean flesh. The very essence of animals is jeopardized: ' "Rabbit" will be a few lines of code, no more important than a set of plans for a 1940 Ford.' He quotes the eschatological opinion of the prominent environmentalist muckraker, Jeremy Rifkin, from probably the most influential popular book on the subject in the 1970s, that 'our children . . . will re-define living things as temporal programmes that can be edited, revised, and re-programmed'.[17] (Advance is rapid. In the autumn of 1997 we were introduced to the headless frog.)

This may be rather paranoid (Anderson dubs Rifkin's position 'biological McCarthyism'), as is the assumption that such research is driven by eugenicist ideology. Nevertheless, those who appraise recent genetic engineering more modestly as a further stage in the evolution of life forms fail to appreciate the extent to which what has been called 'biological and ecological central planning' is dictated by economic rather than natural selection.[18] In 1980 the US Supreme Court supported the corporate interest, judging by a narrow majority (5 to 4) that it was constitutional to patent genetically engineered plants because these were the products of human invention rather than of nature, a ruling extended to animals in 1987. Legal wrangling has followed in Europe over the patenting of the oncomouse (a mouse with an inserted cancer gene) and Astrid the Pig, a pig reared with organs designed for use in human transplants. British scientist Jacqueline McGlade has denounced a proposed European Union directive for the patenting of organisms resulting from biotechnological inventions (as distinct from the processes involved) as 'a charter to enslave nature'.[19]

The nature of animals

Those who feel that the disregard for the distinctive identity of nature that informs genetic engineering is a giant step backwards for humanity in its efforts to begin its dealings with the natural world afresh may be heartened by a different kind of research. The groundwork was laid by the Austrian ethologist Konrad Lorenz and the American psychologist B. F. Skinner in the 1930s and 1940s. Lorenz denied that everything social was cultural, arguing for a physiological basis, shared with animals, for many of our needs. His best-known work, *On Aggression* (often misinterpreted as an apology for violence), posited that we can learn about human behaviour by studying animals. Skinner, who refused to distinguish between social psychology and animal psychology, trained pigeons to direct guided missiles to their targets during the Second World War. This tendentious body of work, which suggests that human and animal behaviour alike stems from environmental considerations rather than from 'within', disregards the distinctive identity of human culture.[20]

   Accordingly, research on animal behaviour that questions the hallowed divide between nature and culture by suggesting common bonds between animals and people also heralds the end of nature. In this respect, however, the end of nature can be regarded as an enormous leap forward: if 'they' are shown to be more like 'us' – not through religiosity or sentimentality but on purely intellectual grounds – then biocentric ecophilosophers might have an easier job persuading other people to include 'them' and their interests within our ethical circle.

Today's altercations over the nature of animals have been prefigured at various times, though, as ever, it is easier to show similarities than to demonstrate connections. Taking the logic of noble savagery to its extreme in the sixteenth century, Montaigne elevated wildlife above humans in an essay written in defence of the natural theologian Raymond Sebond. In accordance with his belief that the 'Book of Nature', properly read, displays truths about God and man, Montaigne created the noble beast with a more highly developed moral code than man, a less violent nature and sometimes greater intelligence. He argued ingeniously, for instance, that tunny fish have a mathematical grasp because they swim in geometric patterns, and that elephants engage in the equivalent of a religious exercise after washing at dawn ('waving their trunks like arms upraised'), standing in devotional pose at regular intervals during the day thereafter. Montaigne deemed man superior to the animals only in his imaginative powers, yet pointed out that some animals even dream (witness the greyhound chasing a hare in its sleep). These fanciful efforts to reunite people with animals (based not on Montaigne's personal observations but on what he had read in the classics) were designed for a purpose that today's animal rights advocates would recognize: to dent human pride and arrogance ('imaginary kingship over other creatures', as he put it).[21]

The leading French philosophers of the seventeenth century, René Descartes and Pierre Gassendi, while seeing eye to eye in many other respects, clashed over whether animals had souls. Descartes denied that even the highest animals had anything in common with mankind. Because speech embodied human rationality as against the thoughtlessness of animals, his case rested on this facility, with speech defined as the vehicle for the expression of thought rather than chatter, and interpreted as an expression of the soul rather than of intelligence:

> It is therefore unbelievable that a monkey or a parrot which was one of the best of its species should not be the equal in this matter of one of the most stupid children, or at least of a child of infirm mind, if their soul were not of a wholly different nature from ours.[22]

Gassendi refused to accept that animals, to be taken seriously, should be expected to exhibit something akin to human language. The case for the immortal souls of animals was reinforced in the late seventeenth century by the German thinker Gottfried Wilhelm von Leibniz, who, as part of his monad theory of 1696 (which holds that individual entities enjoy a co-operative relationship with other substances and that each possesses its own soul), argued that human and animal intelligence differ only in degree. He saw nature as a hierarchy of states of consciousness. At the bottom resided dead matter, fated to eternal sleep; just above this were plants in a passive state, followed by the lower animals; then came the more alert consciousness of the higher animals. Humans perched at the apex of self-consciousness yet remained part of the collective structure.[23]

The so-called 'nature faker' debate in the early twentieth-century United States provides further insight into the controversy over the differences between people and animals. Euro-American fascination with what remained of the nation's original natural profile was reflected in the popularity of wild animal stories, supposedly based on scientific observation in the field. These tales fizzed with unusual activities. Woodcocks, for instance, set their own broken legs in mud casts and orioles tied complicated knots to prevent their suspended nests from falling. The attack on the nature-fakers's anthropomorphic fables gave rise to fundamental questions – debated acrimoniously in the nation's magazines – such as do animals learn? And, if so, from whom? The nature-fakers maintained that their parents taught them, while their opponents insisted on the force of blind instinct.[24]

A. L. Kroeber, an early twentieth-century US anthropologist, was keen to maintain the categorical distinction between animals and people (not least to combat eugenicist assumptions that cultural and historical attainments are the product of race as opposed to culture). But he agreed that differences in the physical and mental realm were relative rather than absolute. So he looked elsewhere to ground his belief in human uniqueness. He found it in culture, denying that anything approaching even a rudimentary culture prevailed among animals (cultural determinism).[25] However, if culture is external to the individual and something that must be acquired, then it is also true that animals learn their behaviour. Lion cubs are taught how to hunt by their parents and buffalo calves are socialized by their uncles and aunts. Urban foxes are more streetwise than their country cousins; there are far fewer squashed foxes on city streets than on rural roads.

Some psychologists still cite speech as 'the rubicon which no animal will ever cross!'[26] But beginning with the work of the Teubers and Wolfgang Koehler on Tenerife in the 1910s, research on chimpanzees has raised popular awareness of their intelligence, focusing on speech facility. (Skinner's *Verbal Behavior* (1957) argued that human language was just another form of communication.) The most famous 'talking' chimp is Washoe, who, in the late 1960s, was taught sign language (Ameslan). By 1975, Washoe had a working vocabulary of 160 signs and could converse, construct sentences and make statements. 'A small doll placed unexpectedly in Washoe's cup', reports the popularizer of science Carl Sagan, 'elicited the response "Baby in my drink."'[27] Another chimpanzee has since been taught computer language (Yerkish), while another has acquired a sense of mathematical proportion (as in being able to tell if a cup is a quarter- or half-full).

The human exceptionalists discount these findings by re-emphasizing Descartes's distinction between language and communication, insisting that while it has been shown that creatures can sometimes understand and act upon spoken commands, they cannot talk themselves. The anti-speciesists, aligning themselves with Gassendi, counter-attack with the evidence that many animals lack the the necessary vocal apparatus; the chimpanzee's voice box, for instance, unlike that of birds, is not suited for human-style speech.

Darwin thought that language facilitated the growth in the size of the human brain relative to that of other primates, insisting, in *The Descent of Man* (1871), that 'there is no fundamental difference between man and the higher mammals in their mental faculties'. He proceeded to assert that 'only a few persons dispute that animals possess some kind of power of reasoning', seeking to refute the belief that they have no power of abstraction, no ability to form general concepts and no sense of self-consciousness by citing the example of his favourite terrier. He explained that when he said 'Hi hi, where is it?', she rushed off into the nearest thicket and then looked up a tree. 'Now do not these actions clearly show that she had in her mind a general idea or concept that some animal is to be discovered and hunted?' If such faculties were more highly developed in humans, then this could be attributed to longer experience with language.[28]

Many species of bird possess forms of communication that we might describe as dialects, with intra-community differences often found within a span of a few hundred metres. But it is whales that the proponents of animal intelligence are most eager to connect us with. Studies of humpback whale 'songs' indicate complex intra-species forms of cultural expression and transmission across vast distances. According to Katherine Payne, wife of Roger Payne the neurophysiologist and whale musicologist who released the first recordings in 1970:

> The whales use a technique very much like one a good composer uses to create beautiful and interesting music. For example, Beethoven sets up rhythmic patterns and musical themes we all recognize and expect to recur. Then he surprises you with a variation. Every humpback whale song I've heard surprises me just the way Beethoven does.[29]

The human exceptionalism represented by tool-making capacity (as distinct from the use of sticks and stones by apes, otters and birds) is frequently cited as additional support for the dichotomy between people and animals.[30] Darwin's efforts to undermine this prop have been seconded by Jane Goodall's research among chimpanzees in Gombe National Park, Tanzania, since 1960. Goodall demonstrated both their capacity for learning ('fishing' for termites with twigs and grass stems) and the length of time it takes to acquire new skills.[31]

Moreover, whereas much animal behaviour has a fixed pattern and is reproduced even in those raised in captivity, songbird research has provided evidence of acculturation: some birds, if raised by foster parents of a different species, will sing the song of their adopted species instead of that of their own – and continue to do so after they hear the song of their own kind.[32] And in view of the latest arguments that the mental capabilities of the corvid (crow) family could be equal to those of higher primates, the day may come when it will be defamatory to use the expression 'bird-brained'.[33]

As for construction activities, prairie dogs build elaborate subterranean cities while beavers erect intricate dams. Leaving aside Katherine Payne's aquatic Beethovens, artistic creativity is another matter, though it should be noted that items of material culture chewed (crafted?) by a pet dog – slippers and cushions – were exhibited in an avant-garde London gallery in 1997. By far the boldest position to date has been taken by Donna Haraway, who wants nothing less than the abolition of the hoary and crippling dualisms of nature/culture, male/female and human/machine. She invites us to transgress these sacred boundaries through the construction of new beings 'from the belly of the [cyborg] monster', thereby emancipating women, among other things, from biologically deterministic reproductive functions.[34]

Other upholders of the sacred distinction between people and animals have pinpointed the ability to think in abstract terms as the critical divide. This was Aristotle's basic point, one generally upheld by medieval thinkers. Still, as the end of the second millennium approaches, we are inclined to take more seriously than ever Sagan's charming wishful thinking: 'The brain mass of a mature sperm whale . . . is almost 9,000 grams, six and a half times that of the average man . . . What does the whale do with so massive a brain? Are there thoughts, insights, arts, sciences and legends of the sperm whale?'[35]

While bearing in mind that brain conformation matters as much as size, it is tempting to think that whales enjoy a non-literate form of culture, if culture is understood to be those aspects of behaviour that are acquired, shared by individual members and orally transmitted down the generations. Perhaps whales have historical consciousness and can record and recollect their experiences. ('Remember when we got chased by a madman with a harpoon, and escaped in the nick of time?')

While we await more conclusive data, implacable hostility will continue to greet the findings and speculations of these researchers, particularly those working on inter-species communications between cetaceans and people.[36] It will do so on broad philosophical and theological grounds (the need to defend the unique status of humankind – John Lilly called dolphins 'humans of the sea') and because of the more immediate need of science and industry to defend the ideological basis of animal experiments and meat-eating. But this work has also fallen foul of many behavioural ecologists, who object to what they see as a blithe disregard for the basic rules of scientific research. (Another bout of fakery?)

The postmodernist challenge

Ask a thoughtful Green what the greatest threat to nature is today and the answer might be 'postmodernism' rather than corporate capitalism, human greed or ignorance. Arran Gare characterizes deep ecologists and ecofeminists as postmodern environmentalists, but many environmentalist thinkers condemn cultural theorists for demoting the natural world from a living entity that requires delicate handling and commands our wonder into something of merely cultural and linguistic construction and significance. For Jean Baudrillard, the desert of the south-western United States is just a metaphor. 'The deserts here', he insists,

> are not part of a Nature defined by contrast with the town. Rather they denote the emptiness, the radical nudity that is the background to every human institution. At the same time, they designate human institutions as a metaphor of that emptiness, and the work of man as a continuum of the desert.

Of the cinematic, geologically dramatic spectacle of Death Valley, Baudrillard writes: 'Nature itself pulled off the finest of its special effects here, long before men came on the scene.' But he continues with the observation that 'it is useless to seek to strip the desert of its cinematic aspects in order to restore its original essence; those features are thoroughly superimposed upon it and will not go away.' The Californian desert impresses him with its 'brilliant, mobile, superficial neutrality, a challenge to meaning and profundity, a challenge to nature and culture, an outer hyperspace, with no origin, no reference-points'. 'Culture itself is a desert there', he remarks of life in California, 'and culture has to be a desert so that everything can be equal and shine out in the same supernatural form.'[37] (These are the sort of people many environmentalists secretly hope will get mauled by a grizzly, stung by poison oak or, in Baudrillard's case, bitten by a rattlesnake.)

In so far as a belief in the necessity and rectitude of human dominion over nature (and extra-European peoples), the blessings of technological innovation and the values of industrialism are key facets of modernity, one might reasonably assume that the future of the earth would be a central concern of postmodernism and that postmodernists would be drawn to environmentalism. This is especially so in view of postmodernist respect for Claude Lévi-Strauss's multiculturalist manifesto and 'decentring' of humanity in *The Savage Mind* (1962).[38] However, the relativism of postmodernism and its stress on the primacy of representation deny the notion of incontestable truth, wisdom and structure, as well as intrinsic value, in nature as in everything else. Aldo Leopold's famous conceit of 'thinking like a mountain' suggests we can crawl inside nature's skin, figure out what it wants and serve as a cipher. But if all claims on truth are perspectival and no perspective (including that of ecological science) has greater veracity than the others, how can we discuss a proper human relationship with nature or insist on a scientific case for biodiversity? It is certainly difficult to present nature as a voice marginalized by the human monopoly on the construction of reality that is struggling to be heard if we cannot agree on nature's identity, and if, as the philosopher Richard Rorty suggests, 'nature has no preferred way of being represented'.[39]

Reckless deconstructionism of this sort cuts the ground from under the argument for the preservation of endangered species. How can we presume to know that a species wishes to avoid extinction? Or that a mountain has not been yearning for the day when a ski resort would break the monotony of the ages? For the postmodernist, the identification of a state of nature, the conception of nature as an externality, and reverence for nature as an unambiguous source of guidance are simply more universalizing metanarratives, more outmoded modernist certainties, dependent on a strict and fatuous separation of culture and nature. According to universally disempowering postmodernist logic, the belief in the existence of a global environmental crisis is just another grand narrative, for cultural theory insists that environmental threats (like everything else) are socially constructed and culturally defined: there are no shared, universal threats – different groups privilege those confronting their own particular interests. Yet it is 'profoundly unhelpful', as Jonathan Bate exclaims,

> To say *'There is no nature'* at a time when our most urgent need is to address and redress the consequences of human civilisation's insatiable desire to consume the products of the earth . . . When there have been a few more accidents at nuclear power stations, when there are no more rainforests, and when every wilderness has been ravaged for its mineral resources, then let us say *'There is no more nature.'*[40]

What the earth's effective defence requires of us, perhaps, is not so much the conquest of the dualism of nature and culture as a heightened sense of nature's otherness, for in its difference lies the basis for respect as well as abuse.

The 'new' ecology

Wilderness aficionados like McKibben remain faithful to the old ecology of Clements and Odum. Whereas McKibben identifies 'unpredictability' as 'the salient characteristic' of the 'new' nature – that affected by climate change and manifested in drought, rising sea-levels, longer growing seasons and warmer winters – the 'salient feature of the old nature was its utter dependability'.[41] The 'new' ecology teaches, however, that even nature unaffected by human agency is mutable: 'wherever we seek to find constancy we discover change . . . nature undisturbed is not constant in form, structure, or proportion, but changes at every scale of time and space'.[42]

Clements and Odum have argued that nature, if undisturbed, tends towards a self-perpetuating climax state of equilibrium. The general validity of this notion is questioned by cases such as the stages of vegetational succession following glacial recession in south-eastern Alaska. Alder are the first colonists, enriching the soil and allowing other trees such as spruce to grow. These newcomers eventually displace the alder, but without the pioneering species the soil loses fertility. So the spruce die, leaving an acidic bog. Another glacial advance and retreat is needed for forest to reappear. Another cardinal tenet of the old ecology was that all forces would endeavour to re-establish the climax stage if it was disturbed. The new ecology, influenced by chaos theory, suggests that we cannot know what state natural systems will work towards. We must think instead of a variety of possible outcomes. Daniel Botkin cites the example of a forest in New Jersey where, by the 1960s, two centuries of fire suppression was replacing the formerly dominant, fire-resistant oak and hickory with sugar maple – a species vulnerable to fire yet protected from it.[43]

These new ideas were brought to the attention of the American thinking public in the *New York Times* (science section) on 31 July 1990, through William K. Stevens's article, 'New Eye on Nature: The Real Constant is Eternal Turmoil'. David Ehrenfeld believes these changes within ecological science are symptomatic of the disintegration of consensus within the wider society and culture, as represented by the upheavals of the Vietnam war, the women's movement, racial disturbances and multiculturalism: 'for twenty years, the idea of a national norm, an equilibrium position, had been breaking up under the influence of repeated disturbances'.[44]

This is where the likes of Botkin can find themselves on common ground with Rorty. How can we let nature be our teacher and provide a cure for culture's ills, and how can we represent its interests, if it is thoroughly mixed with culture and we cannot figure out what it stands for and what it is doing (*and it doesn't even seem to know itself*)? The new ecology of disorder undermines the position of those such as Murray Bookchin, the eco-anarchist, whose views on the congruence of anarchist community ideals and natural systems are predicated on a view of nature as balanced and harmonious. Despite the singular connotations of the word, nature is a plurality and James Proctor reminds us that old-growth forests in the Pacific north-west are not just a 'contested terrain' between environmentalists and loggers, but also between different animal species: northern spotted owls may prefer a mature forest full of decomposing trees but deer and chipmunks, along with certain trees, thrive in the early stages of vegetational succession following felling.[45]

How the new ecology has also generated ideas of nature's potential for rebirth that form an antidote to prophecies of doom can be illustrated with reference to that eco-tragedy incarnate, the oil spill that afflicted Alaska's Prince William Sound in 1989. Livid Americans destroyed their Exxon credit cards and the US media was saturated with distressing images of oil-soaked otters unable to groom themselves chewing off their paws in despair. The books that appeared in the immediate aftermath were understandably sombre and gloom-filled.[46] Writing with the benefit of a little hindsight, in his book *Degrees of Disaster*, Jeff Wheelwright does not deny the severity of short-term impacts. But he contends that we underestimate nature's capacity to recover from such catastrophes. Since natural systems are continually changing, and unpredictably so, it is difficult to disentangle oil as a factor in salmon fry survival rates from a host of other, non-human disturbances. The Nobel Laureate chemist Ilya Prigogine has explained how ecology is shifting from the study of a singular, static, repetitive and universalistic system to one that is multiple, temporal and complex.[47] Wheelwright demonstrates how the notion of nature as community with preordained identity is being replaced by the idea of nature as 'patch' by pointing to apparently identical regions of the intertidal zone in Prince William Sound that host mussels and barnacles respectively.[48]

Nevertheless, Wheelwright retains the time-honoured popular notion of nature as superior authority (summarized by Robert Boyle in 1686 as '*nature* is a most wise being, that *does nothing* in vain; does always that which ... is best to be done'). Accordingly, whatever nature decides to do is preferable to human attempts to determine nature's future. This concept of nature is easily used as an excuse for doing nothing. 'Turn the Valdez Cleanup over to Mother Nature', recommended one politician, while the oil industry hailed the role of heavy winter storms (1989/90) in cleansing shorelines as evidence of nature's healing powers.[49] If change in nature is accepted as the new norm, accusations of destructive, 'unnatural' human interventions lose much of their force. Some have argued that the new ecology, which they align with the ultra-capitalist ideology of the 1980s, presents a licence to exploit.[50]

The old nature

Nature's indomitability has been a favourite literary metaphor since ancient times, with Horace (in a disquisition on the advantages of rural life) jibing that 'you may drive out Nature with a pitchfork, yet she will ever hurry back, and ere you know it, will burst through your foolish contempt in triumph'.[51] A ruin in an otherwise natural setting provided Romantic poets with the perfect motif for the contrast between the brevity and transience of human life and culture on the one hand and nature's enduring qualities on the other. Robert Southey was thrilled by nature's reconquest of man's work through woodbine, moss and weeds, reflecting in 'The Ruined Cottage',

> *So Nature steals on all the works of man,*
> *Sure conqueror she, reclaiming to herself*
> *His perishable piles.*[52]

Environmental historian Donald Worster agrees that nature's powers are too immense for total conquest: 'that is a victory we could never win. Or perhaps I should say that is a crime we are incapable of committing.' Adopting a 'nature bats last'/'nature is dead, long live nature' approach that envisages blades of grass forcing themselves up between the cracks of city pavements, he reminds us of the disintegration of ancient economies and cultures that have outstripped their environmental bases. Modern civilization, he contends, is courting the same fate. Focusing on the Great Plains of the American west, he cites the intensifying crisis of agriculture (not least because underground aquifers are being depleted at an alarming rate), evident in the proliferation of ghost towns, as evidence of the 'ephemeral' nature of the ostensible modern victory over nature. Whereas the 'new' ecologists deny that nature's past can ever be regained, Worster claims that a mere century without human influence would suffice to restore the plains to their condition prior to the white man.[53] Other commentators derive comfort from earthquakes, hurricanes, mudslides, floods and drought, which they interpret – if not as nature's sweet revenge against human misdeeds – at least as evidence of its incomplete capitulation.[54]

Hopeful conceptions of nature's remaining strength, and predictions of its ability to recover from sickness, signal faith in its future (while dying is an irreversible process, ill health is not). Meanwhile, what Nicolson refers to as the 'old truths' of an organic, animate earth that had become 'the language of poets rather than scientists' are reappearing. Rupert Sheldrake detects stirrings among fellow biologists of a 'postmechanistic' world-view, which he attributes not only to global warming but the new conception of earth as a common home for humanity stimulated by the first pictures from space in the 1960s. These bright signs prompt him to herald nature's rebirth ('the revival of animism'). The new ecology of chaos need not be a nihilistic and indifferent force. For Prigogine, the evidence of fluctuation, unpredictability and multiple identity is part of the disintegration of the monolithic, mechanistic view of nature, which opens the way for a new synthesis born of disorder that constitutes the 'renewal of nature'.[55]

As well as putting things that have been taken apart back together again, we must learn to recognize nature beyond what we traditionally think of as the natural world. To say that there is hardly anything or anywhere that is entirely natural anymore does not mean there is no nature left. In the late 1930s, Lewis Mumford argued that to find nature in the city 'one must look overhead, at the clouds, the sun, the moon, when they appear through the jutting towers and building blocks'.[56] Yet as a result of the 'second agricultural revolution' affecting North America and western Europe since 1945, many elements of nature have been increasingly hard to find in rural areas too.[57] The spread of mechanization, insecticides and chemical fertilizers and the accelerated loss of hedgerows, wetlands and grassland as the countryside is converted into a 'food factory' has forced wildlife to seek sanctuary in unlikely spots, notably spaces within the urban environment. Parks, playing fields, university campuses, gardens, vacant lots, cemeteries and other urban oases offer flourishing wildlife habitats, often supporting greater variety and population densities than surrounding countryside. Mature, leafy residential districts are highly desirable living areas for humans, squirrels and foxes alike. Meanwhile, the windowledges of skyscrapers and cooling towers of power stations mimic cliffs for peregrine falcons.[58]

Given that our tastes in nature are manipulated by society and culture – especially the designation of the rare and the valuable – Martin Krieger has argued that there is no limit to the extent to which we can be moulded in our preferences. Since plastic trees are cheaper to make and easier to maintain, more durable, and can be made more readily available than the scarce trees and places we currently treasure, why can't we be trained to enjoy these proxies as much as the real thing? After all, if a forged painting provides the same quality of aesthetic experience as the authentic article, 'why should this bother us?'[59]

Far more important than authenticity or some inscrutable essence of naturalness or wildness is nature's well-being. McKibben laments that 'a child born today might swim in a stream clean of toxic waste, but he won't ever see a natural stream'.[60] Surely we cannot afford to be so punctilious. The crucial question is not how wild or natural nature is, but how *healthy* it is. It does not matter whether a pond is located in an inner-city backyard or a distant national park so long as it hums with dragonflies and teems with tadpoles.

Haraway declares that nature 'is not a physical place to which one can go, nor a treasure to fence in or bank, nor an essence to be saved or violated', and that 'where we need to move is not "back to nature", but *elsewhere*'. She exudes confidence that 'the certainty of what counts as nature' has been 'undermined, probably fatally'. Nevertheless, we remain fixated on the 'authentic' and wild. In the early summer of 1997, BBC Radio 4's *Today* programme reported wryly on the latest culinary fad, wild food. Wild 'foodies', hunting and gathering in playful postmodern fashion, return from their gardens and rural excursions with treasures such as snails and primroses. No matter how much evidence for the cultural construction of natural objects and our feelings for nature accumulates, we appear reluctant to accept Gregg Mitman's existentialist conclusion that 'Nature cannot solve our

problems, it cannot give us guidance, it cannot give us direction . . .
Humans . . . are the sole arbiters of their fate.'[61]

Nostalgia for rural serenity and the unchanging rhythms of nature's
ancien régime ensured the popularity of Gilbert White's *Natural History
of Selborne* (1789) in early nineteenth-century England, when industrialization was disrupting society and rural discontent was vented in the
destruction of farm machinery and the burning of hayricks. The urge to
escape into the past, a past increasingly defined in terms of a sacred
nature, characterized by eternal repetition, outside of, predating
and outliving the profanity of mere history, will grow ever stronger
as the pace, bewilderment and phoniness of life (whether modern or
postmodern) intensify.[62] We remain the 'curious child' in Wordsworth's poem, *The Excursion* (1814), holding a conch to our ears to
learn nature's glad and 'authentic' tidings, desperate for a 'central
peace, subsisting at the heart of endless agitation'. We still crave what
John Clare, in a poem written in 1835, called 'the eternity of nature'
contrasting human transience with the permanence of a daisy plucked
by a child (a timeless activity if ever there was one, at least in temperate
regions).[63] We need a god and nature is a good god, perhaps the only
good god.

In *The Savage Mind*, Lévi-Strauss identified what he called 'the insist-
ence on differentiation', born of a universal need to order and structure
the phenomena of the world through classification, whether on the
basis of colour, sound or form of locomotion (to cite just a few categories). 'All classification', he explained, 'proceeds by pairs of contrasts.'
In the West, at least, there are few more powerful examples of this
'binary opposition' than nature and culture.[64] Succumbing to a hopelessly eighteenth-century and 'certaintist' conception of nature, I am
tempted to conclude that no matter what shape our tomatoes and frogs
assume, the polarity of nature and culture will endure a good deal
longer.

Notes

Preface and Acknowledgements

1 Felipe Fernandez-Armesto, *Millennium: A History of Our Last Thousand Years* (Bantam, London, 1995), p. xiii.
2 *The Poetical Works of Wordsworth*, ed. Thomas Hutchinson (Oxford University Press, London, 1950 [1904]), p. 588. The view across the Bristol Channel to Wales definitely contains more than it did in the 1790s – notably Hinkley Point nuclear power station, a huge box that gleams in the sun to the north-east when you reach the moorland heights.

Chapter 1 The Natures of Nature

1 Raymond Williams, *Keywords: A Vocabulary of Culture and Society* (Oxford University Press, Oxford, 1976), pp. 184, 186; id., 'Ideas of Nature', in *Ecology: The Shaping Inquiry*, ed. Jonathan Benthall (Longman, London, 1972), p. 146. See also Daniel Day Williams, 'Changing Concepts of Nature', in *Earth Might be Fair: Reflections on Ethics, Religion and Ecology*, ed. Ian G. Barbour (Prentice-Hall, Englewood Cliffs, NJ, 1972), pp. 48–61. The most authoritative account of pre-Darwinian times remains Clarence J. Glacken, *Traces on the Rhodian Shore: Nature and Culture in Western Thought from Ancient Times to the End of the Eighteenth Century* (University of California Press, Berkeley, 1967).
2 Quoted in George D. Economou, *The Greek Goddess Natura in Medieval Literature* (Harvard University Press, Cambridge, Mass., 1972), p. 3.
3 Lynn White, Jr., 'The Historical Roots of Our Ecologic Crisis', *Science*, 155 (10 March 1967), pp. 1203–7; reprinted in *Sunshine and Smoke: American Writers and the American Environment*, ed. David D. Anderson (J. B. Lippincott, Philadelphia, Pa., 1971). Citations are taken from this 1971 reprint.

4 Williams, *Keywords*, p. 188.
5 James Thomson, *The Seasons* (John Bumpus, London, 1822), pp. 3–4; Rupert Sheldrake, *The Rebirth of Nature: The Greening of Science and God* (Century, London, 1990), p. 53.
6 Arthur O. Lovejoy and George Boas, *Primitivism and Related Ideas in Antiquity* (Octagon Books, New York, 1965 [1935]), p. 109.
7 Robert Boyle, 'A Free Inquiry into the Vulgarly Received Notion of Nature' (1686), in *Selected Philosophical Papers of Robert Boyle*, ed. M. A. Stewart (Manchester University Press, Manchester, 1979), pp. 179–80.
8 Catherine Albanese, *Nature Religion in America: From the Algonkian Indians to the New Age* (University of Chicago Press, Chicago, 1990), p. 60.
9 Joyce E. Salisbury, *The Beast Within: Animals in the Middle Ages* (Routledge, New York, 1994), p. 62; Bettyann Kevles, *Females of the Species: Sex and Survival in the Animal Kingdom* (Harvard University Press, Cambridge, Mass., 1986), pp. 201–7.
10 Frederick J. E. Woodbridge, *Aristotle's Vision of Nature* (Greenwood Press, Westport, Conn., 1983 [1965]), pp. 52–4, 70, 75; Ralph Waldo Emerson, *Nature* (1836), in *The American Tradition in Literature* (shorter edn), ed. Sculley Bradley et al. (Grosset and Dunlap, New York, 1979), p. 562.
11 As quoted in Clarence J. Glacken, 'Changing Ideas of the Habitable World', in *Man's Role in Changing the Face of the Earth*, ed. William L. Thomas (University of Chicago Press, Chicago, 1956), p. 70. For a discussion of the naturalness of nature, see W. M. Adams, *Future Nature: A Vision for Conservation* (Earthscan, London, 1996), pp. 81–9.
12 *Johnson's Journey to the Western Isles of Scotland and Boswell's Journal of a Tour to the Hebrides with Samuel Johnson*, ed. R. W. Chapman (Oxford University Press, Oxford, 1974 [1775 and 1785]), p. 44. On the Scottish Highlands as a degraded natural environment, see James Hunter, *On the Other Side of Sorrow: Nature and People in the Scottish Highlands* (Mainstream Publishing, Edinburgh, 1995), pp. 149–76.
13 Oliver Rackham, *The History of the Countryside* (J. M. Dent, London, 1986), pp. 358–60.
14 John Stuart Mill, *Collected Works of John Stuart Mill* (University of Toronto Press, Toronto, 1969), vol. 10, p. 377.
15 Michael Howlett and Rebecca Raglon, 'Constructing the Environmental Spectacle: Green Advertisements and the Greening of the Corporate Image, 1910–1990', *Environmental History Review*, 16/4 (Winter 1992), pp. 61–2.
16 C. S. Lewis, 'Nature', in *Studies in Words* (Cambridge University Press, Cambridge, 1960), pp. 45–6.
17 Ty Cashman, 'Epistemology and the Extinction of Species', in *Revisioning Philosophy*, ed. James Ogilvy (State University of New York Press, Albany, 1992), p. 15.
18 Neil Evernden, *The Social Construction of Nature* (Johns Hopkins University Press, Baltimore, Md., 1992), p. 110; Marjorie Hope Nicolson, *Mountain Gloom and Mountain Glory: The Development of the Aesthetics of the Infinite* (W. W. Norton, New York, 1959), p. 1.

19 Susan Hanson, 'Geography and Feminism: Worlds in Collision?', *Annals of the Association of American Geographers*, 82/4 (December 1992), p. 573. The reference is to Thomas Nagel, *The View from Nowhere* (Oxford University Press, New York, 1986), esp. pp. 5–11, 25–7, 60–6.
20 Luther Standing Bear, *Land of the Spotted Eagle* (Houghton Mifflin, Boston, Mass., 1933), p. xix.
21 Johan Goudsblom, *Fire and Civilization* (Penguin, London, 1992), pp. 12–65.
22 George Sessions, 'Shallow and Deep Ecology: A Review of the Philosophical Literature', in *Ecological Consciousness: Essays from the Earthday X Colloquium, University of Denver, April 21–24, 1980*, ed. Robert C. Schultz and J. Donald Hughes (University Press of America, Washington, DC, 1981), pp. 391–462.
23 For a recent example, see A. J. McMichael, *Planetary Overload: Global Environmental Change and the Health of the Human Species* (Cambridge University Press, Cambridge, 1993), pp. 50–1.
24 Anna Bramwell, *Ecology in the 20th Century: A History* (Yale University Press, New Haven, Conn., 1989), pp. 22, 35.
25 Joan DeBardeleben, *The Environment and Marxism-Leninism: The Soviet and East German Experience* (Westview Press, Boulder, Colo., 1985), pp. 81–2.
26 William Cronon, 'Modes of Prophecy and Production: Placing Nature in History', *Journal of American History*, 76/4 (March 1990), p. 1123.
27 Alfred Biese, *The Development of the Feeling for Nature in the Middle Ages and Modern Times* (George Routledge, London, 1905 [1888]), pp. 145, 147–8. Biese's coverage is restricted to art, poetry, novels and gardening. He had previously published *The Development of the Feeling for Nature Among the Greeks* (1882) and *The Development of the Feeling for Nature Among the Romans* (1884). See also Henry Rushton Fairclough, *Love of Nature Among the Greeks and Romans* (Longman, New York, 1930).
28 Yi-Fu Tuan, *Topophilia: A Study of Environmental Perceptions, Attitudes and Values* (Prentice-Hall, Englewood Cliffs, NJ, 1974). Edward O. Wilson's concept of 'biophilia' refers to a more indiscriminate natural affinity for life and sense of kinship with other creatures. See his *Biophilia* (Harvard University Press, Cambridge, Mass., 1984), pp. 1–2, 126–30.
29 Nick Middleton, *The Gobal Casino: An Introduction to Environmental Issues* (Edward Arnold, London, 1995), carries no index entry for 'nature'. For a recent history of natural history and ecological science, see Peter J. Bowler, *The Fontana History of the Environmental Sciences* (Fontana, London, 1992), pp. 139–92, 248–323, 361–78, 503–53.
30 For an introduction to the various positions, see Michael Zimmerman et al. (eds), *Environmental Philosophy: From Animal Rights to Radical Ecology* (Prentice-Hall, Englewood Cliffs, NJ, 1993).
31 A certain depoliticization is evident among second-generation environmental and women's historians. Keen to assert their identity as something more

than a branch of a political and social movement, some scholars distance themselves from 'the struggle'. Many feminists and environmentalists feel betrayed.

32 Myra Reynolds, *The Treatment of Nature in English Poetry between Pope and Wordsworth* (University of Chicago Press, Chicago, 1909), p. v.

33 Roger S. Gottlieb (ed.), *This Sacred Earth: Religion, Nature, Environment* (Routledge, New York, 1996), dedication page; Douglas Davies, 'Introduction: Raising the Issues', in *Attitudes to Nature*, ed. Jen Holm with John Bowker (Pinter, London, 1994), pp. 1–2.

34 Bron Taylor, 'Earth First! From Primal Spirituality to Ecological Resistance', in *This Sacred Earth*, ed. Gottlieb, p. 550; Aldo Leopold, 'Thinking Like a Mountain', in *A Sand County Almanac* (Oxford University Press, New York, 1949), pp. 129–30.

35 For a lucid and refreshingly non-polemical exposition of the ideologies of social ecology, deep ecology and ecofeminism, and the dialogue and disputes between them, see Michael E. Zimmerman, *Contesting Earth's Future: Radical Ecology and Postmodernity* (University of California Press, Berkeley, 1994), pp. 150–83, 233–317.

36 For overviews of the major developments affecting relations with the natural world – fire, agriculture, the growth of trade, urbanization, industrialization, and scientific and technological advance – see Clive Ponting, *A Green History of the World* (Penguin, London, 1991), and I. G. Simmons, *Environmental History: A Concise Introduction* (Basil Blackwell, Oxford, 1993), pp. 1–47.

37 Zimmerman, *Contesting Earth's Future*, p. 364.

38 Ponting, *Green History of the World*, pp. 1–7.

39 William H. TeBrake, 'Air Pollution and Fuel Crises in Preindustrial London', *Technology and Culture*, 16 (1975), pp. 337–59; John Passmore, *Man's Responsibility for Nature: Ecological Problems and Western Traditions* (Duckworth, London, 1980), p. 46.

40 Carolyn Merchant, *The Death of Nature: Women, Ecology and the Scientific Revolution* (HarperCollins, San Francisco, 1990 [1980]), p. 241.

41 René Dubos, *The Wooing of Earth* (Athlone Press, London, 1980), pp. 66, 72.

42 For general introductions, see Donald Worster, 'Appendix: Doing Environmental History', in *The Ends of the Earth: Perspectives on Modern Environmental History*, ed. Donald Worster (Cambridge University Press, Cambridge, 1988), pp. 289–307, and Peter Coates, 'Clio's New Greenhouse', *History Today*, 46/8 (August 1996), pp. 15–22. For a survey stressing the contribution of historical geographers, see Michael Williams, 'The Relations of Environmental History and Historical Geography', *Journal of Historical Geography*, 20/1 (January 1994), pp. 9–15.

43 Peter Burke, 'Overture: The New History, its Past and its Future', in *New Perspectives on Historical Writing*, ed. Peter Burke (Polity Press, Cambridge, 1991), pp. 1, 9.

44 Foucault is quoted in Christopher Manes, *Green Rage: Radical Environmentalism and the Unmaking of Civilization* (Little, Brown, Boston, Mass., 1990), p. 231.
45 For a US perspective, see Richard White, 'American Environmental History: The Development of a New Historical Field', *Pacific Historical Review*, 54 (August 1985), pp. 297–335.
46 Maurice Beresford, *History on the Ground: Six Studies in Maps and Landscapes* (Lutterworth, London, 1957); W. G. Hoskins, *The Making of the English Landscape*, rev. edn, ed. Christopher Taylor (Hodder and Stoughton, London, 1988 [1955]); *Local History in England* (Longman, London, 1959).
47 Michael Aston, *Interpreting the Landscape: Landscape Archaeology in Local Studies* (Batsford, London, 1985); I. G. Simmons and M. J. Tooley (eds), *The Environment in British Prehistory* (Duckworth, London, 1981).
48 As quoted in M. W. Beresford, 'Mapping the Medieval Landscape: Forty Years in the Field', in *The English Landscape: Past, Present and Future*, ed. S. R. J. Woodell (Oxford University Press, Oxford, 1985), p. 112.
49 Rackham, *History of the Countryside*, p. 6.
50 For a critique of this neglect, see Malcolm Chase, 'Can History be Green? A Prognosis', *Rural History*, 3/2 (1992), pp. 243–51.
51 For instance, William C. Brice (ed.), *The Environmental History of the Near and Middle East since the Last Ice Age* (Academic Press, London, 1978).
52 *La longue durée* first appeared in the title of an article in *Annales* (October–December 1958); Fernand Braudel, *The Mediterranean and the Mediterranean World in the Age of Philip II*, vol. 1, rev. edn, trans. Siân Reynolds (Collins, London, 1972 [1949]), p. 16.
53 Braudel, *The Mediterranean*, pp. 29, 243.
54 Karl Marx and Frederick Engels, *The German Ideology*, ed. and introd. C. J. Arthur (Lawrence and Wishart, London, 1970), pp. 58–60.
55 Peter Burke, *The French Historical Revolution: The Annales School, 1929–89* (Polity Press, Cambridge, 1990), pp. 40–1.
56 Emmanuel Le Roy Ladurie, *Times of Feast, Times of Famine: A History of Climate since the Year 1000*, trans. Barbara Bray (Allen and Unwin, London, 1972 [1967]), pp. 18, 20, 22, 17.
57 Ellsworth Huntington, *Civilization and Climate* (Yale University Press, New Haven, Conn., 1915), pp. 278, 294, 6.
58 George Perkins Marsh, *Man and Nature; or, Physical Geography as Modified by Human Action*, ed. David Lowenthal (Harvard University Press, Cambridge, Mass., 1965 [1864]), pp. ix, xxiii–xxiv.
59 Ibid., pp. 36, 29.
60 Roderick Nash, *Wilderness and the American Mind* (Yale University Press, New Haven, Conn., 1982 [1967]); Williams, 'Ideas of Nature', pp. 163, 159. See also Alan Taylor, 'Natural Inequalities: Social and Environmental Histories', *Environmental History*, 1/4 (October 1996), p. 7.
61 William Cronon, 'Kennecott Journey: The Paths Out of Town', in *Under an Open Sky: Rethinking America's Western Past*, ed. William Cronon et al. (W. W. Norton, New York, 1992), pp. 45–8.

62 Alfred W. Crosby, 'The Past and Present of Environmental History', *American Historical Review*, 100/4 (October 1995), p. 1181.

Chapter 2 Ancient Greece and Rome

1 An introductory study can sidestep contentious issues such as the definition and geographical and chronological scope of the ancient/classical world. In this chapter I shall focus mainly on the Hellenistic age and the Roman era from the founding of the empire in 30 BC to imperial collapse in AD 565. There is ample precedent for referring to conflated 'Graeco-Roman' attitudes. All dates and biographical details are from Graham Peake (ed.), *A Dictionary of Ancient History* (Basil Blackwell, Oxford, 1994). I do not provide such levels of information for figures from later periods.

2 Arthur O. Lovejoy and George Boas, *Primitivism and Related Ideas in Antiquity* (Octagon Books, New York, 1965 [1935]), pp. 447–56.

3 Quoted in George D. Economou, *The Goddess Natura in Medieval Literature* (Harvard University Press, Cambridge, Mass., 1972), pp. 4–6.

4 Frederick J. E. Woodbridge, *Aristotle's Vision of Nature* (Greenwood Press, Westport, Conn., 1983 [1956]), p. 49.

5 Fritjof Capra, *The Tao of Physics* (Flamingo, London, 1983 [1975]), p. 24.

6 Woodbridge, *Aristotle's Vision of Nature*, pp. 26–48.

7 Robert Sallares, *The Ecology of the Ancient Greek World* (Duckworth, London, 1991), p. 4.

8 George Perkins Marsh, *Man and Nature; or, Physical Geography as Modified by Human Action*, ed. David Lowenthal (Harvard University Press, Cambridge, Mass., 1965 [1864]), p. 9. Most US conservationists since – especially those sensitized by the Dust Bowl catastrophe that afflicted the American West in the 1930s – have been alert to the lessons of soil mismanagement during classical times. See Paul B. Sears, *Deserts on the March* (University of Oklahoma Press, Norman, 1980 [1935]), pp. 16, 29–31, 66; Vernon O. Carter and Tom Dale, *Topsoil and Civilization* (University of Oklahoma Press, Norman, 1974), pp. 55–155. See also J. Donald Hughes and J. V. Thirgood, 'Deforestation in Ancient Greece and Rome: A Cause of Collapse', *Ecologist*, 12 (1982), pp. 196–208.

9 Mikhail Ivanovich Rostovtzeff, *The Social and Economic History of the Roman Empire*, 2nd, rev., edn (2 vols, Clarendon Press, Oxford, 1957 [1926]), vol. 1, pp. 197, 505, 539. While he recognized the poor condition of soil in parts of the late empire, Rostovtzeff attributed the agrarian crisis largely to social and political factors (ibid., pp. 376–7).

10 J. Donald Hughes, *Pan's Travail: Environmental Problems of the Ancient Greeks and Romans* (Johns Hopkins University Press, Baltimore, Md., 1994), pp. 149–68, esp. pp. 156, 116–25.

11 Quoted in Michael Grant, *The Fall of the Roman Empire: A Reappraisal* (Annenberg School Press, Radnor, Pa., 1976), p. 58.

12 Jerome O. Nriagu, *Lead and Lead Poisoning in Antiquity* (John Wiley, New York, 1983), pp. viii, 253, 262, 318–78, 399–415.

13 The network of ditches and dikes through which Egyptian farmers directed the annual floodwaters of the Nile onto their fields for thousands of years, replenishing soil nutrients and cleansing the soil of salt, serves Donald Worster as a model of sustainable, irrigation-fed agriculture: *The Wealth of Nature: Environmental History and the Ecological Imagination* (Oxford University Press, New York, 1993), pp. 125–6.

14 'The Historical Roots of Our Ecologic Crisis', as reprinted in *Sunshine and Smoke: American Writers and the American Environment*, ed. David D. Anderson (J. B. Lippincott, Philadelphia, 1971), pp. 476–7.

15 Fritz M. Heichelheim, 'Effects of Classical Antiquity on the Land', in *Man's Role in Changing the Face of the Earth*, ed. William L. Thomas (University of Chicago Press, Chicago, 1956), pp. 166, 168.

16 Clarence J. Glacken, *Traces on the Rhodian Shore: Nature and Culture in Western Thought from Ancient Times to the End of the Eighteenth Century* (University of California Press, Berkeley, 1967), pp. 145, 116; id., 'This Growing Second World of Nature within the World of Nature', in *Man's Place in the Island Ecosystem*, ed. Raymond Fosberg (Bishop Museum, Honolulu, 1963), p. 78.

17 Quoted in Glacken, *Traces on the Rhodian Shore*, pp. 138, 140.

18 Quoted ibid., p. 57.

19 René Dubos, 'The Genius of Place', *American Forests* (September 1970), p. 18.

20 J. R. McNeill, *The Mountains of the Mediterranean World: An Environmental History* (Cambridge University Press, Cambridge, 1992), pp. 72–3. See also Heinrich Rubner, 'Greek Thought and Forest Science', *Environmental Review*, 9/4 (Winter 1985), pp. 278–80.

21 Eugene C. Hargrove, *Foundations of Environmental Ethics* (Prentice-Hall, Englewood Cliffs, NJ, 1989), p. 21.

22 J. Donald Hughes, 'Early Greek and Roman Environmentalists', in *Historical Ecology: Essays on Environmental and Social Change*, ed. Lester J. Bilsky (Kennicat Press, Port Washington, NY, 1980), p. 50; id., 'The Environmental Ethics of the Pythagoreans', *Environmental Ethics*, 3 (Fall 1980), pp. 195–213; R. G. Collingwood, *The Idea of Nature* (Clarendon Press, Oxford, 1945), pp. 49–55.

23 Hughes, *Pan's Travail*, pp. 54–5; Ovid, *Metamorphoses*, trans. Mary M. Innes (Penguin, Harmondsworth, 1955), Book 15, p. 337.

24 James Lovelock, *Gaia: A New Look at Life on Earth* (Oxford University Press, Oxford, 1979); James Lovelock and Sidney Epton, 'The Quest for Gaia', *New Scientist*, 65 (1975), p. 304; Lawrence E. Joseph, *Gaia: The Growth of an Idea* (Arkana, London, 1990). On the ancient idea of the earth as goddess and living organism, and the belief in a reciprocal relationship between the earth and its human inhabitants, see J. Donald Hughes, 'Gaia: Environmental Problems in Chthonic Perspective', in *Environmental History: Critical Issues in Comparative Perspective*, ed. Kendall E. Bailes (University Press of America, Lanham, Md., 1985), pp. 64–82 ('chthonic' means 'pertaining to the earth').

25 Lucy Goodison, 'Were the Greeks Green?', *Greening the Planet*, 3 (1992), pp. 24–5; Charlene Spretnak, *Lost Goddesses of Early Greece: A Collection of Pre-Hellenic Myths* (Beacon Press, Boston, Mass., 1984), pp. 17–28.

26 Andrée Collard (with Joyce Contrucci), *Rape of the Wild: Man's Violence against Animals and the Earth* (The Women's Press, London, 1988), p. 27.

27 Janet Biehl (1988), as quoted in Andrew Dobson, *Green Political Thought* (Routledge, London, 1994), p. 198.

28 Hughes, *Pan's Travail*, p. 51.

29 J. Donald Hughes, *Ecology in Ancient Civilizations* (University of New Mexico Press, Albuquerque, 1975), pp. 48–51.

30 Hughes, *Pan's Travail*, p. 171.

31 Hughes, 'Early Greek and Roman Environmentalists', pp. 48–9.

32 J. Donald Hughes, 'How the Ancients Viewed Deforestation', *Journal of Field Archaeology*, 10 (1983), p. 442.

33 Capra, *Tao of Physics*, p. 26.

34 D. S. Wallace-Hadrill, *The Greek Patristic View of Nature* (Manchester University Press, Manchester, 1968), pp. 67, 72.

35 Ibid., pp. 1–3. Feminist philosopher Val Plumwood also traces dualistic thinking to Greek roots: *Feminism and the Mastery of Nature* (Routledge, London, 1993), pp. 72–109.

36 Aristotle, *The Politics*, trans. T. A. Sinclair (Penguin, Harmondsworth, 1962), pp. 64–5, 68–9; Woodbridge, *Aristotle's Vision of Nature*, pp. 38–9; Keith Thomas, *Man and the Natural World: Changing Attitudes in England, 1500–1800* (Penguin, Harmondsworth, 1984), p. 30.

37 Wallace-Hadrill, *Greek Patristic View of Nature*, p. 68.

38 Hughes, *Pan's Travail*, pp. 111, 55.

39 French, *Ancient Natural History: Histories of Nature* (Routledge, London, 1994), pp. x–xi, 10–82, 92–103; Hughes, *Pan's Travail*, pp. 63–5, 108, 186, and 'Theophrastus as Ecologist', *Environmental Review*, 9/4 (Winter 1985), pp. 297–306.

40 Donald Worster, *Nature's Economy: A History of Ecological Ideas* (Cambridge University Press, Cambridge, 1985 [1977]), pp. 2, 81, 180, 378, 29–55.

41 Hughes, *Pan's Travail*, pp. 54–5, 60.

42 Matt Cartmill, *A View to a Death in the Morning: Hunting and Nature through History* (Harvard University Press, Cambridge, Mass., 1993), p. 45.

43 Quoted in Glacken, *Traces on the Rhodian Shore*, p. 32. Raymond Williams noted the dichotomy's ancient roots in *The Country and the City* (Chatto and Windus, London, 1973), p. 9.

44 Archibald Geikie, *The Love of Nature among the Romans: During the Later Decades of the Republic and the First Century of the Empire* (John Murray, London, 1912), pp. 22, 24–5, 27–31, 40–9, 121. For further comments on classic taste in natural beauty, see John Ruskin, *Modern Painters*, vol. 3, in *The Works of John Ruskin* (John B. Alden, New York, 1885), pp. 189–212.

45 Hughes, *Pan's Travail*, pp. 155, 166–7.

46 Quoted in Glacken, *Traces on the Rhodian Shore*, p. 31.

47 For similarities between the ancient myth of a pastoral arcadia and the American version, see Leo Marx, *The Machine in the Garden: Technology and the Pastoral Ideal in America* (Oxford University Press, New York, 1964), pp. 19–24, and 'Pastoral Ideas and City Troubles', in *Western Man and Environmental Ethics*, ed. Ian G. Barbour (Addison-Wesley, New York, 1973), pp. 93–113.
48 Quoted in George Soutar, *Nature in Greek Poetry: Studies Partly Comparative* (Oxford University Press, London, 1939), p. 229.
49 Quoted in Glacken, *Traces on the Rhodian Shore*, p. 29.
50 Soutar, *Nature in Greek Poetry*, pp. 2–3; Wallace-Hadrill, *Greek Patristic View of Nature*, p. 2.
51 Soutar, *Nature in Greek Poetry*, p. 13.
52 Marx, *Machine in the Garden*, pp. 22–3.
53 Soutar, *Nature in Greek Poetry*, pp. 58, 61.
54 Hughes, *Pan's Travail*, pp. 56–8; Geikie, *Love of Nature among the Romans*, p. 198.
55 Wallace-Hadrill, *Greek Patristic View of Nature*, p. 90.
56 Cartmill, *A View to a Death in the Morning*, pp. 32–6; John Kinloch Anderson, *Hunting in the Ancient World* (University of California Press, Berkeley, 1985), p. 29.
57 W. K. C. Guthrie, *The Greeks and their Gods* (Methuen, London, 1950), p. 100. Nemesis, originally a woodland goddess, also took action against those who transgressed her sacred laws, becoming the goddess of retributive justice.
58 J. Donald Hughes, 'Artemis: Goddess of Conservation', *Forest and Conservation History*, 34 (October 1990), pp. 191–7.
59 William E. H. Lecky, *History of European Morals from Augustus to Charlemagne* (2 vols, Longmans Green, London, 1869), vol. 1, p. 297.
60 Hughes, *Pan's Travail*, p. 101; J. M. C. Toynbee, *Animals in Roman Life and Art* (Thames and Hudson, London, 1973), pp. 16–21; George Jennison, *Animals for Show and Pleasure in Ancient Rome* (Manchester University Press, Manchester, 1937), pp. 47, 72–3.
61 Roland Auguet, *Cruelty and Civilization: The Roman Games* (Routledge, London, 1994 [1970]), p. 184.
62 Lecky, *History of European Morals*, vol. 1, p. 298.
63 Auguet, *Cruelty and Civilization*, p. 111; Jennison, *Animals for Show and Pleasure*, pp. 137–53.
64 Sallares, *Ecology of the Ancient Greek World*, pp. 400–1; Hughes, *Pan's Travail*, pp. 96, 102–6, 91.
65 Anderson, *Hunting in the Ancient World*, p. 87; Jennison, *Animals for Show and Pleasure*, p. 52.
66 Hannah Arendt, *Eichmann in Jerusalem: A Report on the Banality of Evil* (Faber and Faber, London, 1963), pp. 23, 49, 93, 134, 231. On inordinate Nazi concern for the humane treatment of dogs, especially German shepherds used for police work, see Daniel J. Goldhagen, *Hitler's Willing Executioners:*

Ordinary Germans and the Holocaust (Abacus, London, 1997), pp. 268–70. Goldhagen interprets this solicitude as crowning evidence of German depravity at this time, but the sentiments of many British pet-lovers today are not much different.

67 Geikie, *Love of Nature among the Romans*, p. 181.
68 Jonathon Porritt, *Seeing Green: The Politics of Ecology Explained* (Basil Blackwell, Oxford, 1984), p. 207. For a critique of this adulation of antiquity, see Val Plumwood, *Feminism and the Mastery of Nature*, pp. 73, 84, 92.

Chapter 3 The Middle Ages

1 Thomas Sharp, *The English Panorama* (Architectural Press, London, 1950 [1936]), p. 28.
2 Derek Pearsall and Elizabeth Salter, *Landscapes and Seasons of the Medieval World* (Elek, London, 1973), pp. 27, 53. Another study stressing the ubiquity of wilderness rather uncritically, this time in Italy, is Vito Fumagalli, *Landscapes of Fear: Perceptions of Nature and the City in the Middle Ages* (Polity Press, Cambridge, 1994), pp. 7, 19, 99, 104, 136.
3 Clarence J. Glacken, *Traces on the Rhodian Shore: Nature and Culture in Western Thought from Ancient Times to the End of the Eighteenth Century* (University of California Press, Berkeley, 1967), p. 321.
4 George D. Economou in *Approaches to Nature in the Middle Ages*, ed. Lawrence D. Roberts (Center for Medieval and Early Renaissance Studies, Binghamton, NY, 1982), pp. 44–5. The context is a critique of Bernard F. Huppé's essay, 'Nature in *Beowulf* and *Roland*', ibid., pp. 3–41.
5 M. W. Beresford, 'Mapping the Medieval Landscape: Forty Years in the Field', in *The English Landscape: Past, Present and Future*, ed. S. R. J. Woodell (Oxford University Press, Oxford, 1985), p. 106.
6 Annie Grant, 'Animal Resources', in *The Countryside of Medieval England*, ed. Grenville Astill and Annie Grant (Basil Blackwell, Oxford, 1988), p. 154; Richard C. Hoffmann, 'Economic Development and Aquatic Ecosystems in Medieval Europe', *American Historical Review*, 101/3 (June 1996), p. 636.
7 W. G. Hoskins, *The Making of the English Landscape*, rev. edn, ed. Christopher Taylor (Hodder and Stoughton, London, 1988 [1955]), pp. 70–1.
8 I. G. Simmons, 'Late Mesolithic Societies and the Environment of the Uplands of England and Wales', *Institute of Archaeology Bulletin*, 16 (1979), p. 111. For the substantial environmental modifications in pre-agricultural England, see also I. G. Simmons, 'The Earliest Cultural Landscapes of England', *Environmental Review*, 12/2 (Summer 1988), pp. 105–16.
9 I. G. Simmons and M. J. Tooley (eds), *The Environment in British Prehistory* (Duckworth, London, 1981), pp. 93, 102–6, 124. Rackham insists that the only burnable tree was pine, and stresses its qualities of self-renewal: *History of the Countryside* (J. M. Dent, London, 1986), pp. 71–2.
10 Rackham, *History of the Countryside*, p. 307.
11 Ibid., pp. 34–6.

12 Hoskins, *Making of the English Landscape*, pp. 40, 38, 17. For a defence of Hoskinian orthodoxy, see Paul Stamper, 'Woods and Parks', in *Countryside of Medieval England*, ed. Astill and Grant, pp. 28–48.

13 Rackham, *History of the Countryside*, pp. 97–100.

14 Hoskins, *Making of the English Landscape*, p. 77; Leonard Cantor, 'Castles, Fortified Houses, Moated Homesteads and Monastic Settlements', in *The English Medieval Landscape*, ed. Leonard Cantor (Croom Helm, London, 1982), p. 146.

15 James Westfall Thompson, *Economic and Social History of the Middle Ages (300–1300)* (D. Appleton, New York, 1928), pp. 609–23, esp. pp. 613, 609.

16 Robin A. Donkin, *The Cistercians: Studies in the Geography of Medieval England and Wales* (Pontifical Institute of Medieval Studies, Toronto, 1978), pp. 39–51, esp. p. 39; Michael Aston, *Interpreting the Landscape: Landscape Archaeology in Local Studies* (Batsford, London, 1985), p. 88.

17 Rackham, *History of the Countryside*, pp. 85, 16, 94; M. E. D. Poole, 'Agriculture, Forestry and the Future Landscape', in *The English Landscape*, ed. Woodell, p. 191; Grant, 'Animal Resources', p. 167.

18 Rackham, *History of the Countryside*, pp. 85, 88.

19 Ibid., p. 293.

20 Angus J. L. Winchester, *Landscape and Society in Medieval Cumbria* (John Donald, Edinburgh, 1987), p. 39.

21 Hubert H. Lamb, 'Climate and Landscape in the British Isles', in *The English Landscape*, ed. Woodell, p. 163; Grenville Astill and Annie Grant, 'The Medieval Countryside: Efficiency, Progress and Change', in *The Countryside of Medieval England*, ed. Astill and Grant, pp. 232–3. An alternative explanation for the demise of vineyards is French competition. Growing grapes in England had always been precarious, both in terms of weather and finances. The labour shortage following the plague must also be taken into account, not to mention a dearth of oak for casks.

22 Robert S. Gottfried, *The Black Death: Natural and Human Disaster in Medieval Europe* (Robert Hale, London, 1983), pp. 163, 54–66, 135–60; Charles R. Bowlus, 'Ecological Crisis in Fourteenth Century Europe', in *Historical Ecology: Essays on Environment and Social Change*, ed. Lester J. Bilsky (Kennikat Press, Port Washington, NY: 1980), p. 86.

23 John Rennie Short, *Imagined Country: Society, Culture and Environment* (Routledge, London, 1991), pp. 67–75; Barbara Bender, 'Stonehenge: Contested Landscapes (Medieval to Present-Day)', in *Landscape: Politics and Perspectives*, ed. Barbara Bender (Berg, Oxford, 1993), p. 245; Sharon Zukin, *Landscapes of Power: From Detroit to Disney World* (University of California Press, Berkeley, 1991), pp. 16–20; C. S. Lewis, *The Abolition of Man* (Oxford University Press, London, 1944), p. 28.

24 Michael Williams, 'Marshland and Waste', in *English Medieval Landscape*, ed. Cantor, pp. 86, 94–7; David C. Douglas, *William the Conqueror: The Norman Impact upon England* (Eyre and Spottiswoode, London, 1964), pp. 371–2. It should be noted that some form of forest law predated the Norman conquest.

25 Rackham, *History of the Countryside*, p. 130; id., 'Ancient Woodland and Hedges in England', in *The English Landscape*, ed. Woodell, p. 73. Proclaiming a forest did not mean that the king appropriated the land itself; he laid claim to its deer and assumed the right to appoint officials and levy fines.

26 Charles R. Young, *Royal Forests of Medieval England* (Leicester University Press, Leicester, 1979), p. 30.

27 *The Anglo-Saxon Chronicle*, ed. Dorothy Whitelock (Eyre and Spottiswoode, London, 1961), p. 165; George Perkins Marsh, *Man and Nature; or Physical Geography as Modified by Human Action*, ed. David Lowenthal (Harvard University Press, Cambridge, Mass., 1965 [1864]), p. 243.

28 Quoted ibid., p. 244.

29 Keith Thomas, *Man and the Natural World: Changing Attitudes in England, 1500–1800* (Penguin, Harmondsworth, 1984), pp. 49–50.

30 Young, *Royal Forests of Medieval England*, pp. 11, 23, 58; Pearsall and Salter, *Landscapes and Seasons of the Medieval World*, pp. 131–2, 220, and illustrations 40a and b.

31 Glacken, *Traces on the Rhodian Shore*, pp. 346–7.

32 As quoted in C. F. D. Moule, *Man and Nature in the New Testament: Some Reflections on Biblical Ecology* (University of London/Athlone Press, London, 1964), p. 1. There is still no consensus on animal welfare issues within the Protestant churches. In 1995 the bishop of Dover participated in protests against the export of live sheep, but in 1990 the Church of England synod had quashed a motion to ban fox-hunting on Church lands.

33 Lynn White, Jr., 'The Historical Roots of our Ecologic Crisis', as reprinted in *Sunshine and Smoke: American Writers and the American Environment*, ed. David D. Anderson (J. B. Lippincott, Philadelphia, Pa., 1971), pp. 472–81. Feminists have compounded White's thesis by arguing that Genesis authorized male dominion over nature and women, both identified with the body and held to be inferior to male spirituality. See Elizabeth Dodson Gray, *Green Paradise Lost: Remything Genesis* (Roundtable Press, Wellesley, Mass., 1981), and Anne Primavesi, *From Apocalypse to Genesis: Ecology, Feminism and Christianity* (Fortress, Minneapolis, Minn., 1991).

34 An accessible summary of the debate over Christianity's ecological merits is David Kinsley, *Ecology and Religion* (Prentice-Hall, Englewood Cliffs, NJ, 1994).

35 Arnold Toynbee, 'The Religious Background of the Present Environmental Crisis', in *Ecology and Religion in History*, ed. David and Eileen Spring (Harper and Row, New York, 1974), pp. 145, 141.

36 The term 'nature' does not appear in the Bible (though 'wilderness' occurs over 300 times). Instead we find words for specific physical entities, the most common term being 'the earth', which meant land-mass. See John Austin Baker, 'Biblical Attitudes to Nature', in *Man and Nature*, ed. Hugh Montefiore (Collins, London, 1975), p. 87.

37 On the fundamentalist beliefs of President Reagan's first Secretary of the Interior (the cabinet official responsible for environmental protection and natural resources), and how they shaped his policies, see Susan Power

Bratton, 'The Ecotheology of James Watt', *Environmental Ethics*, 5 (1983), pp. 225–36.

38 Considerable debate pivots on the precise meaning of 'dominion' in Genesis and the implications of the Hebrew verbs *rada* ('have dominion') and *kabas* ('subdue'). See James Barr, 'Man and Nature: The Ecological Controversy and the Old Testament', *Bulletin of the John Rylands University Library*, 55 (1972), pp. 20–4.

39 David Kinsley, *Ecology and Religion*, as extracted in *This Sacred Earth: Religion, Nature, Environment*, ed. Roger S. Gottlieb (Routledge, New York, 1996), pp. 160, 120. For a discussion of Augustine without green overtones, see Glacken, *Traces on the Rhodian Shore*, p. 198.

40 Convincing cases for the historical significance of the stewardship tradition are John Black, *The Dominion of Man: The Search for Ecological Responsibility* (Edinburgh University Press, Edinburgh, 1970), pp. 44–58; *Man and Nature*, ed. Montefiore, and Robin Attfield, 'Christian Attitudes to Nature', *Journal of the History of Ideas*, 44 (July/September 1983), pp. 369–86.

41 E. P. Evans, *The Criminal Prosecution and Capital Punishment of Animals: The Lost History of Europe's Animal Trials* (Faber and Faber, London, 1987 [1906]), pp. 139–45, 156–9.

42 Ibid., pp. 43–4, 48–9.

43 On the emergence of Christian ecotheology, see Roderick Nash, *The Rights of Nature: A History of Environmental Ethics* (University of Wisconsin Press, Madison, 1989), pp. 87–112.

44 Glacken, *Traces on the Rhodian Shore*, p. 168; John Passmore, *Man's Responsibility for Nature: Ecological Problems and Western Traditions* (Duckworth, London, 1974), chs 1 and 2, esp. pp. 13–17.

45 White, 'Historical Roots of our Ecologic Crisis', p. 480. White first ventured this interpretation in 'Natural Science and Naturalistic Art in the Middle Ages', *American Historical Review*, 52/3 (April 1947), pp. 432–3.

46 As quoted in Gottlieb, *This Sacred Earth*, p. 237.

47 Kinsley, *Religion and Ecology*, p. 121; Nash, *Rights of Nature*, p. 93; Paul Santmire, *The Travail of Nature: The Ambiguous Ecological Promise of Christian Theology* (Fortress Press, Philadelphia, Pa., 1985), 109, 178; Susan Power Bratton, *Christianity, Wilderness, and Wildlife: The Original Desert Solitaire* (University of Scranton Press, Scranton, Pa., 1993), pp. 218–29; Ralph Metzner, 'The Emerging Ecological Worldview', in *Worldviews and Ecology: Religion, Philosophy, and the Environment*, ed. Mary Evelyn Tucker and John A. Grim (Orbis Books, Maryknoll, NY, 1994) p. 168; Edward Armstrong, *Saint Francis: Nature Mystic* (University of California Press, Berkeley, 1973), p. 219. In the Christian tradition, a nature mystic is someone who is spiritually uplifted through the beauty and glory of God as manifest in creation.

48 G. K. Chesterton, *St. Francis of Assisi* (Hodder and Stoughton, London, 1932), pp. 98, 7.

49 Lawrence S. Cunningham, *Saint Francis of Assisi* (Twayne, Boston, Mass., 1976), pp. 55, 122, 54, 124.

50 Roger D. Sorrell, *St. Francis of Assisi and Nature: Tradition and Innovation in Western Christian Attitudes toward the Environment* (Oxford University Press, New York, 1988), pp. 47, 95, 64–5, 68, 138–9.

51 Quoted in Joyce E. Salisbury, *The Beast Within: Animals in the Middle Ages* (Routledge, New York, 1994), p. 177.

52 Sorrell, *St. Francis of Assisi and Nature*, pp. 144–5, 4.

53 Ibid., pp. 14–15.

54 George H. Williams, *Wilderness and Paradise in Christian Thought* (Harper, New York, 1962), pp. ix–x, 38–43; Bratton, *Christianity, Wilderness, and Wildlife*, pp. 161–81. Though Bratton does not make the connection clear, her subtitle, *The Original Desert Solitaire*, refers to the autobiographical *Desert Solitaire* (1968) by the radical US environmentalist and novelist Edward Abbey. This uncompromising eulogy to the desert wilderness of the American south-west has acquired cult status among American wilderness-lovers. Also relevant are Richard D. North, *Fools for God* (Collins, London, 1987) and Derwas J. Chitty, *The Desert, a City: An Introduction to the Study of Egyptian and Palestinian Monasticism under the Christian Empire* (St Vladimir's Seminary Press, Crestwood, NY, 1966), esp. pp. 2–16. For a summary of biblical attitudes to wilderness, see Roderick Nash, *Wilderness and the American Mind* (Yale University Press, New Haven, Conn., 1982 [1967]), pp. 13–20 and Williams, *Wilderness and Paradise*, pp. 3–27. On the role of nature appreciation within the Celtic monastic tradition of the fifth, sixth and seventh centuries, see Bratton, *Christianity, Wilderness, and Wildlife*, pp. 182–216.

55 Quoted in D. S. Wallace-Hadrill, *The Greek Patristic View of Nature* (Manchester University Press, Manchester, 1968), pp. 88–9.

56 For a recent statement of respect for knowing nature through work (part of a reaction against the Western tendency to see human intervention in the natural world in terms of defilement), see Richard White, '"Are You an Environmentalist or Do You Work for a Living?": Work and Nature', in *Uncommon Ground: Toward Reinventing Nature*, ed. William Cronon (W. W. Norton, New York, 1995), pp. 171–85.

57 René Dubos, 'Franciscan Conservation versus Benedictine Stewardship', in *Ecology and Religion in History*, ed. Spring, pp. 126, 131–2. The same self-righteous and edifying conception of the taming of the wild is found among the Puritans who settled New England.

58 Howard Parsons (ed.), *Marx and Engels on Ecology* (Greenwood Press, Westport, Conn., 1977), p. 112.

59 Emmanuel Le Roy Ladurie, *Times of Feast, Times of Famine: A History of Climate Since the Year 1000*, trans. Barbara Bray (Allen and Unwin, London, 1972 [1967]), pp. 2, 23.

60 Evans, *Criminal Prosecution and Capital Punishment of Animals*, p. xxvi.

61 Roberts, *Approaches to Nature*, p. 5; David J. Herlihy, 'Attitudes toward the Environment in Medieval Society', in *Historical Ecology*, ed. Bilsky, pp. 101, 107–9.

62 H. C. Darby, *The Medieval Fenland* (Cambridge University Press, Cambridge, 1940), p. 8.

63 John R. Clark Hall, *Beowulf and the Finnesburg Fragment: A Translation into Modern English Prose* (George Allen and Unwin, London, 1911), p. 88. For a more equivocal approach to wildness, see Richard Bernheimer, *Wild Men in the Middle Ages: A Study in Art, Sentiment, and Demonology* (Harvard University Press, Cambridge, Mass., 1952). Bernheimer (pp. 3–5, 18–20, 106–15, 119) highlights the nobility and innocence associated with wildness, though the medieval wildman tends to emerge as a distant ancestor of Leatherstocking, the character created by nineteenth-century US novelist James Fenimore Cooper, and of Edgar Rice Burroughs's Tarzan.

64 Roberts, *Approaches to Nature*, p. xiii.

65 Brenda Deen Schildgen, 'Dante's Utopian Landscape: The Garden of God', in *The Medieval World of Nature: A Book of Essays*, ed. Joyce E. Salisbury (Garland Publishing, New York, 1993), pp. 203–4.

66 See Chaucer's *Book of the Duchess* for a fine description of a deer garden and his *Parliament of Fowls* ('Assembly of Foules') for a typical high-stone-walled garden: *The Poetical Works of Geoffrey Chaucer in Six Volumes* (Bell and Daldy, London, 1866), vol. 5, pp. 164–71, and vol. 4, pp. 59–74. See also Laura L. Howes, 'Cultured Nature in Chaucer's Early Dream-Poems', in *Medieval World of Nature*, ed. Salisbury, pp. 188–95.

67 As quoted in Pearsall and Salter, *Landscapes and Seasons of the Medieval World*, p. 173.

68 Ibid., p. 87. Lorris wrote the first part of the poem, which was continued by Jean de Meun.

69 Howes, 'Cultured Nature in Chaucer's Early Dream-Poems', p. 193.

70 George D. Economou, *The Goddess Natura in Medieval Literature* (Harvard University Press, Cambridge, Mass., 1972), pp. 2, 141, viii.

71 Glacken, *Traces on the Rhodian Shore*, pp. 203–5; Passmore, *Man's Responsibility for Nature*, p. 15; White, 'Historical Roots of our Ecologic Crisis', p. 478.

72 Salisbury, *Beast Within*, p. 9.

73 White, 'Natural Science and Naturalistic Art in the Middle Ages', pp. 424–5.

74 A. C. Crombie, *Medieval and Early Modern Science*, vol. 1 (Doubleday, Garden City, NY, 1959), p. 15. On the shift from symbolism to representationalism, see also John Huizinga, *The Waning of the Middle Ages* (Edward Arnold, London, 1924), pp. 182–200.

75 Willene B. Clark and Meredith T. McMunn (eds), *Beasts and Birds of the Middle Ages: The Bestiary and its Legacy* (University of Pennsylvania Press, Philadelphia, Pa., 1989), pp. 1–11, 180–1, 184–7; Nona C. Flores, 'The Mirror of Nature Distorted: The Medieval Artist's Dilemma in Depicting Animals', in *Medieval World of Nature*, ed. Salisbury, pp. 3–45.

76 Robin S. Oggins, 'Falconry and Medieval Views of Nature', in *Medieval World of Nature*, ed. Salisbury, pp. 47–8, 56.

77 Flores, 'Mirror of Nature Distorted', pp. 3, 8–10, 36–8; Otto Pächt, 'Early Italian Nature Studies and the Early Calendar Literature', *Journal of the Warburg and Courtauld Institutes*, 13/1–2 (1950), pp. 30–2.

78 Salisbury, *Beast Within*, p. 128.

79 Thomas, *Man and the Natural World*, p. 64.

80 Herlihy, 'Attitudes toward the Environment in Medieval Society', p. 110. Extravagant claims for the new mentality have been made by Tina Stiefel, who hails a group of twelfth-century thinkers (*moderni*) as 'true scientists', the precursors of the modern idea and process of scientific rationality. See Stiefel's *The Intellectual Revolution in Twelfth-Century Europe* (Croom Helm, London, 1985), pp. 106, 1–4, 16–18, 24–8, 34–7, 72–3.

81 Hoffmann, 'Economic Development and Aquatic Ecosystems', pp. 631, 638, 640–52.

82 White, 'Historical Roots of our Ecologic Crisis', p. 476.

83 E. M. Carus-Wilson, 'An Industrial Revolution of the Thirteenth Century' (1941), in *Essays in Economic History*, vol. 1, ed. E. M. Carus-Wilson (Edward Arnold, London, 1954), pp. 41–60; Jean Gimpel, *The Medieval Machine: The Industrial Revolution of the Middle Ages* (Victor Gollancz, London, 1977).

84 Herlihy, 'Attitudes toward the Environment in Medieval Society', p. 112.

85 Bowlus, 'Ecological Crisis in Fourteenth Century Europe', pp. 94–5. Glacken estimates that, in France between 1050 and 1350, eighty cathedrals, 500 large churches and tens of thousands of smaller churches were erected (*Traces on the Rhodian Shore*, p. 350).

86 Marie-Dominique Chenu, *Nature, Man, and Society in the Twelfth Century: Essays on New Theological Perspectives in the Latin West* (University of Chicago Press, Chicago, 1968 [1957]), pp. 43–5.

87 Karen Jolly, 'Father God and Mother Earth: Nature-Mysticism in the Anglo-Saxon World', in *Medieval World of Nature*, ed. Salisbury, pp. 224, 248, 226; Ian Wei, personal communication, 28 October 1997.

88 G. E. Hutchinson, 'Attitudes towards Nature in Medieval England: The Alphonso and Bird Psalters', *Isis*, 65 (1974), pp. 5–37.

89 Matt Cartmill, *A View to a Death in the Morning: Hunting and Nature through History* (Harvard University Press, Cambridge, Mass., 1993), pp. 58–9.

90 Kenneth Clark, *Landscape into Art* (Penguin, Harmondsworth, 1949), pp. 19, 31, 43.

91 Ibid., p. 23. See also, H. C. Hollway-Calthrop, *Petrarch: His Life and Times* (Methuen, London, 1907), p. 67, and Alfred Biese, *The Development of the Feeling for Nature in the Middle Ages and Modern Times* (George Routledge, London, 1905), pp. 118–21. I say that Petrarch 'apparently' climbed the mountain because some Petrarch scholars not only argue that the famous letter describing the event was an allegory, but dispute the very fact of his ascent, explaining it simply as a metaphor for the ascent of the soul to God.

92 Geoffrey Chaucer, *The Franklin's Tale from the Canterbury Tales*, ed. Gerald Morgan (Hodder and Stoughton, London, 1980), p. 57.

93 Jacob Burckhardt, *The Civilization of the Renaissance in Italy*, trans. S. G. C. Middlemore, introd. Peter Burke (Penguin, London, 1990 [1860]), pp. 193–5; Nash, *Wilderness and the American Mind*, pp. 19–20; Clark, *Landscape into Art*, p. 23.

94 Quoted in Marjorie Hope Nicolson, *Mountain Gloom and Mountain Glory: The Development of the Aesthetics of the Infinite* (W. W. Norton, New York, 1963 [1959]), p. 50.

Chapter 4 The Advent of Modernity

1 Huston Smith, 'Tao Now: An Ecological Testament', in *Earth Might be Fair: Reflections on Ethics, Religion, and Ecology*, ed. Ian G. Barbour (Prentice-Hall, Englewood Cliffs, NJ, 1972), p. 64.

2 For the various ways in which Anglo-American humanities scholars have diagnosed the intellectual roots of the ecological crisis in the wake of White's 1967 essay, see Roderick S. French, 'Is Ecological Humanism a Contradiction in Terms? The Philosophical Foundations of the Humanities under Attack', in *Ecological Consciousness: Essays from the Earthday X Colloquium, University of Denver, April 21–24, 1980*, ed. Robert C. Schultz and J. Donald Hughes (University Press of America, Washington, DC, 1981), pp. 43–82.

3 Theodore Roszak, *Where the Wasteland Ends: Politics and Transcendence in Postindustrial Society* (Faber and Faber, London, 1973), pp. 7–8, 17–18, 127, 133, 179–80, 193, 225, 172; John Opie, 'Renaissance Origins of the Environmental Crisis', *Environmental Review*, 11 (Spring 1987), pp. 3, 5, 15.

4 Carolyn Merchant, *The Death of Nature: Women, Ecology and the Scientific Revolution* (HarperCollins, San Francisco, 1990 [1980]), pp. xxi, 61; Merchant, *Radical Ecology: The Search for a Livable World* (Routledge, London, 1992), pp. 58, 47. See also Max Oelschlaeger, *The Idea of Wilderness: From Prehistory to the Age of Ecology* (Yale University Press, New Haven, Conn., 1991), pp. 76–96; Donald Worster, *Nature's Economy: A History of Ecological Ideas* (Cambridge University Press, Cambridge, 1985 [1977]), p. 40.

5 John Gray, *Enlightenment's Wake: Politics and Culture at the Close of the Modern Age* (Routledge, London, 1995), pp. 145, 167, 178, 182–3. See also Andrew Dobson, *Green Political Thought* (Routledge, London, 1990), pp. 8–9, and C. Fred Alford, *Science and the Revenge of Nature: Marcuse and Habermas* (University Press of Florida, Gainesville, 1985), pp. 2, 11, 15–17, 142. For a spirited defence of the *philosophes* against postmodernism's charges, see Robert Darnton, 'George Washington's False Teeth', *New York Review of Books*, 44/5 (27 March 1997), pp. 34–8.

6 Robert Nisbet, *History of the Idea of Progress* (Heinemann, London, 1980), pp. 104, 112–17. This is not the place to discuss issues such as the definition of industrialism, the timing of the Industrial Revolution, or the legitimacy of the concept of an industrial revolution. And though I am aware of the absence of consensus as to when and where the Renaissance began and ended, and that some scholars question the very notion of a Renaissance superseding the Middle Ages, I cannot enter here into debates over periodization. The generalist tracing a single thread across time will inevitably fall foul of the specialist and be accused of unravelling the intricate fabric of specific eras.

7 Jacob Burckhardt, *The Civilization of the Renaissance in Italy*, trans. S. G. C. Middlemore, introd. Peter Burke (Penguin, London, 1990 [1860]), esp. pp. 98–104, 120–3, 185–92, 198–213.

8 Burckhardt's study, according to Peter Burke, is 'easy to criticize' (not least on account of its hostility to medieval civilization) 'but . . . also difficult to replace' (*Civilization of the Renaissance in Italy*, introduction, p. 14). For a thoughtful restatement of faith in the essential validity of the 'Promethean' interpretation, see William J. Bouwsma, 'The Renaissance in the Drama of Western History', *American Historical Review*, 84 (1979), pp. 1–15, esp. pp. 10, 13–14. On the economic context for Renaissance individualism, see Alfred von Martin, *Sociology of the Renaissance* (Harper and Row, New York, 1963 [1932]), pp. 1–2, 47, 57–62, 82–3.

9 Belief in divine/natural retribution survives among Christian fundamentalists in the United States. Californian Republican congresswoman Andrea Seastrand, a prominent anti-abortionist up for re-election in 1996, interpreted her state's glut of natural disasters over recent years – earthquakes, floods and fires – as God's precision punishment for Californian immorality.

10 Ernst Cassirer, *The Individual and the Cosmos in Renaissance Philosophy*, trans. Mario Domandi (University of Pennsylvania Press, Philadelphia, Pa., 1972 [1927]), p. 56; R. G. Collingwood, *The Idea of Nature* (Clarendon Press, Oxford, 1945), p. 95; Burckhardt, *Civilization of the Renaissance*, pp. 192–8, 103.

11 Michael Levey, *Early Renaissance* (Penguin, Harmondsworth, 1967), pp. 75–6.

12 Richard Lewinsohn (Morus), *Animals, Men and Myths: A History of the Influence of Animals on Civilization and Culture* (Victor Gollancz, London, 1954), p. 172.

13 White, 'The Historical Roots of our Ecologic Crisis', as reprinted in *Sunshine and Smoke: American Writers and the American Environment*, ed. David D. Anderson (J. B. Lippincott, Philadelphia, Pa., 1971), pp. 473, 479; David S. Landes, *The Unbound Prometheus: Technological Change and Industrial Development in Western Europe from 1750 to the Present* (Cambridge University Press, London, 1969), pp. 21–8, esp. p. 21.

14 White, 'Historical Roots of our Ecologic Crisis', pp. 474–5.

15 Lewis Mumford, *The Myth of the Machine*, vol. 2, *The Pentagon of Power* (Harcourt Brace Jovanovich, New York, 1970), pp. 77–94, 105–29; Gray, *Enlightenment's Wake*, pp. 146, 158, 163, 177–8; Rupert Sheldrake, *The Rebirth of Nature: The Greening of Science and God* (Century, London, 1990), pp. 29–32, 37–41; Jonathon Porritt, *Seeing Green: The Politics of Ecology Explained* (Basil Blackwell, Oxford, 1984), p. 105; Kirkpatrick Sale, *The Conquest of Paradise: Christopher Columbus and the Columbian Legacy* (Penguin, New York, 1990), p. 81; Jeremy Rifkin, *Entropy: A New World View* (Viking, New York, 1980), pp. 19–25.

16 As quoted in David Pepper, *The Roots of Modern Environmentalism* (Routledge, London, 1986), p. 47.

17 Oelschlaeger, *Idea of Wilderness*, p. 78. See also Pepper, *Roots of Modern Environmentalism*, pp. 48–50; Mumford, *Pentagon of Power*, pp. 51–65.

18 Francis Bacon, *The New Organon and Related Writings*, ed. Fulton H. Anderson (Liberal Arts Press, New York, 1960 [1620]), p. 39. For the abbre-

viation, see Mumford, *Pentagon of Power*, p. 118. The original postmodernist treatment is Max Horkheimer and Theodor W. Adorno, *Dialectic of Enlightenment*, trans. John Cumming (Seabury, New York, 1972), pp. 3–42. For a view of Bacon as less modern, assured and arrogant than environmentalist and postmodern critiques have made him out to be, see Charles Whitney, *Francis Bacon and Modernity* (Yale University Press, New Haven, Conn., 1986), pp. 1–19 (esp. pp. 2–11 and 15–16), 105–25, 168. Whitney also challenges his reputation as a phallocentric, capitalist apologist (pp. 123, 167–8).

19 William Leiss, *The Domination of Nature* (Braziller, New York, 1972), p. 105. See also Roszak, *Where the Wasteland Ends*, pp. 144–74, 236. The classic postmodern treatment of the relationship between knowledge and power is Michel Foucault, *Discipline and Punish*, trans. Alan Sheridan (Harmondsworth, Penguin, 1979), esp. p. 27.

20 Francis Bacon, *A Critical Edition of the Major Works*, ed. Brian Vickers (Oxford University Press, Oxford, 1996), p. 482.

21 Glanvill quoted in Merchant, *Death of Nature*, p. 189; Bacon, *Critical Edition of the Major Works*, p. 480. See also Brian Easlea, *Science and Sexual Oppression: Patriarchy's Confrontation with Women and Nature* (Weidenfeld and Nicolson, London, 1981), p. 70. The idea of progress already existed, as Robert A. Nisbet explains in *History of the Idea of Progress* (Heinemann, London, 1980), pp. 3–100. But prior to Bacon it was less clearly articulated in the sense in which I have used it.

22 Merchant, *Radical Ecology*, p. 47; id., *Death of Nature*, pp. 294, 186.

23 Marjorie Hope Nicolson, *The Breaking of the Circle: Studies in the Effect of the 'New Science' upon Seventeenth Century Poetry* (Northwestern University Press, Evanston, Ill., 1950), esp. pp. xvii–xxi, 65, 89, 103–4, 107, 110–11, 134; id., *Mountain Gloom and Mountain Glory: The Development of the Aesthetics of the Infinite* (W. W. Norton, New York, 1963 [1959]), pp. 159–63; Merchant, *Death of Nature*, p. xxi; Evelyn F. Keller, *Reflections on Gender and Science* (Yale University Press, New Haven, Conn., 1985), p. 7.

24 Merchant, *Death of Nature*, pp. 171–2; Leiss, *Domination of Nature*, 60; Ken Wilbur, *Up from Eden: A Transpersonal View of Human Evolution* (Shambhala, Boulder, Colo., 1983), p. 287. Ecofeminist contentions raise vital questions. Can men who respect nature participate in the subjection of women? Is a society with a mechanistic view of nature necessary for the subjugation of women? One is tempted to answer yes to the first question and no to the second. For a critique of ecofeminist assumptions, see Dobson, *Green Political Thought*, pp. 192–204.

25 Merchant, *Death of Nature*, pp. 33, 38–41.

26 Ibid., pp. 10, 189–90.

27 Vandana Shiva, *Staying Alive: Women, Ecology and Development* (Zed Books, London, 1989), pp. 16–20; Judith Plant (ed.), *Healing the Wounds: The Promise of Ecofeminism* (Green Print, London, 1989), pp. 28, 255; Fritjof Capra, *The Turning Point: Science, Society and the Rising Culture* (Flamingo, London, 1993), pp. 24, 41, 46. Others, as indicated in chapter 2, prefer to trace the problem to antiquity.

28 Opie, 'Renaissance Origins of the Environmental Crisis', p. 11; Francis Bacon, 'The Wisdom of the Ancients' (1609), in *The Essays* (Harmondsworth, Penguin, 1985), p. 270. Prometheus was an ancient Greek demigod who made man from clay, stole fire from Zeus and used it to empower man.

29 René Descartes, 'Discourse on Method', in *Philosophical Essays*, trans. Laurence J. LaFleur (Bobbs-Merrill, Indianapolis, Ind., 1964), pp. 4, 24, 25, 35, 42, 44; David Ray Griffin, 'Whitehead's Deeply Ecological Worldview', in *Worldviews and Ecology: Religion, Philosophy, and the Environment*, ed. Mary Evelyn Tucker and John A. Grim (Orbis Books, Maryknoll, NY, 1994), p. 196.

30 Val Plumwood, *Feminism and the Mastery of Nature* (Routledge, London, 1993), pp. 108, 114–15.

31 Descartes, 'Discourse on Method', pp. 41–3; Peter Singer, *Animal Liberation: A New Ethics for our Treatment of Animals* (Avon Books, New York, 1975), p. 209; Bacon, *Critical Edition of the Major Works*, p. 482. As is often the case, however, Descartes's disciples were more zealous than their mentor.

32 Keith Thomas, *Man and the Natural World: Changing Attitudes in England 1500–1800* (Penguin, Harmondsworth, 1984), p. 34.

33. Karl Marx, *Capital: A Critical Analysis of Capitalist Production*, vol. 1, trans. Samuel Moore and Edward Aveling (Lawrence and Wishart, London, 1974 [1867]), p. 368; John Passmore, *Man's Responsibility for Nature: Ecological Problems and Western Traditions* (Duckworth, London, 1974), p. 21.

34 Singer, *Animal Liberation*, pp. 207–9.

35 Descartes, 'Discourse on Method', p. 45. Descartes has his defenders among professional philosophers. James Collins, *Descartes' Philosophy of Nature* (Basil Blackwell, Oxford, 1971), denies that his concept of nature as a great machine alienated people from nature or divested the natural world of its wonder (pp. 29–30, 92–3). Gordon Baker and Katherine J. Morris dispute whether Descartes himself really believed in 'Cartesian dualism', arguing that his attitudes to animals were complex. While he denied them reason, thought and soul, he did not preclude bodily sensations: *Descartes's Dualism* (Routledge, London, 1996), pp. 2–4. In the early 1950s it was possible to write a large book on Descartes's legacy (Albert G. A. Balz, *Descartes and the Modern Mind* (Yale University Press, New Haven, Conn., 1952)) without a single index reference to animals. Even if Descartes's own stance was at odds with the 'legend' of Cartesian dualism, I am more concerned with the dominant lay interpretation, however simplistic.

36 Merchant, *Radical Ecology*, p. 55; Porritt, *Seeing Green*, p. 105; Maurice Berman, *The Reenchantment of Nature* (Cornell University Press, Ithaca, NY, 1981), pp. 16, 41.

37 *Guardian*, 1996, otherwise undated clipping; Fritjof Capra, *The Tao of Physics* (Flamingo, London, 1983 [1975]), pp. 27–8, 63–9; *The Turning Point*, pp. 37–62. 'Tao' is equivalent to 'nature' in its broadest sense: the cosmos and laws of nature that determine phenomena such as the seasons, phases of the moon and vegetational growth.

38 *Times Higher Education Supplement*, 15 November 1996, pp. 18–19.

39 Merchant, *Death of Nature*, pp. 56–61; William H. TeBrake, *Medieval Frontier: Culture and Ecology in Rijnland* (Texas A & M University Press, College Station, Tex., 1985); id., 'Land Drainage and Public Environmental Policy in Medieval Holland', *Environmental Review*, 12/3 (Fall 1988), pp. 75–93.

40 Merchant, *Death of Nature*, pp. 2–3, 28–41, 56–61, 68.

41 G. M. Trevelyan, *English Social History: A Survey of Six Centuries, Chaucer to Queen Victoria* (Longman, London, 1944), pp. 125, 236, 237–8. Trevelyan was a prominent campaigner for the protection of areas of outstanding natural beauty during the interwar period. See David Cannadine, *G. M. Trevelyan: A Life in History* (HarperCollins, London, 1992), pp. 153–6, 178–9.

42 The expression 'landscape of hell' is from Archie Clow, 'The Influence of Technology on Environment', in *Ecology, The Shaping Inquiry*, ed. Jonathan Benthall (Longman, London, 1972), p. 79. Bernard W. Clapp, *An Environmental History of Britain since the Industrial Revolution* (Longman, London, 1994), is essentially an economic history of natural resource extraction/use and energy production. Despite his title, Clapp does not relate this material to the wider currents or historiography of environmental history.

43 Trevelyan, *English Social History*, pp. 400–1.

44 John J. Compton, 'Science and God's Action in Nature', in *Earth Might Be Fair*, ed. Barbour, p. 44.

45 Alfred North Whitehead, *Science and the Modern World* (Cambridge University Press, Cambridge, 1926), pp. 77, 272–4. See also Griffin, 'Whitehead's Deeply Ecological Worldview', pp. 192, 194, 196, 200.

46 Alfred W. Crosby, 'A Renaissance Change in European Cognition', *Environmental History Review*, 14/1–2 (Spring/Summer 1990), p. 28. Crosby's *The Measure of Reality: Quantification and Western Society, 1250–1600* (Cambridge University Press, New York, 1997), discusses how western Europeans came to calculate, measure and have control over the physical world by dividing reality into equal but arbitrary units, focusing on the shift from qualitative to quantitative perceptions of time, space and the material world (pp. xi, 3–19, 49, 58, 75–93, 227).

47 Passmore, *Man's Responsibility for Nature*, p. 19.

48 Bacon, *The New Organon and Related Writings*, p. 15.

49 Leiss, *Domination of Nature*, p. 50.

50 Basil Willey, *The Eighteenth-Century Background: Studies on the Idea of Nature in the Thought of the Period* (Chatto and Windus, London, 1949), p. 5. William Leiss is particularly interested in how Bacon formulated his ideas to harmonize with Christianity (*Domination of Nature*, pp. 48–71).

51 Passmore, *Man's Responsibility for Nature*, p. 21.

52 Worster, *Nature's Economy*, p. 37.

53 Ibid., pp. 22–3.

54 Merchant, *Death of Nature*, p. 64; Collingwood, *Idea of Nature*, pp. 8–9.

55 Collingwood, *Idea of Nature*, p. 9.

Chapter 5 The World Beyond Europe

1 *Guardian*, 9 August 1996.
2 Donald Worster, 'The Vulnerable Earth', in *The Ends of the Earth: Perspectives on Modern Environmental History*, ed. Donald Worster (Cambridge University Press, Cambridge, 1988), pp. 11–12; 'Toward an Agroecological Perspective in History', *Journal of American History*, 76/4 (March 1990), p. 1097.
3 Donald Worster, *The Wealth of Nature: Environmental History and the Ecological Imagination* (Oxford University Press, New York, 1993), pp. 214–18.
4 Simon Schama, *Landscape and Memory* (HarperCollins, London, 1995), p. 13.
5 Hesther Lynch Piozzi, *Anecdotes of the Late Samuel Johnson, LL.D., During the Last Twenty Years of his Life*, ed. S. C. Roberts (Cambridge University Press, Cambridge, 1925), p. 66.
6 The debate over the euro was reported on the *Today* programme, BBC Radio 4, 13 December 1996. Trevelyan is quoted in David Cannadine, *G. M. Trevelyan: A Life in History* (HarperCollins, London, 1992), pp. 155–6. Archetypical scenes of pastoral British countryside appeared on recruitment posters during the First World War ('Your Britain, fight for it now'). See George L. Mosse, 'The Appropriation of Nature', in his *Fallen Soldiers: Reshaping the Memory of the World Wars* (Oxford University Press, New York, 1990), pp. 108–9.
7 Michel de Montaigne, 'Of Coaches' (Des Coches), in *The Essayes of Michael, Lord of Montaigne, The Third Booke*, trans. John Florio (Grant Richards, London, 1908 [1603]), p. 175. The coach served Montaigne as a symbol of luxury, to be contrasted with the wheelless simplicity of American Indian cultures.
8 Samuel Eliot Morison et al., *A Concise History of the American Republic* (Oxford University Press, New York, 1977), p. 10.
9 Carolyn Merchant, 'Reinventing Eden: Western Culture as a Recovery Narrative', in *Uncommon Ground: Toward Reinventing Nature*, ed. William Cronon (W. W. Norton, New York, 1995), p. 145.
10 Simon Schama, otherwise unidentified 1992 clipping from the *Guardian*.
11 Neil Evernden, *The Natural Alien: Humankind and the Environment* (Toronto University Press, Toronto, 1985), p. 23; Francis Bacon, *A Critical Edition of the Major Works*, ed. Brian Vickers (Oxford University Press, Oxford, 1996), p. 487.
12 Richard White, 'Discovering Nature in North America', *Journal of American History*, 79/3 (December 1992), p. 879. This misidentification was aggravated by the problems of conceptualization and description faced by all Europeans whose encounters with the New World prompted assessment of the strange in terms of the familiar.
13 Max Oelschlaeger, *The Idea of Wilderness: From Prehistory to the Age of Ecology* (Yale University Press, New Haven, Conn., 1991), pp. 6, 8–24 (quotation on p. 28). For glorification of the hunter-gatherer, see also Richard B. Lee and Irven DeVore (eds), *Man the Hunter* (Aldine, Chicago, 1968), and Paul Shepard, *The Tender Carnivore and the Sacred Game* (Scribner, New York, 1973).

14 Clive Ponting, *A Green History of the World* (Penguin, London, 1991), pp. 37–87.
15 Christopher Manes, *Green Rage: Radical Environmentalism and the Unmaking of Civilization* (Little, Brown, Boston, Mass., 1990), pp. 228, 237.
16 These admirers skate over the reality that few indigenes made a living purely from hunting and gathering.
17 J. Donald Hughes, *American Indian Environments* (1983), as quoted in Roger S. Gottlieb (ed.), *This Sacred Earth: Religion, Nature, Environment* (Routledge, New York, 1996), p. 131. For representative statements by environmentalists, see Fred Fertig, 'Child of Nature: The American Indian as Ecologist', *Sierra Club Bulletin*, 55/8 (August 1970), pp. 4–7, and Peter Marshall, *Nature's Web: Rethinking Our Place on Earth* (Paragon House, New York, 1994), pp. 137–48.
18 Hughes, *American Indian Environments*, as quoted in Gottlieb, *This Sacred Earth*, p. 135. David Rothenburg reports that German schoolchildren are required to learn the text by heart ('Will the Real Chief Seattle Please Speak Up?', *Resurgence*, 178 (September/October 1996), p. 5). Though usually referred to as the Point Elliott Treaty speech, and believed to have been delivered on the occasion of that treaty's signing in 1855, it was actually addressed to the new Governor and Commissioner of Indian Affairs for Washington territory in 1854.
19 J. Baird Callicott, 'Traditional American Indian and Western European Attitudes to Nature: An Overview', in *Defense of the Land Ethic: Essays in Environmental Philosophy*, ed. J. Baird Callicott (State University of New York Press, Albany, 1989), p. 201; id., 'American Indian Land Wisdom?: Sorting Out the Issues', ibid., pp. 207–10.
20 Robert Boyle, *A Free Enquiry into the Vulgarly Receiv'd Notion of Nature* (1686), as quoted in Peter J. Bowler, *The Fontana History of the Environmental Sciences* (Fontana, London, 1992), p. 89.
21 For a withering assault on the norm of the ecological Indian, see Bernard W. Powell, 'Were these America's First Ecologists?', *Journal of the West*, 26 (1987), pp. 17–25.
22 Carolyn Merchant, *Ecological Revolutions: Nature, Gender, and Science in New England* (University of North Carolina Press, Chapel Hill, 1989), p. 1; Elinor G. K. Melville, 'Global Developments and Latin American Environments', in *Ecology and Empire: Environmental History of Settler Societies*, ed. Tom Griffiths and Libby Robin (Keele University Press, Edinburgh, 1997), pp. 187–90.
23 Kirkpatrick Sale, *The Conquest of Paradise: Christopher Columbus and the Columbian Legacy* (Penguin, New York, 1990), pp. 293–317, esp. 318–19; Brian Fagan, 'If Columbus had not Called', *History Today*, 42 (May 1992), pp. 30–4.
24 Andy Smith, 'For All Those who were Indian in a Former Life', in *Ecofeminism and the Sacred*, ed. Carol J. Adams (Continuum, New York, 1993), pp. 168–71. As the title of Alvin Josephy's book indicates, there were at least 500 Indian nations in North America in 1492: Josephy, *500 Nations:*

An Illustrated History of North American Indians (Hutchinson, London, 1995), pp. 8, 444.

25 The case for a substantial Indian contribution is put by George L. Cornell, 'The Influence of Native Americans on Modern Conservationists', *Environmental Review*, 9/2 (Summer 1985), pp. 105–17, and Calvin Martin, 'The American Indian as Miscast Ecologist', in *Ecological Consciousness: Essays from the Earthday X Colloquium, University of Denver, April 21–24 1980*, ed. Robert C. Schultz and J. Donald Hughes (University Press of America, Washington, DC, 1981), pp. 137, 145.

26 As quoted in Roderick Nash (ed.), *Environment and Americans: The Problem of Priorities* (Holt Dryden, New York, 1972), p. 77.

27 Calvin Martin, *Keepers of the Game: Indian–Animal Relationships in the Fur Trade* (University of California Press, Berkeley, 1978).

28 S. F. Cook and W. Borah, *Essays in Population History* (University of California Press, Berkeley, 1971–9), vol. 3, pp. 129–76.

29 BBC TV, *Horizon*, transcript, 'In Search of the Noble Savage' (Broadcasting Support Services, London, 1992), pp. 12–15. The programme was broadcast on 27 January 1992.

30 Sale, *Conquest of Paradise*, pp. 317, 320; Paul S. Martin, 'The Discovery of America', *Science*, 179/4077 (9 March 1973), pp. 969–70, 972–4; BBC, 'In Search of the Noble Savage', pp. 5–6; Michael P. Hoffman, 'Prehistoric Ecological Crises', in *Historical Ecology: Essays on Environment and Social Change* ed. Lester J. Bilsky (Kennikat Press, Port Washington, NY, 1980), pp. 33–7.

31 The reports of Euro-American explorers, soldiers, missionaries, fur traders and settlers – the most readily available source for the study of American Indians – though prone to ethnocentrism (like American Indian accounts), should not be dismissed lightly.

32 Shepard Krech III, 'Ecology and the American Indian', *Ideas*, 3/1 (Summer 1994), pp. 17–19.

33 BBC, 'In Search of the Noble Savage', p. 10. Rows of upper teeth sitting on top of lower rows suggest that the skulls decayed and collapsed *in situ*, indicating that neither head nor skin were removed.

34 Callicott, 'Indian and Western European Attitudes to Nature', p. 195.

35 The term 'land wisdom' is from Stewart L. Udall, *The Quiet Crisis and the Next Generation* (Peregrine Smith, Salt Lake City, 1988), p. 3.

36 John Baden, Richard Stroup and Walter Thurman, 'Myths, Admonitions and Rationality: The American Indian as Resource Manager', *Economic Inquiry*, 19 (January 1981), p. 142; Eric L. Jones, 'The History of Natural Resource Exploitation in the Western World', *Research in Economic History*, 13 (1991), pp. 235–52.

37 Richard D. North, *Life on a Modern Planet: A Manifesto for Progress* (Manchester University Press, Manchester, 1995), pp. 201–3.

38 Hughes, *American Indian Environments*, as quoted in Gottlieb, *This Sacred Earth*, p. 135; Rudolf Kaiser, '"A Fifth Gospel, Almost": Chief Seattle's Speech(es): American Origins and European Reception', in *Indians and*

Europe: An Interdisciplinary Collection of Essays, ed. Christian F. Feest (Rader Verlag, Aachen, 1987), pp. 505–26; Rothenburg, 'Will the Real Chief Seattle Please Speak Up?', p. 5.

39 Frederic H. Wagner et al., *Wildlife Policies in the U.S. National Parks* (Island Press, Washington, DC, 1995), p. 141.

40 William M. Denevan, 'The Pristine Myth: The Landscape of the Americas in 1492', *Annals of the Association of American Geographers*, 82/3 (1992), pp. 369–85; Karl W. Butzer, 'The Indian Legacy in the American Landscape', in *The Making of the American Landscape*, ed. Michael P. Conzen (Routledge, New York, 1994), pp. 27–50.

41 William E. Doolittle, 'Agriculture in North America on the Eve of Contact: A Reassessment', *Annals of the Association of American Geographers*, 82/3 (1992), pp. 386–7, 398, 392–3.

42 Jones, 'History of Natural Resource Exploitation', p. 240; Doolittle, 'Agriculture in North America on the Eve of Contact', pp. 389–90.

43 James J. Parsons, 'Raised Field Farmers as Pre-Columbian Landscape Engineers: Looking North from the San Jorge (Columbia)', in *Prehistoric Intensive Agriculture in the Tropics*, ed. I. S. Farrington (British Archaeological Reports, International Series 232, Oxford, 1985), p. 161.

44 Callicott, 'American Indian Land Wisdom?', p. 205.

45 Michael Williams, *Americans and their Forests: An Historical Geography* (Cambridge University Press, New York, 1989), p. 46.

46 For an open-minded world tour, which concludes that no single religious tradition holds the cure, see Mary Evelyn Tucker and John A. Grim (eds), *Worldviews and Ecology: Religion, Philosophy, and the Environment* (Orbis Books, Maryknoll, NY, 1994). A useful summary of how Eastern philosophies have featured in Western discussions of environmental ethics since 1967 is Eugene C. Hargrove's foreword to *Nature in Asian Traditions of Thought: Essays in Environmental Philosophy*, ed. J. Baird Callicott and Roger T. Ames (State University of New York Press, Albany, 1989), pp. xiii–xxi.

47 Henry David Thoreau, *Walden* (Penguin, London, 1983), p. 346.

48 Daisetz T. Suzuki, 'The Role of Nature in Zen Buddhism', *Eranos-Jahrbuch*, 22 (1953), pp. 291–321.

49 Lynn White, 'The Historical Roots of our Ecologic Crisis', as reprinted in *Sunshine and Smoke: American Writers and the American Environment*, ed. David D. Anderson (J. B. Lippincott, Philadelphia, Pa., 1971), p. 479. White's views on Asian religions are echoed by US environmental historian Roderick Nash, *Wilderness and the American Mind* (Yale University Press, New Haven, Conn., 1982 [1967]), pp. 20–2.

50 For these terms, see Callicott and Ames, 'Introduction: The Asian Traditions as Conceptual Resources for Environmental Philosophy', in *Nature in Asian Traditions of Thought*, p. 7.

51 For Buddhism's relevance to conservation, see Allan Hunt Badiner (ed.), *Dharma Gaia: A Harvest of Essays in Buddhism and Ecology* (Parallax Press, Berkeley, 1990).

52 E. F. Schumacher, *Small is Beautiful: A Study of Economics as if People Mattered* (Blond and Briggs, London, 1973), pp. 48–56; Kenneth E. Boulding, *Human Values on the Spaceship Earth* (National Council of Churches, New York, 1966), pp. 6, 14.

53 Vandana Shiva, *Staying Alive: Women, Ecology and Development* (Zed Books, London, 1989), pp. 38–41, 67–77; Madhav Gadgil and Ramachandra Guha, *This Fissured Land: An Ecological History of India* (Oxford University Press, Delhi, 1992), pp. 223–4; Ramachandra Guha, *The Unquiet Woods: Ecological Change and Peasant Resistance in the Himalaya* (Oxford University Press, Delhi, 1989). Chipko tactics and ideology have influenced direct action protests against road-building in Britain over recent years.

54 Ian White, 'Buddhism', in *Attitudes to Nature*, ed. Jean Holm with John Bowker (Pinter, London, 1994), pp. 23, 25.

55 Richard Lewinsohn (Morus), *Animals, Men and Myths: A History of the Influence of Animals on Civilization and Culture* (Victor Gollancz, London, 1954), pp. 80–1.

56 Aldous Huxley, *Letters of Aldous Huxley*, ed. Grover Smith (Chatto and Windus, London, 1969), pp. 578–9; Xinzhong Yao, 'Chinese Religions', in *Attitudes to Nature*, ed. Holm with Bowker, p. 155.

57 As quoted in Xinzhong Yao, 'Chinese Religions', pp. 138, 136; ibid., p. 154. For an equally flattering account of pre-Western values, see Wenhui Hou, 'Reflections on Chinese Traditional Ideas of Nature', *Environmental History*, 2/4 (October 1997), pp. 482–93.

58 For this approach, see Anuradha Roma Choudhury, 'Hinduism', in *Attitudes to Nature*, ed. Holm with Bowker, pp. 68–9.

59 O. P. Dwivedi, '*Satyagraha* for Conservation: Awakening the Spirit of Hinduism', in *Ethics of Environment and Development: Global Challenge, International Response*, ed. J. Ronald Engel and Joan Gibb Engel (Belhaven Press, London, 1990), pp. 201, 210–11.

60 Lester J. Bilsky, 'Ecological Crisis and Response in Ancient China', in *Historical Ecology*, ed. Bilsky, pp. 61, 65–6.

61 Yi-Fu Tuan, 'Discrepancies between Environmental Attitude and Behaviour: Examples from Europe and China' (1968), in *Ecology and Religion in History*, ed. David and Eileen Spring (Harper and Row, New York, 1974), pp. 102, 111; id., 'Our Treatment of the Environment in Ideal and Actuality', *American Scientist*, 58 (1970), pp. 244–9. For a critique of Europeans as the 'makers of history', see J. M. Blaut, *The Colonizer's Model of the World: Geographical Diffusionism and Eurocentric History* (Guilford Press, New York, 1993), esp. p. 1.

62 Robert B. Marks, 'Commercialization without Capitalism: Processes of Environmental Change in South China, 1550–1850', *Environmental History*, 1/1 (January 1996), pp. 72–4.

63 E. H. Schafer, 'The Conservation of Nature under the T'ang Dynasty', *Journal of Economic and Social History of the Orient*, 5 (1962), pp. 299–300.

64 Ramachandra Guha, 'Radical American Environmentalism and Wilderness Preservation: A Third World Critique', *Environmental Ethics*, 11 (Spring

1989), pp. 76–8. Despite the fact that it was not a Judaeo-Christian culture, China was far in advance of Europe technologically and scientifically until the seventeenth century. See Thomas S. Derr, 'Religion's Responsibility for the Ecological Crisis: An Argument Run Amok', *World View*, 18 (1975), p. 43.

65 Fernand Braudel, *The Mediterranean and the Mediterranean World in the Age of Philip II*, vol. 1, rev. edn, trans. Siân Reynolds (Collins, London, 1972 [1949]), pp. 16, 20.

66 Merchant inserts a gender dimension absent from much environmental history. When men took over and commercialized dairying, poultry-raising and horticulture, traditionally women's spheres, they marginalized women in the economy beyond the home. See her *Ecological Revolutions*, pp. 167–72, 190–7.

67 Alfred W. Crosby, *The Columbian Exchange: Biological and Cultural Consequences of 1492* (Greenwood Press, Westport, Conn., 1972), p. 64. See also his *Ecological Imperialism: The Biological Expansion of Europe, 900–1900* (Cambridge University Press, Cambridge, 1986), and *Germs, Seeds and Animals: Studies in Ecological History* (Sharpe, Armonk, NY, 1994).

68 William Cronon, 'Modes of Prophecy and Production: Placing Nature in History', *Journal of American History*, 76/4 (March 1990), p. 1128; id., *Changes in the Land: Indians, Colonists, and the Ecology of New England* (Hill and Wang, New York, 1983), pp. 135–7.

69 Blaut, *The Colonizer's Model of the World*, p. 186; David Arnold, *The Problem of Nature: Environment, Culture and European Expansion* (Basil Blackwell, Oxford, 1996), p. 85.

70 Arnold, *Problem of Nature*, p. 165; Gadgil and Guha, *This Fissured Land*, pp. 116–23.

71 Lucile H. Brockway, *Science and Colonial Expansion: The Role of the British Royal Botanical Gardens* (Academic Press, New York, 1979), pp. xi, 6–7, 8–11, 14–15, 77–102, 188–96.

72 Richard Grove, *Green Imperialism: Colonial Expansion, Tropical Island Edens and the Origins of Environmentalism, 1600–1860* (Cambridge University Press, Cambridge, 1995), pp. 176, 485, 6, 1, 15; Arnold, *Problem of Nature*, pp. 152–3.

73 Grove, *Green Imperialism*, pp. 2, 472; id., 'The Origins of Environmentalism', *Nature*, 345 (3 May 1990), p. 11.

74 Perry Miller, 'Nature and the National Ego', in his *Errand into the Wilderness* (Harvard University Press, Cambridge, Mass., 1956), p. 209; id., *Nature's Nation* (Harvard University Press, Cambridge, Mass., 1967), pp. 175–83.

75 As reprinted in Merle Curti et al. (eds), *American Issues: The Social Record* (J. B. Lippincott, Chicago, 1960), p. 228.

76 Nash, *Wilderness and the American Mind*, p. 68.

77 Thomas Jefferson, *The Complete Jefferson*, ed. Saul K. Padover (Duell, Sloan and Pearce, New York, 1943), p. 891. See also Ralph N. Miller, 'American Nationalism as a Theory of Nature', *William and Mary Quarterly*, 12/1 (January 1955), pp. 74–81; Daniel Boorstin, *The Lost World of Thomas Jefferson* (Beacon Press, Boston, 1948), pp. 100–4.

78 Frances Trollope, *Domestic Manners of the Americans* (Vintage, New York, 1960 [1832]), p. 33.

79 Quoted in Alfred Runte, *National Parks: The American Experience* (University of Nebraska Press, Lincoln, 1979), p. 22.

80 As quoted in Larzer Ziff, *Literary Democracy: The Declaration of Cultural Independence in America* (Penguin, Harmondsworth, 1982), p. 62. See also Benjamin Spencer, *The Quest for Nationality: An American Literary Campaign* (Syracuse University Press, Syracuse, NY, 1957), pp. 79, 198.

81 Henry David Thoreau, 'Walking', in *The Portable Thoreau*, ed. Carl Bode (Penguin, Harmondsworth, 1977), pp. 607–8.

82 By the late nineteenth century Australia too was sufficiently established and urbanized to feel nostalgic about its pioneer heritage, of which the landscape was also an indispensable ingredient. See John Rennie Short, *Imagined Country: Society, Culture and Environment* (Routledge, London, 1991), p. 206.

83 James Thomas Flexner, *History of American Painting*, vol. 3, *That Wilder Image (The Native School from Thomas Cole to Winslow Homer)* (Dover, Mineola, NY, 1970), p. 58. See also Stephen Daniels, *Fields of Vision: Landscape Imagery and National Identity in England and the United States* (Princeton University Press, Princeton, NJ, 1993), pp. 146–73.

84 Neil Evernden, *The Social Construction of Nature* (Johns Hopkins University Press, Baltimore, Md., 1992), p. 120. On the tendency to ignore scenes of devastation, see Nancy K. Anderson, ' "The Kiss of Enterprise": The Western Landscape as Symbol and Resource', in *The West as America: Reinterpreting Images of the Frontier, 1820–1920*, ed. William H. Truettner (Smithsonian Institution, Washington, DC, 1991), p. 241.

85 James Fenimore Cooper, *The Pioneers* (Holt, Rinehart and Winston, New York, 1967 [1823]), p. 249, and *The Prairie* (Holt, Rinehart and Winston, 1967 [1827]), p. 80. For exaggerated claims on Cooper's behalf, see Fred Erisman, 'Western Fiction as an Ecological Parable', *Environmental Review*, 6 (1978), pp. 15–16, 18, and William W. Bevis, '*The Prairie*: Cooper's Desert Ecology', *Environmental Review*, 10/1 (Spring 1986), pp. 3, 7–8, 14.

86 Tim Bonyhady, 'Artists with Axes', *Environment and History*, 1/2 (1995), pp. 221–39.

87 Catherine L. Albanese, *Nature Religion in America: From the Algonkian Indians to the New Age* (University of Chicago Press, Chicago, 1990), p. 54.

88 Marcia B. Kline, *Beyond the Land Itself: Views of Nature in Canada and the United States* (Harvard University Press, Cambridge, Mass., 1970), pp. 25–6, 33.

89 Northrop Frye quoted in Carl F. Klinck (ed.), *Literary History of Canada: Canada's Literature in English* (University of Toronto Press, Toronto, 1965), p. 843. More recent scholarship suggests a common North American outlook. Lawrence Buell stresses the 'family resemblances' of cultural nationalisms based on nature throughout the white settler colonies: *The Environmental Imagination: Nature Writing and the Formation of American Culture* (Harvard University Press, Cambridge, Mass., 1995), pp. 55–62.

90 Philip J. Pauly, 'The Beauty and Menace of the Japanese Cherry Trees: Conflicting Visions of American Ecological Independence', *Isis*, 87 (1996), pp. 53, 61, 70–3.

Chapter 6 Nature as Landscape

1 Ronald Hepburn, 'Aesthetic Appreciation of Nature', in *Aesthetics in the Modern World*, ed. Harold Osborne (Thames and Hudson, London, 1968), pp. 51–2.
2 Kenneth R. Olwig, 'Reinventing Common Nature: Yosemite and Mount Rushmore – A Meandering Tale of a Double Nature', in *Uncommon Ground: Toward Reinventing Nature*, ed. William Cronon (W. W. Norton, New York, 1995), p. 388; W. J. T. Mitchell, 'Imperial Landscapes', in *Landscape and Power*, ed. W. J. T. Mitchell (University of Chicago Press, Chicago, 1994), p. 14.
3 Donald Meinig, foreword to *The Making of the American Landscape*, ed. Michael P. Conzen (Routledge, London, 1994), p. xv; J. Wreford Watson, *Mental Images and Geographical Reality in the Settlement of North America* (University of Nottingham Press, Nottingham, 1967), p. 9; Simon Schama, *Landscape and Memory* (HarperCollins, London, 1995). The Conzen collection encompasses petrol (gas) stations and dams as well as substantially natural scenes.
4 J. B. Jackson, 'The Vernacular Landscape', in *Landscape Meanings and Values*, ed. Edmund C. Penning-Rowsell and David Lowenthal (Allen and Unwin, London, 1986), p. 68.
5 Kenneth R. Olwig, 'Sexual Cosmology: Nation and Landscape at the Conceptual Interstices of Nature and Culture; or, What does Landscape Really Mean?', in *Landscape: Politics and Perspectives*, ed. Barbara Bender (Berg, Oxford, 1993), p. 327, (see also pp. 317–20); John Barrell, *The Idea of Landscape and the Sense of Place 1730–1840: An Approach to the Poetry of John Clare* (Cambridge University Press, Cambridge, 1972), pp. 1–3.
6 John Rennie Short, *Imagined Country: Society, Culture and Environment* (Routledge, London, 1991), p. 67; Tom Williamson, *Polite Landscapes: Gardens and Society in Eighteenth-Century England* (Alan Sutton, Stroud, 1995), pp. 100–18. Michael Bunce, *The Countryside Ideal: Anglo-American Images of Landscape* (Routledge, London, 1994), explores love of and nostalgia for the countryside in all its manifestations, from British television series such as *All Creatures Great and Small* (based on James Heriot's books about veterinary surgeons in the Yorkshire Dales between the 1930s and 1950s) to the Edwardian children's literature of Beatrix Potter.
7 Schama, *Landscape and Memory*, pp. 7, 9; Olwig, 'Reinventing Common Nature', pp. 381–2, 384, 390, 396.
8 Short, *Imagined Country*, p. 75. Short criticizes the National Trust, which began to acquire rural houses and estates in the 1930s, for preserving the landscape of the rich in symbolic form (p. 80). For a defence of preservation on aesthetic grounds, see Williamson, *Polite Landscapes*, pp. 166–7.

9 As quoted in Karl Marx, *Capital: A Critical Analysis of Capitalist Production*, vol. 1, trans. Samuel Moore and Edward Aveling (Lawrence and Wishart, London, 1974 [1867]), p. 682. Oliver Rackham believes over-population was the fundamental issue and contends that the greatest human exoduses were post-Clearance: *History of the Countryside* (J. M. Dent, London, 1986), p. 320. Short refers to the 'Balmorality' of a landscape which became a royal playground (*Imagined Country*, pp. 74–5). On the creation of 'wilderness' in the Scottish Highlands, see Karen Fog Olwig and Kenneth Olwig, 'Underdevelopment and the Development of "Natural" Park Ideology', *Antipode: A Radical Journal of Geography*, 11/2 (1979), pp. 18–20.

10 Short, *Imagined Country*, p. 67.

11 W. G. Hoskins, *The Making of the English Landscape*, rev. edn, ed. Christopher Taylor (Hodder and Stoughton, London, 1988 [1955]), p. 118.

12 Alluding to the 'Enclosure-Act Myth', Rackham argues that the substantial impact of eighteenth-century enclosure was largely restricted to central England: *History of the Countryside*, pp. 88, 94.

13 Daniel Defoe, *A Tour Through the Whole Island of Great Britain* (Penguin, Harmondsworth, 1971), p. 156.

14 Carolyn Merchant, *The Death of Nature: Women, Ecology and the Scientific Revolution* (HarperCollins, San Francisco, 1990 [1980]), pp. 56–61; H. C. Darby, *The Draining of the Fens* (Cambridge University Press, Cambridge, 1940), pp. 53–82. 'Adventurers' is invariably capitalized in contemporary references.

15 Anne Barton, 'The Village Genius', *New York Review of Books*, 43/20 (19 December 1996), pp. 42–3, 46–8; Barrell, *The Idea of Landscape*, pp. 189–215, 115; *The Poems of John Clare*, ed. J. W. Tibble (2 vols, J. M. Dent, London, 1935), vol. 1, p. 155.

16 *Poems of John Clare*, vol. 1, p. 72; Barton, 'The Village Genius', p. 48.

17 Paul Stamper, 'Woods and Parks', in *The Countryside of Medieval England*, ed. Grenville Astill and Annie Grant (Basil Blackwell, Oxford, 1988), p. 147.

18 Jane Austen, *Mansfield Park* (Oxford University Press, Oxford, 1990 [1814]), p. 220.

19 Harry Hopkins, *The Long Affray: The Poaching Wars, 1760–1914* (Secker and Warburg, London, 1985), pp. 66–7.

20 Stamper, 'Woods and Parks', p. 147.

21 John Ginger, *The Notable Man: The Life and Times of Oliver Goldsmith* (Hamish Hamilton, London, 1977), pp. 264–6.

22 Hoskins, *Making of the English Landscape*, pp. 134–5; Maurice Beresford, *History on the Ground: Six Studies in Maps and Landscapes* (Lutterworth, London, 1957), pp. 198–203; Christopher Taylor, *Dorset* (Hodder and Stoughton, London, 1970), p. 160.

23 Francis Bacon, 'Of Gardens', in *A Critical Edition of the Major Works*, ed. Brian Vickers (Oxford University Press, Oxford, 1996), pp. 430–3; Derek Clifford, *A History of Garden Design* (Faber and Faber, London, 1962), p. 92; Geoffrey Jellicoe et al. (eds), *The Oxford Companion to Gardens* (Oxford University Press, Oxford, 1986), pp. 33, 604.

24 Keith Thomas, *Man and the Natural World: Changing Attitudes in England, 1500–1800* (Penguin, Harmondsworth, 1984), p. 239.
25 Myra Reynolds, *The Treatment of Nature in English Poetry between Pope and Wordsworth* (University of Chicago Press, Chicago, 1909), pp. 252, 257–8.
26 For a 'new' garden history that stresses the socio-economic context rather than the aesthetic/philosophical milieu, see Williamson, *Polite Landscapes*, esp. pp. 118–40.
27 Kenneth Woodbridge, *The Stourhead Landscape* (National Trust, London, 1996), p. 9. For a more extended treatment, see his *Landscape and Antiquity: Aspects of English Culture at Stourhead, 1718 to 1838* (Oxford University Press, Oxford, 1970).
28 Schama, *Landscape and Memory*, p. 539.
29 As quoted in Alfred Biese, *The Development of the Feeling for Nature in the Middle Ages and Modern Times* (George Routledge, London, 1905 [1888]), p. 369. See also D. G. Charlton, *New Images of the Natural in France: A Study in European Cultural History, 1750–1800* (Cambridge University Press, Cambridge, 1984), pp. 32–4.
30 How consciously artistic a decision this was is open to debate. It certainly helps to bear in mind that the house was of modest size and not intended for day-to-day living. The main Hoare home was in Clapham.
31 Woodbridge, *Stourhead Landscape*, pp. 31, 19–20.
32 Ibid., pp. 25, 31. For further information on the Hoares, see C. G. A. Clay, 'Henry Hoare, Banker, his Family, and the Stourhead Estate', in *Landowners, Capitalists, and Entrepreneurs: Essays for Sir John Habakkuk*, ed. F. M. L. Thompson (Clarendon Press, Oxford, 1994), pp. 114–21.
33 As quoted in Olwig, 'Sexual Cosmology', p. 313.
34 Schama, *Landscape and Memory*, p. 539; Christopher Thacker, *The Wildness Pleases: The Origins of Romanticism* (Croom Helm, London, 1983), pp. 32–3.
35 Raymond Williams, *The Country and the City* (Chatto and Windus, London, 1973), p. 106. See also Olwig, 'Sexual Cosmology', p. 333.
36 Raymond Williams, 'Ideas of Nature', in *Ecology: The Shaping Inquiry*, ed. Jonathan Benthall (Longman, London, 1972), pp. 159–60; id., *Country and the City*, pp. 105–6; Olwig, 'Reinventing Common Nature', pp. 387–8; Ann Bermingham, *Landscape and Ideology: The English Rustic Tradition, 1740–1860* (University of California Press, Berkeley, 1986), pp. 13–14.
37 Williams, 'Ideas of Nature', p. 159.
38 Gray Brechin, 'Grace Marchant and the Global Garden', in *The Meaning of Gardens*, ed. Mark Francis and Randolph T. Hester, Jr. (MIT Press, Cambridge, Mass., 1990), pp. 227–8. Nothing remains of the Barron estate or gardens, which have been completely consumed by the town of Menlo Park. (I am grateful to David Hoch for ferreting out various details about Barron Garden.) Cinnabar tailings still leach mercury from the old New Almaden mines into the streams and reservoirs of what is now a state park on the edge of San Jose, hence the 'No Fishing' and 'No Swimming' signs.
39 R. E. M. Peach, *The Life and Times of Ralph Allen* (D. Nutt, London, 1895), pp. 76, 81–2; Anthony Mitchell, *Prior Park Landscape Garden* (National Trust,

London, 1996), pp. 4–5. In *Mansfield Park*, Jane Austen pokes fun at the so-called 'Wilderness' at Sotherton – a planted, 2-acre wood, which 'though laid out with too much regularity, was darkness and shade, and natural beauty, compared with the bowling-green and the terrace' (p. 82).

40 Reynolds, *Treatment of Nature*, p. 267; Williamson, *Polite Landscapes*, p. 148.

41 Woodbridge, *Stourhead Landscape*, p. 8; Williamson, *Polite Landscapes*, p. 109. That landed aristocrats were spending increasing amounts of time in London may also have encouraged the adoption of the new simplicity. For what was the point of having an elaborate garden if you were only there on occasion?

42 Reynolds, *Treatment of Nature*, p. 263. Shenstone, a poet, owned the Leasowes estate in Warwickshire.

43 Stephen Daniels, *Fields of Vision: Landscape Imagery and National Identity in England and the United States* (Princeton University Press, Princeton, NJ, 1993), p. 83.

44 As quoted in Hoskins, *Making of the English Landscape*, p. 138.

45 Ann Leighton, *American Gardens in the Eighteenth Century* (Houghton Mifflin, Boston, Mass., 1976), p. 359; Edward Hyams, *Capability Brown and Humphry Repton* (J. M. Dent, London, 1971), pp. 39–40, 109; Charles A. Miller, *Jefferson and Nature: An Interpretation* (Johns Hopkins University Press, Baltimore, Md., 1988), pp. 116–17.

46 John Muir, from *The Mountains of California*, in *John Muir: The Eight Wilderness Discovery Books* (Diadem Books, London, 1992), p. 296.

47 Merrill D. Peterson (ed.), *The Portable Thomas Jefferson* (Viking, New York, 1975), p. 397.

48 Eugene Hargrove, *Foundations of Environmental Ethics* (Prentice-Hall, Englewood Cliffs, NY, 1988), p. 63.

49 John Locke, *Two Treatises of Government: The Second Treatise* (Cambridge University Press, Cambridge, 1988 [1690]), p. 288.

50 *Poems of John Clare*, p. 419.

Chapter 7 Reassessments of Nature: Romantic and Ecological

1 Charles A. Reich, *The Greening of America* (Penguin, London, 1971 [1970]), pp. 220–1.

2 Anthony, earl of Shaftesbury, *Characteristics*, ed. John M. Robertson (2 vols, Grant Richards, London, 1900 [1711]), vol. 2, p. 125. The case for Shaftesbury as the father of Romanticism is made by Christopher Thacker, *The Wildness Pleases: The Origins of Romanticism* (Croom Helm, London, 1983), pp. 12–18, 77.

3 P. R. Hay, 'The Contemporary Environment Movement as Neo-Romanticism: A Re-Appraisal from Tasmania', *Environmental Review*, 12/4 (Winter 1988), pp. 39–59. By contrast, Meredith Veldman's *Fantasy, the Bomb, and the Greening of Britain: Romantic Protest, 1945–1980* (Cambridge University Press, Cambridge, 1994) makes a strong case for the connections

between the Romantic intellectual tradition and the recent green movement. See esp. pp. 1–36, 246–310.

4 Theodore Roszak, *Where the Wasteland Ends: Politics and Transcendence in Postindustrial Society* (Faber and Faber, London, 1973), pp. 277–345, 400–1; Wordsworth quotations on p. 316. For originals, see *The Poetical Works of Wordsworth*, ed. Thomas Hutchinson (Oxford University Press, London, 1950 [1904]), pp. 501, 509 (I. 562–6 and III. 127–32).

5 Lawrence John Zillman (ed.), *Shelley's Poetic Vision: The Text and the Drafts* (Yale University Press, New Haven, Conn., 1968), p. 95.

6 Basil Willey, *The Eighteenth Century Background: Studies on the Idea of Nature in the Thought of the Period* (Chatto and Windus, London, 1940), p. 2.

7 Stephen Horigan, *Nature and Culture in Western Discourses* (Routledge, London, 1988), pp. 2–4.

8 Willey, *Eighteenth Century Background*, p. 2.

9 Thomas Hobbes, *Leviathan* (Penguin, London, 1985), p. 186.

10 Willey, *Eighteenth Century Background*, pp. 161, 164.

11 Arthur O. Lovejoy and George Boas, *Primitivism and Related Ideas in Antiquity* (Octagon Books, New York, 1965 [1935]), p. 7.

12 Quoted ibid., pp. 46–7.

13 The first use of 'noble savage' is often attributed to John Dryden. In his play, *The Conquest of Granada* (1670), Almanzor (a Moor), declares 'I am as free as Nature first made man, 'ere the base Laws of Servitude began, when wild in woods the noble Savage ran.' (*Dryden: The Dramatic Works* (6 vols, Gordian Press, New York, 1968), vol. 3, p. 34.

14 Jean-Jacques Rousseau, *The Social Contract and Discourses*, trans. G. D. H. Cole (Dent, London, 1973), pp. 5, 9, 44–113.

15 Thacker, *Wildness Pleases*, pp. 155–8; see also pp. 153–80.

16 Gilbert F. LaFreniere, 'Rousseau and the European Roots of Environmentalism', *Environmental History Review*, 14/4 (Winter 1990), pp. 52–3.

17 LaFreniere believes Rousseau's direct and indirect influence on the better-known nineteenth-century American precursors of conservation and environmentalism has been under-appreciated: ibid., pp. 41–2. For a comprehensive discussion of the new ways of looking at and depicting nature current at this time, see Donald Geoffrey Charlton, *New Images of the Natural in France: A Study in European Cultural History, 1750–1800* (Cambridge University Press, Cambridge, 1984) (pp. 41–65 for 'wild sublimity').

18 William Godwin, *St. Leon: A Tale of the Sixteenth Century* (Henry Colburn and Richard Bentley, London, 1831 [1799]), pp. 36, 90–1, 85.

19 William Wordsworth, *Descriptive Sketches*, ed. Eric Birdsall (Cornell University Press, Ithaca, NY, 1984 [1793]), p. 88; Jonathan Bate, *Romantic Ecology: Wordsworth and the Environmental Tradition* (Routledge, London, 1991), p. 25.

20 George Gordon Byron, *The Poetical Works of Lord Byron* (Oxford University Press, London, 1921), p. 213; Marjorie Hope Nicolson, *Mountain Gloom and Mountain Glory: The Development of the Aesthetics of the Infinite* (W. W. Norton, New York, 1963 [1959]), p. 1.

21 Keith Thomas, *Man and the Natural World: Changing Attitudes in England 1500–1800* (Penguin, Harmondsworth, 1984), p. 259; Nicolson, *Mountain Gloom and Mountain Glory*, pp. 63–6.

22 John Ruskin, *Modern Painters*, vol. 4, in *The Works of John Ruskin* (Alden, New York, 1885), pp. 339, 367; see also, vol. 3, pp. 189–271.

23 The case for advances in scientific understanding as the driving force behind changes in aesthetic appreciation of nature is put by Allen Carlson, 'Nature and Positive Aesthetics', *Environmental Ethics*, 6 (1984), p. 33.

24 Thomas Burnet, *The Sacred Theory of the Earth* (Centaur Press, London, 1965 [1684]), pp. 13, 15–17, 23–129; Willey, *Eighteenth Century Background*, p. 41.

25 Mary Midgley, *Animals and Why They Matter* (University of Georgia Press, Athens, 1984), p. 62.

26 Gilpin's guide to the River Wye (1782), as quoted in Myra Reynolds, *The Treatment of Nature in English Poetry between Pope and Wordsworth* (University of Chicago Press, Chicago, 1909), p. 236.

27 Ibid., p. 237. Gilpin found Snowdon, the highest peak in England and Wales, so wanting by his criteria that he did not bother climbing to the top.

28 Immanuel Kant, *Observations on the Feeling of the Beautiful and Sublime*, trans. John T. Goldthwait (University of California Press, Berkeley, 1960 [1764]), pp. 46–7.

29 Edmund Burke, *A Philosophical Inquiry into the Origin of our Ideas of the Sublime and Beautiful*, ed. and introd. J. T. Boulton (Routledge and Kegan Paul, London, 1958 [1757]), pp. 57, lvi.

30 Anthony, earl of Shaftesbury, *Characteristics*, vol. 2, p. 125.

31 Byron, *Poetical Works*, pp. 386–7.

32 Jean-Jacques Rousseau, *Confessions* (Book 4), trans. J. M. Cohen (William Glaisher, London, 1953), p. 132. The Romantic imperative also pervaded landscape painting. Even John Constable, who much preferred the pastoral farmscapes busy with human activity of his native Suffolk, felt obliged to tour and paint the Lake District in the autumn of 1806. See Louis Hawes, *Presences of Nature: British Landscape, 1780–1830* (Yale Center for British Art, New Haven, Conn. 1982), pp. 10, 16.

33 Donald Worster, *Nature's Economy: A History of Ecological Ideas* (Cambridge University Press, Cambridge, 1985 [1977]), pp. 58–111; Bate, *Romantic Ecology*, pp. 8–11.

34 See especially *The Excursion*, IV. 941–1324, in *The Poetical Works of Wordsworth*, ed. Hutchinson, pp. 636–41; Bate, *Romantic Ecology*, p. 67.

35 Bate, *Romantic Ecology*, p. 48.

36 Samuel Taylor Coleridge, *The Poems of Samuel Taylor Coleridge* (Oxford University Press, London, 1935), p. 379; *William Wordsworth: Selected Prose*, ed. John O. Hayden (Penguin, Harmondsworth, 1988), p. 91.

37 Willey, *Eighteenth Century Background*, p. 292.

38 Quoted ibid.

39 Ralph Waldo Emerson, *Nature*, in *The American Tradition in Literature* (shorter edn) ed. Sculley Bradley et al. (Grosset and Dunlap, New York, 1979), pp. 564, 562, 566, 563, 572, 570. For admiration of Emerson by a 'new

age', 'post-mechanistic' biologist, see Rupert Sheldrake, *The Rebirth of Nature: The Greening of Science and God* (Century, London, 1990), pp. 50–1.

40 Peter Iver Kaufman, 'The Instrumental Value of Nature', *Environmental Review*, 4/1 (1980), p. 34.

41 Emerson, *Nature*, pp. 596, 565; Michael Pollan, *Second Nature: A Gardener's Education* (Dell, New York, 1991), pp. 116, 123, 127, 133.

42 Gertrude Reif Hughes, *Emerson's Demanding Optimism* (Louisiana State University Press, Baton Rouge, 1984), p. 136.

43 Emerson, *Nature*, p. 563.

44 Harriet Ritvo takes the story of the growing affection for animals and the humane movement's motivations and achievements into the nineteenth century: *The Animal Estate: The English and other Creatures in the Victorian Age* (Harvard University Press, Cambridge, Mass., 1987), pp. 82–202.

45 Midgley, *Animals and Why They Matter*, p. 13.

46 Lisa Mighetto, 'Wildlife Protection and the New Humanitarianism', *Environmental Review*, 12/1 (Spring 1988), pp. 46–7; David Evans, *A History of Nature Conservation in Britain* (Routledge, London, 1992), pp. 32–3.

47 Peter Singer, *Animal Liberation: A New Ethic for our Treatment of Animals* (Avon Books, New York, 1975), p. 179.

48 *Johnson's Journey to the Western Isles of Scotland and Boswell's Journal of a Tour to the Hebrides with Samuel Johnson*, ed. R. W. Chapman (Oxford University Press, Oxford, 1974 [1775 and 1785]), pp. 30, 35–6, 407.

49 John Bowlby, *Charles Darwin: A New Biography* (Pimlico, London, 1991), p. 420; Adrian J. Desmond and James Moore, *Darwin* (Michael Joseph, London, 1991), p. 615; George Hendrick, *Henry Salt: Humanitarian Reformer and Man of Letters* (University of Illinois Press, Urbana, 1977), pp. 59–60, 120–1.

50 Charles Darwin, *The Origin of Species* (Mentor, New York, 1958 [1859]), pp. 82–3.

51 Thomas H. Huxley, 'On The Origin of Species', in *Man's Place in Nature and The Origin of Species* (n.d., as quoted in Clarence J. Glacken, 'This Growing Second World within the World of Nature', in *Man's Place in the Island Ecosystem*, ed. Raymond Fosberg (Bishop Museum, Honolulu, 1963), p. 90.

52 For the debate over 'man's place in nature', see Robert M. Young, *Darwin's Metaphor: Nature's Place in Victorian Culture* (Cambridge University Press, Cambridge, 1985), pp. 164–247.

53 Desmond and Moore, *Darwin*, pp. 243–4, 593.

54 Singer, *Animal Liberation*, pp. 219–20.

55 Worster, *Nature's Economy*, pp. 172–3.

56 Desmond and Moore, *Darwin*, p. 314.

57 Young, *Darwin's Metaphor*, pp. 1–22.

58 Singer, *Animal Liberation*, p. 213.

59 Florence Emily Hardy, *The Life of Thomas Hardy, 1840–1928* (Macmillan, London, 1962), p. 349.

60 Aldo Leopold, *A Sand County Almanac* (Oxford University Press, New York, 1949), p. 109.

61 Lewis Mumford, *The Myth of the Machine*, vol. 2, *The Pentagon of Power* (Harcourt Brace Jovanovich, New York, 1970), pp. 387–93, esp. p. 388. Mumford oversimplifies a complex matter, claiming that Darwin 'sturdily opposed' vivisection (p. 388).

62 Kenneth Heuer (ed.), *The Lost Notebooks of Loren Eiseley* (Little, Brown, Boston, Mass., 1987), p. 129.

63 Anna Bramwell, *Ecology in the 20th Century: A History* (Yale University Press, New Haven, Conn., 1989), pp. 43–5.

64 David H. DeGrood, *Haeckel's Theory of the Unity of Nature* (Christopher Publishing, Boston, Mass., 1965), pp. 38–9.

65 Quoted in Anne Chisholm, *Philosophers of the Earth: Conversations with Ecologists* (Sidgwick and Jackson, London, 1972), pp. 18, 50–1; Ernest Haeckel, *The Riddle of the Universe*, trans. Joseph McCabe (Harper, New York, 1901), p. 291.

66 Haeckel, *Riddle of the Universe*, p. 244; James M. Gillis, *False Prophets* (Macmillan, New York, 1930), p. 108.

67 Bettyann Kevles, *Females of the Species: Sex and Survival in the Animal Kingdom* (Harvard University Press, Cambridge, Mass., 1986), pp. 17–19, 201–7. Kevles also locates incest, abortion, rape ('forced insemination'), prostitution (sex for food), polyandry and sisterhood in the animal kingdom, pointing out that monogamy is stressful because the partners have to learn to live with each other beyond the mating act (pp. 112–16, 108–9, 159–61, 116–18, 97–9, 183–93, 101–3).

68 The seminal work is Thomas S. Kuhn, *The Structure of Scientific Revolutions* (University of Chicago Press, Chicago, 1962), pp. 1–9. On the myth of a value-free science, see also Peter J. Bowler, *The Fontana History of the Environmental Sciences* (Fontana, London, 1992), pp. 547–53.

69 Donald Worster, 'The Ecology of Order and Chaos', *Environmental History Review*, 14/1–2 (Spring/Summer 1990), pp. 3–7.

70 Gregg Mitman, *The State of Nature: Ecology, Community and American Social Thought, 1900–1950* (University of Chicago Press, Chicago, 1992), pp. 7–8. Allee's associationalist views lost ground in American ecology during the 1950s, when they became linked to the justification of totalitarian regimes.

Chapter 8 The Disunited Colours of Nature

1 Malcolm Chase, 'Can History be Green? A Prognosis', *Rural History*, 3/2 (1992), p. 243.

2 Aristotle, *The Politics*, trans. T. A. Sinclair (Penguin, Harmondsworth, 1962), p. 69; Edmund Burke, *Reflections on the Revolution in France* (Holt Rinehart and Winston, New York, 1950 [1790]), pp. 103, 117–18, 57–8.

3 See Richard Hofstadter, *Social Darwinism in American Thought* (Beacon, Boston, Mass., 1944), and Mike Hawkins, *Social Darwinism in European and American Thought, 1860–1945: Nature as Model and Nature as Threat* (Cambridge University Press, Cambridge, 1997).

4 David Pepper, *Eco-Socialism: From Deep Ecology to Social Justice* (Routledge, London, 1993), p. 89. Sociobiology is by no means identical with Social Darwinism, however.

5 Ibid., p. 9.

6 John Stuart Mill, *Collected Works of John Stuart Mill* (University of Toronto Press, Toronto, 1969), vol. 10, pp. 373–462, esp. p. 377.

7 Friedrich Engels, *Herr Eugen Dühring's Revolution in Science (Anti-Dühring)* (Martin Lawrence, London, 1937), p. 129.

8 Peter Kropotkin, *Mutual Aid: A Factor of Evolution* (Freedom Press, London, 1987 [1902]), pp. 12–19, 21–73, esp. pp. 12–13, 43–50, 72–3.

9 On Marx and Engels as important forerunners (as distinct from founders) of human/social/political ecology, see Jean-Guy Vaillancourt, 'Marxism and Ecology: More Benedictine than Franciscan', *Capitalism, Nature, Socialism*, 3/1 (1992), pp. 19–35, esp. pp. 27–8, 32, 35. (Founded in 1988, *Capitalism, Nature, Socialism* is dedicated to demonstrating the relevance of Marxism to efforts to cope with the environmental crisis.) On recent Marxist environmentalism in the West, see also Arran E. Gare, *Postmodernism and the Environmental Crisis* (Routledge, London, 1994), pp. 80–6.

10 Karl Marx, *Grundrisse: Foundations of the Critique of Political Economy*, trans. Martin Nicolaus (Allen Lane, London, 1973 [1857/8]), p. 410; id., 'On the Jewish Question', in *Early Political Writings*, ed. Joseph O'Malley (Cambridge University Press, Cambridge, 1994 [1844]), p. 54; id., *Capital: A Critical Analysis of Capitalist Production*, vol. 1, trans. Samuel Moore and Edward Aveling (Lawrence and Wishart, London, 1974 [1867]), pp. 474–5. Donald Worster uses this famous quotation to open his book about America's best-known twentieth-century ecological catastrophe: *Dust Bowl: The Southern Plains in the 1930s* (Oxford University Press, New York, 1979), p. 3.

11 Marx, *Capital: A Critique of Political Economy*, vol. 3 (Lawrence and Wishart, London 1974 [1894]), p. 812.

12 Joan DeBardeleben, *The Environment and Marxism-Leninism: The Soviet and East German Experience* (Westview Press, Boulder, Colo., 1985), p. 87.

13 Friedrich Engels, *The Condition of the Working Class in England* (Oxford University Press, Oxford, 1993 [1845]), pp. 61–6.

14 Friedrich Engels, *Dialectics of Nature*, trans. Clemens Dutt (Foreign Languages Publishing House, Moscow, 1954 [1925]), pp. 239–46, esp. p. 242.

15 Anna Bramwell, *Ecology in the 20th Century: A History* (Yale University Press, New Haven, Conn., 1989), p. 33.

16 Marx, 'Economo-Philosophical Manuscripts of 1844', in *The Portable Karl Marx*, ed. Eugene Kamenka (Penguin, London, 1983), p. 138; *Capital*, vol. 1, p. 175.

17 Engels, *Herr Eugen Dühring's Revolution in Science*, p. 129; id., *Dialectics of Nature*, p. 306.

18 William Cronon, *Nature's Metropolis: Chicago and the Great West* (W. W. Norton, New York, 1993), pp. xvii, 402, 149–50.

19 Marx, *Capital*, vol. 1, p. 175; Donald Worster, *The Wealth of Nature: Environmental History and the Ecological Imagination* (Oxford University Press, New

York, 1993), pp. ix–x, 203–19; Madhav Gadgil and Ramachandra Guha, *This Fissured Land: An Ecological History of India* (Oxford University Press, Delhi, 1992), pp. 12–13. With reference to the idea of natural capital, Cronon is careful to note that value is never intrinsic. For instance, Native Americans and white settlers evidently assessed the buffalo's value differently (*Nature's Metropolis*, p. 424).

20 Bramwell, *Ecology in the 20th Century*, p. 33–4.
21 Howard Parsons (ed.), *Marx and Engels on Ecology* (Greenwood, Westport, Conn., 1977), pp. 84–6.
22 Donald Worster, 'The Vulnerable Earth', in *The Ends of the Earth: Perspectives on Modern Environmental History*, ed. Donald Worster (Cambridge University Press, Cambridge, 1988), p. 17.
23 Parsons, *Marx and Engels on Ecology*, pp. 90–2.
24 Murray Bookchin, 'Ecology and Revolutionary Thought', *Antipode: A Radical Journal of Geography*, 10/3–11/1 (1979), p. 22.
25 Quoted in Albert E. Burke, 'Influence of Man upon Nature: the Russian View', in *Man's Role in Changing the Face of the Earth*, ed. William L. Thomas, Jr. (University of Chicago Press, Chicago, 1956), p. 1048.
26 Quoted in DeBardeleben, *The Environment and Marxism-Leninism*, p. 92. Though Soviet interest in ecology was largely tied to economic development, a subsidiary strand focused on nature protection in 'no-go areas' (*zapovedniki*). See Douglas R. Weiner, 'The Changing Face of Soviet Conservation', in *The Ends of the Earth*, ed. Worster pp. 252–3.
27 Martin Heidegger, 'The Question Concerning Technology' (1953), in *Basic Writings: Martin Heidegger*, ed. David Farrell Krell (Routledge, London, 1993), pp. 311–41. For a Frankfurt School approach, see Alfred Schmidt, *The Concept of Nature in Marx* (New Left Books, London, 1971).
28 Max Horkheimer, *The Eclipse of Reason* (Oxford University Press, New York, 1947), pp. 100–1.
29 Jonathon Porritt, *Seeing Green: The Politics of Ecology Explained* (Basil Blackwell, Oxford, 1984), pp. 43–4, 48. For the essential difference of the ecological thrust, despite some congruence with socialism, see Arne Naess, *Ecology, Community and Lifestyle: An Outline of an Ecosophy*, trans. and rev. David Rothenberg (Cambridge University Press, Cambridge, 1989), pp. 157–60.
30 Naess's leading US disciples are Bill Devall and George Sessions, whose *Deep Ecology: Living as if Nature Mattered* (Peregrine Smith, Salt Lake City, Utah, 1985) laid out the principles, while Devall's *Simple in Means, Rich in Ends: Practising Deep Ecology* (Merlin Press, London, 1990) explained how to implement them.
31 Pepper, *Eco-Socialism*, pp. 91, 244–8; Andrew Dobson, *Green Political Thought* (Routledge, London, 1990), pp. 29–32, 175–92.
32 Pepper, *Eco-Socialism*, p. 118; Murray Bookchin, 'Social Ecology versus Deep Ecology', *Socialist Review*, 12 (July–September 1988), pp. 12–14; Andrew Ross, *Strange Weather: Culture, Science, and Technology in the Age of Limits* (Verso, London, 1991), p. 166.

33 Derek Wall (ed.), *Green History: A Reader in Environmental Literature, Philosophy and Politics* (Routledge, London, 1994), p. 13 (see also p. 2).
34 Peter Marshall, *Nature's Web: Rethinking our Place on Earth* (Cassell, London, 1995), pp. 300–4, 287–8, 312–14. Marshall is also author of *Demanding the Impossible: A History of Anarchism* (1992), and biographer of Godwin.
35 Peter C. Gould, *Early Green Politics: Back to Nature, Back to the Land, and Socialism in Britain, 1880–1900* (Harvester Press, Brighton, 1988), p. 161. Gould's reference is to Porritt, *Seeing Green*, pp. 216–17.
36 Gould, *Early Green Politics*, p. 15.
37 William Morris, *News from Nowhere* (Longmans Green, London, 1907 [1891]), pp. 7, 80, 220, 44–5, 7, 214–16.
38 Edward Carpenter, *My Days and Dreams: Being Autobiographical Notes* (Allen and Unwin, London, 1916), pp. 141–2. See also Chushichi Tsuzuki, *Edward Carpenter, 1844–1929: Prophet of Human Fellowship* (Cambridge University Press, Cambridge, 1980), pp. 79–80.
39 George Hendrick, *Henry Salt: Humanitarian Reformer and Man of Letters* (University of Illinois Press, Urbana, 1977), pp. 22, 25; Henry S. Salt, *Seventy Years among Savages* (George Allen and Unwin, London, 1921), p. 74. See also George Hendrick, 'Henry S. Salt and the Late Victorian Socialists, and Thoreau', *New England Quarterly*, 50 (1977), pp. 409–22.
40 Michael Pollan, *Second Nature: A Gardener's Education* (Dell, New York, 1991), p. 223; William Cronon, 'The Trouble with Wilderness; or, Getting Back to the Wrong Nature', *Environmental History*, 1/1 (January 1996), pp. 7–28; Elizabeth Larson, 'Granola Boys, Ecodudes, and Me', *Ms*, 2 (July/August 1991), pp. 96–7. On the appeal of wilderness to 'bourgeois culture', see C. Rojek, *Ways of Escape: Modern Transformations in Leisure and Travel* (Macmillan, Houndmills, 1993), pp. 196–9.
41 William Cronon (ed.), *Uncommon Ground: Toward Reinventing Nature* (W. W. Norton, New York, 1995), pp. 79, 114–31, 401; Laura Pulido, *Environmentalism and Economic Justice: Two Chicano Struggles in the Southwest* (University of Arizona Press, Tucson, 1996). The refusal to privilege outstanding (canonical) aspects of nature and the desire to reinvest the ordinary and representative with significance can create the impression that there is little to choose between the Lake District and Yosemite, and an overgrown, abandoned city lot where children pick dandelions and make dens.
42 Jim Schwab, *Deeper Shades of Green: The Rise of Blue-Collar and Minority Environmentalism in America* (Sierra Club Books, San Francisco, 1994), p. 55.
43 Giovanna di Chiro, 'Nature as Community: The Convergence of Environment and Social Justice', in *Uncommon Ground*, ed. Cronon, pp. 319–20; Alexander Wilson, *The Culture of Nature: The North American Landscape from Disney to the Exxon Valdez* (Basil Blackwell, Oxford, 1992), p. 17.
44 Basil Willey, *The Eighteenth Century Background: Studies of the Idea of Nature in the Thought of the Period* (Chatto and Windus, London, 1940), pp. 253–70.
45 Wordsworth, 'On the Projected Kendal and Windermere Railway', in *The Poetical Works of Wordsworth*, ed. Thomas Hutchinson (Oxford University Press, London, 1950 [1904]), p. 224.

46 *William Wordsworth: Selected Prose*, ed. John O. Hayden (Penguin, Harmondsworth, 1988), pp. 89, 84. The new line opened in the spring of 1847, bringing the first Mancunians, but it was the coming of the M6 motorway in the 1960s that really opened up the Lake District.

47 Wilson, *Culture of Nature*, p. 27.

48 John Taylor, *A Dream of England: Landscape, Photography and the Tourist's Imagination* (Manchester University Press, Manchester, 1994), p. 275, and colour plate between pp. 272 and 273. See also Stephen Daniels, *Fields of Vision: Landscape Imagery and National Identity in England and the United States* (Princeton University Press, Princeton, NJ, 1993), p. 7, and Phil Kinsman, 'Landscape, Race and National Identity: The Photography of Ingrid Pollard', *Area*, 27/4 (December 1995), pp. 300–10. On nature and landscape as key ingredients of conservative English identity, see David Lowenthal, 'British National Identity and the English Landscape', *Rural History*, 2/2 (1991), pp. 213–22.

49 William Hazlitt, *The Complete Works of William Hazlitt*, ed. P. P. Howe (J. M. Dent, London, 1930 [1817]), vol. 4, pp. 19–20; Jonathan Bate, *Romantic Ecology: Wordsworth and the Environmental Tradition* (Routledge, London, 1991), pp. 19–20, 33, 50, 53.

50 Bate, *Romantic Ecology*, pp. 53–4. For a further example of these sentiments, see Gillian Darley, *Octavia Hill: A Life* (Constable, London, 1990), p. 309.

51 Robert Blatchford, *Merrie England* (Clarion, London, 1894), p. 23.

52 Ibid., p. 22.

53 Gould, *Early Green Politics*, p. 39.

54 Walter Harding and Michael Meyer, *The New Thoreau Handbook* (New York University Press, New York, 1980), p. 219.

55 G. Williams, *The Royal Parks of London* (Constable, London, 1978), p. 205.

56 Gould, *Early Green Politics*, pp. 88–103.

57 Frederick Law Olmsted, *Walks and Talks of an American Farmer in England* (University of Michigan Press/UMI, Ann Arbor, 1967 [1852]), p. 54. Nevertheless, lots inside Birkenhead Park were reserved for private villas. For the Salt quotation, see Hendrick, *Henry Salt*, p. 42.

58 M. Hill, *Freedom to Roam: The Struggle for Access to Britain's Moors and Mountains* (Moorland Publishing, Ashbourne, Derbyshire, 1980).

59 David Prynn, 'The Clarion Clubs, Rambling and the Holiday Associations in Britain since the 1890s', *Journal of Contemporary History*, 11/2–3 (July 1976), pp. 68–71.

60 David Evans, *A History of Nature Conservation in Britain* (Routledge, London, 1992), p. 41.

61 Raymond H. Dominick, *The Environmental Movement in Germany: Prophets and Pioneers, 1871–1971* (Indiana University Press, Bloomington, 1992), pp. 61–3.

62 Gould, *Early Green Politics*, p. 47.

63 George Orwell, *The Road to Wigan Pier* (Secker and Warburg, London, 1956), pp. 207–8.

64 Thomas Carlyle, 'Signs of the Times', in *The Works of Thomas Carlyle in Thirty Volumes* (Chapman and Hall, London, 1899), vol. 27, pt 2, pp. 59–60; *The Letters of Thomas Carlyle to his Brother Alexander (with Related Family Letters)*, ed. Edwin W. Marrs, Jr. (Belknap Press, Cambridge, Mass., 1968), pp. 177–8.

65 Bate, *Romantic Ecology*, pp. 61, 55, 58.

66 John Ruskin, *Unto this Last and Other Writings* (Penguin, London, 1985), pp. 224–6.

67 Wall, *Green History*, pp. 14, 178–9.

68 Carolyn Merchant, 'The Women of the Progressive Conservation Crusade, 1900–1915', in *Environmental History: Critical Issues in Comparative Perspective*, ed. Kendall E. Bailes (University Press of America, Lanham, Md., 1985), pp. 153–75; Vera Norwood, *Made From This Earth: American Women and Nature* (University of North Carolina Press, Chapel Hill, 1993), pp. 37–8; John Sheail, *Nature in Trust: The History of Nature Conservation in Britain* (Blackie, Glasgow, 1976), pp. 4–5, 12–16, 22–4.

69 Andrée Collard (with Joyce Contrucci), *The Rape of the Wild: Man's Violence against Animals and the Earth* (The Women's Press, London, 1988), p. 137. With the advent of insidious new pollutants, the status of 'home' as a refuge from the outer world was eroded. See Norwood, *Made From This Earth*, pp. 155–6, for household metaphors in Rachel Carson's writings. Schwab also views the often predominantly female leadership of and involvement in contemporary grassroots social and racial justice environmentalism as an extension of their traditional roles as protectors of home and family (*Deeper Shades of Green*, p. 418).

70 Evans, *History of Nature Conservation*, pp. 43–4.

71 Wall, *Green History*, p. 229; Bramwell, *Ecology in the 20th Century*, pp. 104–32.

72 Simon Schama, *Landscape and Memory* (HarperCollins, London, 1995), pp. 102–3.

73 Dominick, *Environmental Movement in Germany*, pp. 22–3, 87.

74 Elim Papadakis, *The Green Movement in West Germany* (Croom Helm, London, 1984), p. 2; Peter D. Stachura, *The German Youth Movement, 1900–1945: An Interpretative and Documentary History* (Macmillan, London, 1981), pp. 13–37, 44. For nature's appeal to Germans discontented with civilization, see Martin Green, *Mountain of Truth: The Counterculture Begins; Ascona, 1900–1920* (University Press of New England, Hanover, NH, 1986), pp. 1–2, 123–4, 156–60, 185–6.

75 Lewis Mumford, *The Myth of the Machine*, vol. I, *Technics and Human Development* (Harcourt Brace Jovanovich, New York, 1967), p. 283; *The Myth of the Machine*, vol. 2, *The Pentagon of Power* (Harcourt Brace Jovanovich, New York, 1970), pp. 248–53; Anna Bramwell, 'Was this Man Father of the Greens?', *History Today*, 34 (September 1984), pp. 7–13.

76 Anna Bramwell, *Blood and Soil: Richard Walther Darré and Hitler's 'Green Party'* (The Kensal Press, Bourne End, 1985), pp. 20–1, 172–5, 54–62; Dominick, *Environmental Movement in Germany*, p. 95.

77 We should note Bramwell's own admiration for the vanishing yeoman farmer and that she places organic farming at the heart of 'ecologism' (*Ecology in the 20th Century*, p. xii).

78 George L. Mosse, *Fallen Soldiers: Reshaping the Memory of the World Wars* (Oxford University Press, Oxford, 1990), pp. 87–9.

79 Robert Jan van Pelt and Deborah Dwork, *Auschwitz: 1270 to the Present* (Yale University Press, New Haven, Conn. 1996), pp. 156–9; Gert Groening and Joachim Wolschke-Bulmahn, 'Some Notes on the Mania for Native Plants in Germany', *Landscape Journal*, 11 (1992), 121–4, esp. p. 123.

80 Bramwell, 'Was this Man Father of the Greens?', p. 11; *Blood and Soil*, p. 12.

81 Michael Zimmerman, 'Toward a Heideggerian Ethos for Radical Environmentalism', *Environmental Ethics*, 5/2 (September 1983), pp. 99–131; id., 'Marx and Heidegger on the Technological Domination of Nature', *Philosophy Today*, 23 (Summer 1979), pp. 99–112.

82 Dominick, *Environmental Movement in Germany*, p. 111.

83 Robert A. Pois, *National Socialism and the Religion of Nature* (Croom Helm, London, 1986), pp. 79, 82–3.

84 Bramwell, *Ecology in the 20th Century*, pp. 161–2, 170–1, 180.

85 Pois, *National Socialism*. Pois takes the views of a few members of the inner core to be representative of Nazism as a whole and overstates the prominence of nature mysticism in Nazi ideology. See John Stroup, 'Nazis as Nature Mystics? A Review Essay on Robert A. Pois's *National Socialism and the Religion of Nature*', *This World: A Journal of Religion and Public Life*, 23 (Fall 1988), pp. 99–114.

86 Pois, *National Socialism*, p. 129.

87 Adolf Hitler, *Mein Kampf*, introd. D. C. Watt, trans. Ralph Manheim (Hutchinson, London, 1969), p. 261; see also pp. 258–62.

88 Ibid., p. 363; Pois, *National Socialism*, pp. 55, 53, 87.

89 Ibid., pp. 123, 131.

90 As quoted in Joachim C. Fest, *The Face of the Third Reich: Portraits of the Nazi Leadership*, trans. Michael Bullock (Weidenfeld and Nicolson, 1970 [1963]), p. 121.

91 Pois, *National Socialism*, p. 126.

92 Dominick, *Environmental Movement in Germany*, p. 92. That love of animals and dislike of people enjoy a certain symbiosis, however, is suggested by the British T-shirt slogan 'The more people I meet, the more I love my dog.'

93 Quoted in Pois, *National Socialism*, p. 132.

94 Murray Bookchin, *Which Way for the Ecology Movement?* (AK Press, Edinburgh, 1994), p. 27; James Lovelock, *The Ages of Gaia: A Biography of our Living Earth* (Oxford University Press, Oxford, 1988), p. 212; John Gray, *Enlightenment's Wake: Politics and Culture at the Close of the Modern Age* (Routledge, London, 1995), p. 183.

95 Bookchin, *Which Way for the Ecology Movement?*, pp. 7–8. The new French 'eco-right' also seeks to discredit ecocentrism by connecting it to Nazi love of nature and animals. See Luc Ferry, *The New Ecological Order*, trans. Carol Volk (University of Chicago Press, Chicago, 1995 [1992]), p. 91; Verena

Andermatt Conley, *Ecopolitics: The Environment in Poststructuralist Thought* (Routledge, London, 1997), pp. 12–13, 19.

96 Richard L. Rubenstein, *The Cunning of History: Mass Death and the American Future* (Harper and Row, New York, 1975), p. 90.

97 Bookchin, *Which Way for the Ecology Movement?*, pp. 6–7, 40–1.

98 Miss Ann Thropy, 'Is AIDS the answer to an environmentalist's prayer?', *Earth First! Journal* (1987), as quoted in Susan Zakin, *Coyotes and Town Dogs: Earth First! and the Environmental Movement* (Penguin, London, 1995), p. 350.

99 Edward Abbey, *Desert Solitaire* (Ballantine, New York, 1968), p. 20.

Chapter 9 The Future of Nature

1 Francis Fukuyama, 'The End of History?', *The National Interest*, 16 (Summer 1989), pp. 3–18. References below are to the subsequent book, *The End of History and the Last Man* (Penguin, London, 1992).

2 Fukuyama, *End of History*, pp. xi, xii, xiv, 3–4, 83.

3 Richard White, 'Environmental History, Ecology and Meaning' *Journal of American History* (special issue on environmental history), 76/4 (March 1990), p. 1115.

4 David J. Herlihy, 'Attitudes toward the Environment in Medieval Society', in *Historical Ecology: Essays on Environment and Social Change*, ed. Lester J. Bilsky (Kennikat Press, Port Washington, NY, 1980), p. 105.

5 Ibid., p. 103. Such views hardly fit with Lynn White's portrait of a triumphalist Christianity impelling a brash remodelling of nature.

6 Quoted in Victor Harris, *All Coherence Gone* (University of Chicago Press, Chicago, 1949), p. 95.

7 Ibid., pp. 10, 33, 137, 147.

8 Ibid., p. 59.

9 Marjorie Hope Nicolson, *The Breaking of the Circle: Studies in the Effect of the 'New Science' upon Seventeenth Century Poetry* (Northwestern University Press, Evanston, Ill., 1950); id., *Mountain Gloom and Mountain Glory: The Development of the Aesthetics of the Infinite* (W. W. Norton, New York, 1963 [1959]); Carolyn Merchant, *The Death of Nature: Women, Ecology and the Scientific Revolution* (HarperCollins, San Francisco, 1990 [1980]).

10 Bill McKibben, *The End of Nature* (Penguin, London, 1990), pp. 7, 43, 54, 57, 194.

11 Fukuyama, *End of History*, p. 88.

12 McKibben, *End of Nature*, p. 43; Michael Pollan, *Second Nature: A Gardener's Education* (Delta, New York, 1991), p. 5. For an earlier expression of the same sentiments as Pollan's, see John Passmore, *Man's Responsibility for Nature: Ecological Problems and Western Traditions* (Duckworth, London, 1974), pp. 36–7. For a critique of the idea of nature as a reality divorced from any cultural and historical context, see the various essays in William Cronon (ed.), *Uncommon Ground: Toward Reinventing Nature* (W. W. Norton, New York, 1995). Perhaps only an American cultural perspective hooked on wilderness as the supreme manifestation of nature, and shaped by the comparative recency of the large-scale transformation of the natural world

in North America, has to work so hard to grasp the absence of clear boundaries between nature and culture.

13 Pollan, *Second Nature*, pp. 3, 130–3.

14 For the need to cherish the familiar, 'near' landscape as much as remote wilderness ('what ground could be more hallowed?'), see Frank Fraser Darling's closing statement in his Reith Lectures of 1969, 'Wilderness and Plenty': *Wilderness and Plenty: The Reith Lectures, 1969* (BBC, London, 1970), p. 87. See also René Dubos, 'The Genius of Place', *American Forests* (September 1970), pp. 16–19, 61–2, and W. M. Adams, *Future Nature: A Vision for Conservation* (Earthscan, London, 1996), pp. 110–11.

15 For a thoughtful, measured treatment, see Dieter T. Hessel, 'Now that Animals can be Genetically Engineered: Biotechnology in Theological-Ethical Perspective', *Theology and Public Policy*, 5/1 (1993), pp. 284–99. See also Walter Truett Anderson, *To Govern Evolution: Further Adventures of the Political Animal* (Harcourt Brace Jovanovich, New York, 1987), pp. 131–6.

16 Sheldon Krimsky, *Biotechnics and Society: The Rise of Industrial Genetics* (Praeger, New York, 1991), opens with the famous quotation from Francis Bacon cited in chapter 4. See also ibid., pp. 84–5; Anderson, *To Govern Evolution*, pp. 77–8.

17 McKibben, *End of Nature*, pp. 152, 197, 151, 155. The book in question is Ted Howard and Jeremy Rifkin, *Who Should Play God?* (Dell, New York, 1977). McKibben's introduction of a second end of nature detracts from the impact of his thesis regarding climate change.

18 Anderson, *To Govern Evolution*, p. 135; Herman E. Daly and John R. Cobb, *For the Common Good: Redirecting the Economy toward Community, the Environment and a Sustainable Future* (Green Print, London, 1990), p. 204.

19 Krimsky, *Biotechnics and Society*, pp. 48, 50–7; *Times Higher Education Supplement*, 15 December 1995, and 21 February 1997 (for McGlade's quotation). Some 'genetech' species are ecologically advantageous, not least the oil-eating microbes that were the subject of the 1980 ruling. For the big money invested in biotechnology, see Paul Rauber, 'Better Nature through Chemistry', *Sierra*, 76/4 (July/August 1991), pp. 32–4.

20 Richard I. Evans, *Konrad Lorenz: The Man and his Ideas* (Harcourt Brace Jovanovich, New York, 1975), pp. 24–5, 99; James A. Schellenberg, *Masters of Social Psychology: Freud, Mead, Lewin, and Skinner* (Oxford University Press, New York, 1978), pp. 89–94, 105; Anna Bramwell, *Ecology in the 20th Century: A History* (Yale University Press, New Haven, Conn., 1989), pp. 57–60.

21 Michel de Montaigne, 'An Apology for Raymond Sebond' and 'On Cruelty', in *The Essays of Michel de Montaigne*, ed. M. A. Screech (Allen Lane, London, 1991), pp. 509, 534, 522, 536, 487.

22 René Descartes, 'Discourse on Method', in *Philosophical Essays*, trans. Laurence J. LaFleur (Bobbs-Merrill, Indianapolis, Ind., 1964), p. 43.

23 Richard Lewinsohn (Morus), *Animals, Men and Myths: A History of the Influence of Animals on Civilization and Culture* (Victor Gollancz, London, 1954), pp. 185–8; Merchant, *The Death of Nature* pp. 258–68.

24 Ralph H. Lutts, *The Nature Fakers: Wildlife, Science and Sentiment* (Fulcrum, Golden, Colo., 1990), pp. 32–6, 76–83, 112–14, 62–4, 145–61.

25 Carol P. MacCormack and Marilyn Strathern (eds), *Nature, Culture and Gender* (Cambridge University Press, Cambridge, 1980), pp. 20–3; Stephen Horigan, *Nature and Culture in Western Discourses* (Routledge, London, 1988), pp. 4–5, 20–4.

26 Lewinsohn, *Animals, Men and Myths*, pp. 301, 303.

27 Carl Sagan, *The Dragons of Eden: Speculations on the Evolution of Human Intelligence* (Random House, New York, 1977), pp. 110–11. For chimpanzee research, see ibid., pp. 107–24, and Horigan, *Nature and Culture in Western Discourses*, pp. 84–101. Even if we concede that Washoe's medium of communication qualifies as talk, it is still by no means clear that this talk can be put to any significant use.

28 Charles Darwin, *The Descent of Man and Selection in Relation to Sex* (John Murray, London, 1874), pp. 98–9, 114, 121, 127–8, 134–7. Darwin's terrier sounds at least as bright as Washoe and may well have possessed a far greater natural intelligence. I am grateful to John Anderson for encouraging me to think more critically about the findings of the animal behaviourists, and for suggesting some connections with wider themes addressed in this book.

29 David Day, *The Eco Wars* (Harrap, London, 1980), p. 114. The imposition of human concepts such as 'song' and 'music' onto animal sounds is more problematic than the Paynes suggest. The celebration of these composers of the ocean depths contains, perhaps, a generous dose of wish fulfilment, reminiscent of the qualities that white environmentalists have discovered in American Indians.

30 Alice E. Ingerson, 'Tracking and Testing the Nature–Culture Dichotomy', in *Historical Ecology: Cultural Knowledge and Changing Landscapes*, ed. Carole L. Crumley (School of American Research Press, Santa Fe, NM, 1994), p. 57.

31 Darwin, *Descent of Man*, pp. 123–6; Jane van Lawick-Goodall, *In the Shadow of Man* (Collins, London, 1974 [1971]), pp. 43–5; see also pp. 217–27. Research showing how dolphins use sponges to protect the tips of their noses from stingrays as they cruise along the seabed fishing was widely reported in the media in the autumn of 1997. Accomplishments that initially strike us as impressive appear more mundane on further reflection. Goodall's chimps have acquired a high level of proficiency at 'fishing' but how great is their potential command of the ordinary skills at the disposal of stone age man?

32 The example is that of a male zebra finch imitating the song of a male Bengalese finch. See P. Reynolds, *The Evolution of Human Behavior* (University of California Press, Berkeley, 1981), p. 23. Again, we need to treat research of this kind with caution. There are plenty of case studies indicating less adaptability.

33 Candace Savage, *Bird Brains: The Intelligence of Crows, Ravens, Magpies and Jays* (Sierra Club Books, San Francisco, 1995).

34 Donna J. Haraway, 'The Promises of Monsters: A Regenerative Politics for Inappropriate/d Others', in *Cultural Studies*, ed. Lawrence Grossberg, Cary Nelson and Paula Treichler (Routledge, London, 1992), pp. 296–8, 310, 313, 320, 329; id., 'A Cyborg Manifesto' and 'The Biopolitics of Postmodern

Bodies', in *Simians, Cyborgs and Women: The Reinvention of Nature* (Free Association, London, 1991), pp. 151–2, 177–8, 210–11. Others contend that if we are serious about eliminating the divide between nature and culture, then we must be prepared to accept that 'man's works (yes, including H-bombs and gas chambers) are as natural as those of bower birds and beavers'. See R. Watson, 'A Critique of Non-Anthropocentric Biocentrism', *Environmental Ethics*, 3 (1983), p. 252. Ecocentrics refute this by arguing that environmentally destructive behaviour perverts our naturally benign relationship with nature.

35 Anderson, *To Govern Evolution*, pp. 39–40.

36 John C. Lilly, *Communications between Man and Dolphin: The Possibility of Talking with other Species* (Crown, New York, 1961); id., *Lilly on Dolphins: Humans of the Sea* (Anchor Press, Garden City, NY, 1975); Ted Crail, *Apetalk and Whalespeak: The Quest for Interspecies Communication* (Contemporary Books, Chicago, 1983). After the human, the dolphin is the species with the largest brain mass relative to body weight. On pet ownership as a force corrosive of the nature–culture dichotomy at a practical level, see James Serpell, *In the Company of Animals: A Study of Human–Animal Relationships* (Cambridge University Press, Cambridge, 1996), esp. pp. ix, 235–6. What ultimately matters most from the historian's standpoint (especially in view of this book's special interest in the literature of advocacy) is not the scientific validity of research promoting the cause of big mammal intelligence, but how it serves the western urge to find 'us' in 'them'.

37 Arran E. Gare, *Postmodernism and the Environmental Crisis* (Routledge, London, 1995), p. 87; Jean Baudrillard, *America* (Verso, London, 1988), pp. 99, 5, 8, 30, 63, 69, 124, 126.

38 Claude Lévi-Strauss, *The Savage Mind* (Weidenfeld and Nicolson, London 1966 [1962]). Albert Borgmann, *Crossing the Postmodern Divide* (University of Chicago Press, Chicago, 1992) is one of relatively few 'green' postmodern texts. But Borgmann is another victim of the conceit that wilderness is an unimpeachable reality, that speaks with a clear and eloquent voice 'because it shows no traces of human intonation' (p. 120). Neil Evernden, too, for all his emphasis on cultural contingency, craves a truly ahistorical other, also locating it in culturally unmediated wilderness: *The Social Creation of Nature* (Johns Hopkins University Press, Baltimore, Md., 1992), p. 10). For an attempt to highlight the ecological ramifications of postmodernism (the 'theories of 1968'), see Verena Andermatt Conley, *Ecopolitics: The Environment in Poststructuralist Thought* (Routledge, London, 1997), esp. pp. 1–12, 42–55.

39 Richard Rorty, *Philosophy and the Mirror of Nature* (Princeton University Press, Princeton, NJ, 1979), p. 300. While recognizing its neglect of ecological issues, Arran Gare believes postmodernism can inspire an 'effective' environmental movement: *Postmodernism and the Environmental Crisis*, pp. 1–3, 5–8, 86–107.

40 Jonathan Bate, *Romantic Ecology: Wordsworth and the Environmental Tradition* (Routledge, London, 1991), p. 56. A good example of the postmodern

discourse that annoys Bate is David Demeritt, 'Ecology, Objectivity and Critique in Writings on Nature and Human Societies', *Journal of Historical Geography*, 20/1 (1994), pp. 22–37.

41 McKibben, *End of Nature*, p. 88.

42 Daniel Botkin, *Discordant Harmonies: A New Ecology for the Twenty-First Century* (Oxford University Press, New York, 1990), p. 62.

43 Ibid., p. 53.

44 David Ehrenfeld, *Beginning Again: People and Nature in the New Millennium* (Oxford University Press, New York, 1993), p. 143.

45 James D. Proctor, 'Whose Nature? The Contested Moral Terrain of Ancient Forests', in *Uncommon Ground*, ed. Cronon, pp. 269–97, esp. pp. 276, 283–4, 288, 295.

46 Art Davidson, *In the Wake of the Exxon Valdez* (Sierra Club Books, San Francisco, 1990); John Keeble, *Out of the Channel* (HarperCollins, New York, 1991).

47 Jeff Wheelwright, *Degrees of Disaster: Prince William Sound: How Nature Reels and Rebounds* (Simon and Schuster, New York, 1994); Ilya Prigogine and Isabelle Stengers, *Order Out of Chaos: Man's New Dialogue with Nature* (William Heinemann, London, 1984), pp. 11, 13, xxvii, 291–312.

48 Wheelwright, *Degrees of Disaster*, p. 46.

49 Robert Boyle, *Selected Philosophical Papers of Robert Boyle*, ed. M. A. Stewart (Manchester University Press, Manchester, 1979), p. 183; Wheelwright, *Degrees of Disaster*, pp. 108, 112.

50 For criticism of the new ecology on these grounds, see Donald Worster, *The Wealth of Nature: Environmental History and the Ecological Imagination* (Oxford University Press, New York, 1993), pp. 150–3, 166–7.

51 'Epistles' (Book 1), as quoted in Clarence J. Glacken, *Traces on the Rhodian Shore: Nature and Culture in Western Thought from Ancient Times to the End of the Eighteenth Century* (University of California Press, Berkeley, 1967), p. 31.

52 Robert Southey, *Poems of Robert Southey*, ed. Maurice H. Fitzgerald (Oxford University Press, London, 1909), p. 415.

53 Donald Worster, 'A Country Without Secrets', in *Under Western Skies: Nature and History in the American West* (Oxford University Press, New York, 1992), pp. 246, 239.

54 John McPhee, *The Control of Nature* (Farrar Straus Giroux, New York, 1989).

55 Nicolson, *Mountain Gloom*, p. 161; Rupert Sheldrake, *The Rebirth of Nature: The Greening of Science and God* (Century, New York, 1990), pp. 61–75, 123–36; Prigogine and Stengers, *Order Out of Chaos*, pp. xxvii, 312–13.

56 Lewis Mumford, *The Culture of Cities* (Secker and Warburg, London, 1938), p. 252.

57 Marion Shoard, *The Theft of the Countryside* (Temple Smith, London, 1980), pp. 11–20.

58 Eric G. Bolen and William L. Robinson, *Wildlife Ecology and Management* (Prentice-Hall, Englewood Cliffs, NJ, 1995), pp. 354–80.

59 Martin H. Krieger, 'What's Wrong with Plastic Trees?', *Science*, 179/4072 (2 February 1973), pp. 448, 453, 450.

60 McKibben, *End of Nature*, p. 55.
61 Haraway, 'The Promises of Monsters', pp. 296, 313; 'A Cyborg Manifesto', pp. 152–3; Gregg Mitman, *The State of Nature: Ecology, Community and American Social Thought, 1900–1950* (University of Chicago Press, Chicago, 1992), p. 212.
62 For the distinction between 'profane' historical time and 'sacred' ancient time beyond historical time, and the desire for the 'abolition' of time, see Mircea Eliade, *The Myth of the Eternal Return*, trans. Willard R. Trask (Pantheon Books, New York, 1954 [1949]), pp. 20–1, 35–6, 57, 62, 90, 153, 157–8.
63 *The Poetical Works of Wordsworth*, ed. Thomas Hutchinson (Oxford University Press, London, 1950 [1904]), p. 639; *The Poems of John Clare*, ed. J. W. Tibble (2 vols, J. M. Dent, London, 1935), vol. 2, pp. 12–15.
64 Lévi-Strauss, *The Savage Mind*, pp. 39–40, 42, 66, 75, 217. This binary approach to nature and culture has been dismissed as a Western peculiarity. See MacCormack and Strathern, *Nature, Culture and Gender*, pp. 5–11, 176–82.

Index